D0182413

Provided
You Don't Kiss Me

20 YEARS WITH BRIAN CLOUGH

DUNCAN HAMILTON

FOURTH ESTATE · *London*

First published in Great Britain in 2007 by
Fourth Estate
An imprint of HarperCollins*Publishers*
77–85 Fulham Palace Road
London W6 8JB
www.4thestate.co.uk

Visit our authors' blog: www.fifthestate.co.uk

A catalogue record for this book is
available from the British Library

ISBN-13 978-0-00-724710-3

Typeset in ITC Century Book by
Rowland Phototypesetting Ltd, Bury St Edmunds, Suffolk

Printed in Great Britain by Clays Ltd, St Ives plc

In memory of my parents
James and Jenny Hamilton

If only football could be that much fun...

The best account of what it is like to be a football reporter was written by B. S. Johnson, an experimental novelist and poet who regularly covered matches for *The Observer*. His novel *The Unfortunates*, published in the late 1960s, is Johnson's 'book in a box', an example of modernist literature. It consists of twenty-seven unbound chapters which, except for the first and the last, can be read in any order. The idea, argued Johnson, was to convey the arbitrary nature of thought.

Johnson was a lugubrious man. *The Unfortunates* is the mournful story of an unnamed narrator (actually Johnson himself) who arrives by train at an unnamed city (coincidentally Nottingham) to cover a football match. He takes a plunge into his past. The surroundings – 'I know this city' – awaken in him rich slices of memory that rise up and wash over him like waves. And thus, improbable as it may sound, on a grey Saturday afternoon he drifts from meditations on football and football writing into reflections on life and death. Unlike Bill Shankly, he comes to the conclusion that life is more important than football can ever be.

The sections of the book about football are evocative.

1

Johnson's narrator reports on a match between City and United – names chosen, I'd imagine, because they represent the game's Everyman – and slowly peels away the misconceptions about the free seat in the press box. Johnson is miserable and unforgiving, and he has an acid tongue.

Given the number of matches a reporter is obliged to sit through over the course of a season – in my experience, anywhere between sixty and a hundred – and the number of words he has to write about each of them, it isn't difficult to become, like Johnson's character, so disillusioned with the trade that cynicism sets in and hardens like cement.

To the outsider, football reporting, like much of what happens inside newspaper offices, gives off a strong glow of romance and glamour, recalling old movies about the press: a hard-bitten, tough-guy, trilby-wearing Bogart balancing a drooping cigarette on the edge of his lip in *Deadline USA*, or a workaholic Jack Hawkins beating himself into exhaustion in *Front Page Story*. It's a world of typewriters, eyeshades and braces, saloon bars and harassed men in belted trench coats bellowing down black, megaphone-sized telephones to a pouting blonde copy-taker. Amid the clatter of the keyboards and the twisted vines of cigarette smoke, each day is a swirl of gripping, unforgettable events.

If only. The truth, especially in the provinces, is that newspaper reporting is often a mundane, repetitive slog: season after season of unbearably joyless matches, one so indistinguishable from another that it becomes impossible – without examining the statistics of teams and goalscorers in *Rothmans Football Yearbook* – to tell them apart. I came into journalism specifically for the free seat. I wanted to watch sport without paying for the privilege, and sports writing seemed like a decent alternative to real work. Soon I began to understand what Robert Louis

Stevenson meant when he wrote that it is a better thing to travel hopefully than to arrive.

The beautiful game can seem ugly and dull when viewed through tired and jaded eyes. It looks worse when in early March you find yourself recycling phrases, already soiled by overuse, that you originally wrote in August or September. Worse still, after a while you learn to routinely fabricate an emotional response to something about which you feel absolutely nothing. This is exactly what Johnson conveys so well in *The Unfortunates*:

> Always, at the start of each match, the excitement, often the only moment of excitement, that this might be the ONE match, the match in which someone betters Payne's ten goals, where Hughie Gallacher after being floored nods one in while sitting down, where the extraordinary happens, something that makes it stand out, the match one remembers and talks about for years afterwards, the rest of one's life. The one moment, the one match. A new beginning, is it? But already I suspect the worst . . . have to be prepared, as always, in everything, to settle for less.

Even a cursory flick through Jonathan Coe's biography of Johnson, *Like A Fiery Elephant*, reveals a man not only at odds with life but tragically soured by it. His bitter dissatisfactions, frustrations and, eventually, profound unhappiness led to his suicide in 1973. None of this devalues Johnson's opinions. Whatever his demons, the darts he threw from the pages of *The Unfortunates* always fell near, or directly inside, the bullseye. He *knew*. He had been there and felt it.

When Johnson buys a football paper, bowed by the weight of

stale phrases such as 'star-studded forward line' and 'shooting boots', he says, relieved: 'I don't have to write that sort of preliminary speculative meaningless crap. Just my own kind of crap.'

Handed the attendance figure on a slip of paper, he laments: '24,833 poor sods have paid good money to see this rubbish', and later tartly adds: 'Not even a bloody quote from the crowd ... cowed by seeing rubbish like this nearly every week, I should think.'

He complains about the press box dirt that 'blows across my pages' and the 'cramped seat'. He is scathing about the 'Heavy Mob' – his sobriquet for red-top tabloid reporters, who are castigated as 'the well paid pseuds ... armed to the teeth (with) Colour and Metaphor'.

Most significantly, however, he puts across the monotonous grind of weekly football reporting and its ritualistic language – the words manufactured in a mechanical, depressing way as if by a blank-eyed factory worker turning out rivets. In a single sentence he sums up the way I often felt towards the end of a season, sometimes in the middle of it: 'Bollocks to this stinking match.'

Johnson was lucky – he was a part-timer. His football reporting supplemented the serious work of creating novels and poems. Although Johnson complained about it – and about the subeditors who, he thought, desecrated his copy with crass, overzealous use of the blue pencil – he pressed on with football writing because he was at heart a football man. He arrived at a ground each Saturday hoping that he wouldn't be disappointed again.

How well I knew that feeling. For seventeen years I covered football for two freelance agencies, one national newspaper and for the *Nottingham Evening Post*. Apart from one season covering Notts County (which, because of its manager, Jimmy Sirrel, was like dropping into the Fifth Circle of Dante's Hell), I followed Nottingham Forest.

A word or two about Sirrel. He looked like a garden gnome that had been roughed up a bit. He had bug eyes and his nose was bent and flat, as if someone had struck him in the face with an iron. I found him devoid of charm and uncooperative, to the extent that I could barely get a word out of him. Once, pleading for a story, I fell back on the weakest of all arguments: 'Well, Jim, the fans will want to know what's going on.' Sirrel, a Glaswegian, replied, 'Aw, fuck the fans.'

My morning phone call to him had previously gone one of two ways.

'Morning Jim. Lovely day.'

'If you think so, you write it,' he'd reply.

Or, 'Good morning Jim. Lovely day.'

'Aye, but not if you're dead, is it, eh?'

I couldn't explore the 'What if . . .' scenario with Sirrel either. 'Aye,' he'd say, 'if ma granny had a dicky than she would'nae be my granny.'

I can't imagine that any football reporter has physically strangled to death the manager of the club he covered. But there were a lot of occasions when I would gladly have put my hands around Sirrel's neck, squeezed hard and taken my chances. I longed to escape across the River Trent. That's where you found Brian Clough. Although he was frightening and obstreperous, Clough would give you a line – provided, of course, he was prepared to speak to you in the first place. And after that one season covering Notts County, my wish came true.

I can only guess at the number of Nottingham Forest matches I watched. At a rough calculation, it was possibly more than a thousand at all levels: first team and reserves, and occasionally the youth side too, which meant getting lime from the still-damp touchline markings on my best (and usually only) pair of shoes, on a pitch in a park. The youth games, normally played in front of the proverbial dog and a few retired men with nothing better to do, were a miniature exhibition of Clough's peculiarities. Unpredictable is not the half of it.

Often I watched these games standing beside Clough. When he yelled at full volume it was like being pressed against the speakers at an Iron Maiden concert. I could feel my bones vibrate. Some of the opposition youth-team players were so tremblingly afraid of that volcanic bark, and kept such a distance from him, that you could build a small house on the part of the pitch near where Clough stood. Entire matches were played in midfield. If the worst happened, and the ball went out of play, he had a habit of retrieving it from the bushes and hurling it back with great force, aiming the ball directly at the groin of the unfortunate player sent to take the throw-in. 'I aim at the bollocks,' he said to me with a mischievous grin. 'It keeps 'em on their toes.'

With Clough, you could take nothing for granted. Like a hornet, he stung people indiscriminately. I didn't mind, though; he wasn't Jimmy Sirrel. I spent many waking hours of my life with Clough in his office, in cars or coaches, trains or planes – so many, in fact, that if you strung them together they would certainly add up to a year or two. And I count myself as very fortunate. Unlike B. S. Johnson, I saw a lot of memorable matches, *the* matches that stay with you for the rest of your life.

On an August night in Barcelona, after a downpour so intense that the rain seemed to hang from the sky in a single flat sheet, I saw the stubby-framed Diego Maradona perform juggling and conjuring tricks in a pre-season friendly. Maradona was two months short of his twenty-fourth birthday, and three years away from the football immortality – and notoriety – that the 1986 World Cup would guarantee him.

I can still see him now. He sets off on a slanting fifteen-yard run across the Nou Camp, flicking the ball up with the toe of his boot because it refuses to roll on the water-drenched surface. It's like a one-man game of keepy-uppy. The white ball glistens under the lights as if it's been highly polished. Three red-shirted defenders dive in and are casually beaten. The defenders turn in open-mouthed incredulity at what's happened to them before setting off in fruitless pursuit, as if chasing a pickpocket down a street. But it's too late. Maradona reaches the box and, finishing his work with a flourish, he lifts the ball with his toe for the last time and volleys it into the net. He raises his left hand in a modest salute. It is the hand that will punch a goal past Peter Shilton, the hand that will eventually hold the World Cup.

On successive Saturdays in September 1986, I saw Forest comprehensively dismantle first Aston Villa and then Chelsea. This pair of results, 6–0 and 6–2, were beautifully described as looking on paper like a routine first-round match for Martina Navratilova.

I saw Forest claw back a two-goal deficit in a European Cup semi-final against Cologne on a ploughed field of a pitch. The City Ground mud clung to the players' boots like glue, yet John Robertson, Garry Birtles and Tony Woodcock seemed to be running on silk. The match finished 3–3.

A year later, in 1980, I saw Forest retain the European Cup on a May evening in Madrid against Hamburg. The air was heavy, the sky like glass. I remember afterwards briefly holding one of the handles of the silver trophy, reaching out for it the way a wide-eyed infant would stretch to touch a coloured bauble on a Christmas tree.

I was there when Forest played West Ham at home at the end of the 1985–86 season and a Dutchman called Johnny Metgod – one of the players I regarded as a friend – hit the ball so hard that I thought it would burst. Metgod took a free kick to the right of the box, about twenty yards out. The ball appeared to me to travel in a straight, rising line of white light before it filled the net. The crowd, in stunned disbelief, were mute for a moment, but then the noise began, so loud it could have perforated eardrums.

And each Saturday I saw the skills of John Robertson, the grace of Trevor Francis and Martin O'Neill, and I watched Peter Shilton save shots that looked unreachable for mere mortals.

There was a downside. I spent too much of my time on motorways. I ate too much takeaway food and sandwiches in plastic wrapping. I stood hunched in car parks in the blowing rain waiting for a pimply-skinned player to toss me a cliché. I wrote match reports in the early hours of cold, midweek mornings, the fierce glare of the office lights burning my eyes, the nightly vacuuming of the carpet roaring in my ears.

Despite his eccentricities – and there were an awful lot of them – Clough made it all interesting and, for the most part, worthwhile. A football reporter in the provinces is in a position which is privileged yet at times almost impossible. He is privileged because representing the local paper is a golden key that opens most doors. You can build up an unrivalled relationship with the manager and the players because you are in contact with them every day. A spurious intimacy evolves between you. You share so much with the characters you write about that you can pretty much corner the market in quotes.

Of course, that access comes at an exorbitant cost. Closeness to the team, and any emotional attachment to it, horribly distorts the line between candid reporting and scarf-waving support. Too many journalists succumb, seduced by the insider knowledge fed to them, and begin to identify with the glory or misfortune of *their* team. The football world soon divides into 'them and us'. It is all too easy to become overprotective or self-censoring, so that criticism is either wrapped in cotton wool or disguised in nebulous, worn euphemisms. Contacts become friends, and human nature takes over. You don't want to lose your place at the manager's table.

A reporter even half-decent at his job is guaranteed to gather a notebook's-worth of information which has been given to him in the strictest confidence. He is privy to so much that for various reasons has to go unreported. The manager knows that the reporter will not break his trust: the consequences would be too dire. The reporter has daily space to fill, yet another deadline or back-page lead to write. The editor back at the office probably neither understands nor, even if he does, is sympathetic to the shaky high-wire act you perform, and which obliges you to find the balance between diplomacy and full disclosure – something, in other words, which benefits both the newspaper and the club.

If you do upset anyone – and a mild falling-out usually happened at least twice a month in my case – the golden key is snatched out of your hand. You are shut out or banned. A total ban arrived for me, like Christmas, once a year. The most spectacular of them came after I had written a report critical of a Saturday League match. Clough regarded the report as a 'bag of shit'. After the next game, a Wednesday-night UEFA Cup tie which Forest won without overtaxing themselves, Clough sent a breathless apprentice to the press box to summon me to the dressing room. Inside, Clough came at me like a bullet. Emerging out of the steam that poured from the showers, he pointed to the wall. He had cut out my match report and pinned it there. The headline read: REDS MORALE NOSE DIVES.

Clough's eyes widened, his nostrils flared. He leaned right over me, his hot breath on my face. 'I didn't need a fucking motivational talk tonight. I just had to show them the shit you'd written. Now, I've got a message for you. Take your fucking portable typewriter and stick it up your arse. You're banned. You're fucking banned for ever from this ground. Fucking for ever.'

The captain, Ian Bowyer, still wrapped in a towel, looked at me pityingly and shook his head. The goalkeeper, Hans van Breukelen – who hadn't played that night – pressed his index finger silently to his lips to dissuade me from replying. I remember Garry Birtles staring at his bare feet and then sensibly moving away. He gave me the sort of supportive sideways glance that I took to mean, 'Just tough it out. The storm will pass.'

However, it carried on for half a minute more, which for me was like an hour. Clough's voice grew louder and I thought he might spontaneously combust. I was standing in the centre of the dressing room, pathetically limp and embarrassed, with my notebook redundant in my hand. I wanted the steam from the showers to descend like a fog and hide me. 'You come into this club and we treat you like a friend,' Clough raged. 'And you fucking insult us. You know fuck all about this game. Fuck all. Don't stand there, just fuck off!'

I exited – downcast, angry, silent, and feeling as though I had been scalded by a branding iron. As I walked the two and a quarter miles back to the office, I thought about his machine-gun use of the F-word. This was, after all, the man who had once tried to dissuade his own supporters from using bad language by erecting a sign at the City Ground that read 'Gentleman, no swearing please'.

Two days later, on a Friday lunchtime when I ought to have been collecting team news, I was sitting at my desk trying to think if there was anything already in my notebook that I might turn into a readable story for the following night's edition. The phone rang.

'Where are you, shithouse?' asked Clough. (He used the word 'shithouse' as frequently as other people use 'please' and 'thank you'. 'It's an affectionate term,' he'd explain – though he didn't always use it that way.)

'Er, you banned me. You told me never to come back to the ground,' I said, and heard in return a sigh of mock exasperation.

'Fucking hell, fucking hell. Don't be such a stupid bugger. Get your arse down here. I didn't mean it. Spur of the moment thing. Gone and forgotten now. Come down and we'll have a drink. I've a got a story for you. Fancy a glass of champagne?'

I paused. 'OK,' I said. 'Provided you don't kiss me.'

'You're too fucking ugly for that,' he said, and slammed the phone down.

He was waiting for me at the door. 'There's a Scotch for you,' he said. 'Get it down you and I'll fetch the champagne.'

I stayed well into the late autumn afternoon and left hopelessly drunk on Bell's Whisky. We never got to the champagne. My notebook was choked with stories.

Of course, no football reporter knows everything. A fair amount of what he writes is largely intelligent guesswork, a decent stab at trying to understand what is happening from the evidence – first hand or empirical – that he has gathered from various sources. Clough, being Clough, took a different view.

'If you're going to work with me, and we're going to build a relationship, I'll tell you the lot,' he said at the beginning, which was a blatant untruth. What he meant was that I would be told 90 per cent of what was going on 85 per cent of the time – but that wasn't a bad return.

And so it began, an extraordinary journey with a contradictory, Chinese box of a man – idiosyncratic, eccentric, wholly unpredictable from one blink of an eye to the next, and unfathomably difficult to burrow to the core of. I saw him at his very best and at his very worst.

On the one hand, Clough was capable of being unforgivably rude, unnecessarily cruel, appallingly bombastic and arrogant, and so downright awkward that I wanted to drop something large and heavy on his big head. On the other hand, he could be extravagantly generous, emollient and warm, ridiculously kind, and loyal to whoever he thought warranted it, and he often went out of his way to be no bother to anybody. Ken Smales, Forest's secretary, said that Clough could be like a sheep in wolf's clothing or a wolf in sheep's clothing, but that 'mostly he was just himself', a description which perfectly encapsulated my problem in the minute or two before our daily meetings: which Brian Clough was going to turn up?

Flowers were sent as routinely as other people posted greetings cards. Friends found gambling debts, mortgage arrears and bills paid anonymously. Even strangers, if he got to hear about their plight and regarded it as unjust, might find themselves bailed out of financial difficulty. He did it quietly and on the strict understanding that there would be no publicity involved.

I stammered, sometimes badly. One morning, forcing out a question took me longer than usual. 'Young man,' he said impatiently, 'do you stammer with me, or do you stammer with everyone?' I told him boldly, and with no hesitation in my voice, that he shouldn't feel privileged because I stammered to all and sundry. 'What's the cure?' he asked. I said there wasn't one;

once a stammerer, nearly always a stammerer. He pressed on: 'When do you stammer the most?' I said that talking on the phone was always difficult because you couldn't use the natural pauses that punctuate face-to-face conversation to your advantage. 'I'll phone you every day for two weeks,' he said. 'We'll crack this.' He almost kept to his word. My stammer didn't vanish, but it gradually became less severe.

When he was at his worst, and especially when drinking brought out the darker side of his personality, covering Forest was like being ordered around at gunpoint. All the same, I followed Clough with the growing astonishment that Boswell must have felt walking with Johnson across the Western Isles. What Boswell said about Johnson also fitted Clough to a tee: he had 'a great ambition to excel', and a 'jealous independence of spirit, and impetuosity of temper'. Not much, he did.

Looking back, and putting what I saw into context, Clough's eighteen years at the City Ground was a period of madness punctuated by wonderful bursts of sanity. I don't know how I survived it without (a) becoming an alcoholic or (b) being confined to a padded cell at some point.

Since the spit and polish of Sky TV reinvented the game, everyone has a team to support, colours to wear, a result to search for on a Saturday evening or Sunday afternoon. Everyone is suddenly an expert too, from the strategy of 4–4–2 and the sweeper system to set pieces and diagonal runs from 'the hole.' It wasn't always like that. Given today's obsession with football, and the way it is anchored in social and cultural life, it can be difficult to imagine what the game was like before the convulsions of the 1990s turned it into a designer sport.

In the 1970s, when hooliganism ran across it like a ghastly scar, football wasn't just out of kilter with fashion. It was regarded as faintly repellent, like a sour smell, by most of those who never passed through the turnstiles. I knew a lot of people who genuinely believed that the scene before a typical Saturday afternoon game resembled Lowry's melancholic painting *Going to the Match*: dark, whippet-thin fans in flat caps and mufflers, bent into a slicing wind, and the skyline around each ground smudged by smoke from factory chimneys. Football to them was crude, a prehistoric pastime, and redolent of a distant past featuring dubbin, cheap liniment and steel-toecapped boots. Even by the 1980s, when the implications of the tragedies at Heysel, Bradford and Hillsborough were absorbed and football began to look at itself afresh, it was still a struggle to weld together a convincing argument for its future health.

In each decade Clough significantly promoted football through the strength of his personality; as a character instantly recognisable to those who didn't habitually watch the game. He was a guest on *Parkinson*. Mike Yarwood impersonated him with a jabbing finger and a 'now young man, listen to me' routine, which Clough found immensely flattering. 'True fame is when the newspapers spell your name right in Karachi – and ordinary fame is when Yarwood does you,' he once told me. 'Yarwood did me a favour. He made me popular. He advanced my cause.'

Clough was so skilled at self-promotion that I felt he didn't need anyone to beat a drum on his behalf. TV and newspapers adored him because you seldom had to look underneath his words to find the hidden meaning (though the motive was often of labyrinthine complexity). Each sentence was plain and pointed, like a spear. He didn't rely on qualifying terms such as 'perhaps' or 'might' or 'maybe'. He didn't dissolve into banality. He hated yawning politeness, and didn't mind being portrayed as a snarling malcontent.

A sport's back-page lead, aimed primarily at a popular audience, is necessarily limited in scope. My own pieces tended for obvious reasons to be variations on a single theme: Clough's opinions. He sold newspapers. I would sit at the keyboard and write: 'Brian Clough today . . .' and then press on with the guts of the story.

Every day on the back of the *Nottingham Evening Post*, Clough 'demanded' or 'insisted' or 'attacked' or 'appealed' or (less often) 'made a plea' or 'sent a message' to someone or other. The quotes justifying the first paragraph began to run from the third. The rest was as straightforward as joining the dots in a child's puzzle book. The basic principle was to make sure his name appeared in the intro because, as Hollywood says, the lead always gets the close-up.

Good quotes are the diamonds of popular journalism, and Clough represented the richest and the deepest seam. He was an inexhaustible mine of one-liners. He took pride in being an agitator, and gratuitously provocative. He didn't care – at least not very much – about the way he was perceived, whether or not anyone liked him or how his opinions would play politically, except, naturally, when it suited his own agenda. It meant that enemies gathered in battalions, a fact Clough acknowledged sanguinely.

'That bunch of shithouses at the Football Association – who know nowt – want me to shut up,' he said from behind his cluttered desk, showing me a letter with the FA's embossed shield on it. The FA had written to admonish him for a comment he had made about wanting to 'kick' one of his own players. 'Let's you and me write a piece and tell them to fuck off – in the nicest possible way. You'll pick the right words . . . Make it up for me.' He trusted you to do your job the way he trusted a player on a Saturday afternoon. If you didn't shape up . . . well, a bollocking followed.

Stories about his epic drinking, the rages like forked lightning, and the 'bungs' are draped like a black cape across the
sad last acts of his career. But a man's life has to be seen in
the full to appreciate it. He shouldn't be judged on the last
flickerings of the candle. The good years were pure gravy for
Clough, filled with silverware and respect, and not purely
because his name was there in the record books as having
won the League Championship and European Cup twice
apiece. His legacy went beyond the business of winning
trophies.

When Clough became a manager at Hartlepool in 1965, aged
only thirty, his contemporaries were predominantly conven-
tional figures with a 1940s or 1950s ideology. Most were middle-
aged or approaching it and maintained a staid, regulation
collar-and-tie approach to football. Clough was iconoclastic.
Very early on he recognised the value of publicity and how to
make it work for him. He had the loudest voice, the magnetic
pull of the fairground barker and an understanding of how the
mechanics of the media functioned. He knew how to exploit it
for himself.

As a player at Middlesbrough, Clough had deliberately leaked
his dissatisfaction with the club's attitude towards him so that
he could gain the upper hand in the struggle to either force a
transfer or improve his salary. He was eventually sold. As a
manager, with Peter Taylor, he had the prescience to realise
that two men, personally compatible but with contrasting
talents, could do the manager's job better than one. He pioneered the idea of a short break mid-season for the team, and
proved himself innovative in his handling of players and in his
approach to coaching.

Clough was also lucky. His break into management came at
the time when television began to embrace football more firmly,

chiefly because of England's World Cup win in 1966. He eventually became emblematic of the period when managers began to dominate the headlines as much as, if not more than, players – and he was one of the main reasons why the cult of the manager developed in the way it did. Clough made sure that he – not the players, and certainly not the chairman who bankrolled it – was the axis on which the club always turned. Open dissent against someone or something, or merely going against the grain, pushed him to centre stage. The strategy of yelling his contempt and kicking up dust whenever he could for the sake of it proved profitable. Clough soon became more important than whichever team he managed, and then more important than the club itself. Profile was everything to him because it was accompanied by power.

As a manager, Clough enjoyed the advantage of relative youth, which helped him to glamorise management in the late 1960s and early 1970s and give it an almost film-star sheen. When he secured promotion to the First Division for Derby in 1969, he was thirty-four years old. His contemporaries were ancient by comparison. Joe Mercer (Manchester City) was fifty-five. Bill Shankly (Liverpool) was fifty-four, and Bertie Mee (Arsenal) and Joe Harvey (Newcastle) were both fifty-one. Bill Nicholson (Tottenham) and Harry Catterick (Everton) were fifty. Don Revie was forty-two, but looked ten years older; perhaps it was the pressure of managing Leeds. When Clough took Forest into the First Division eight years later, all but one of those managers (Revie) had retired.

Clough didn't merely represent the start of a new generation, he shaped it too. In the early 1980s, after Forest's two European Cup wins, the lower divisions seemed to me to be awash with Clough clones. I met one who came to the City Ground in the manner of a pilgrim worshipping at a shrine. He looked like a very bad insomniac, gaunt and hollow-eyed with a putty-coloured complexion. As I listened to him talk about discipline, as though a big stick was enough to guarantee quivering obedience, I realised how badly he wanted to *be* Clough, but what was also clear was his utter failure to appreciate the people skills of the man he venerated. He had, perhaps unknowingly, begun to imitate some of Clough's gestures, and the inflections in his voice and a few of his expressions had infiltrated his vocabulary. I thought of the old line about one Shakespeare and many Hamlets.

Clough got some things horribly wrong. His fear that live TV would soon kill football was quickly discredited. His criticism of successive England managers stemmed from the suppurating wounds that the Football Association inflicted on him. No one, he felt, could do a better job with England than the face he saw every morning in the shaving mirror. His criticism of players and other managers was frequently unfair.

But another thing about him, and a major reason to admire the man, was his refreshing philosophy about how the game ought to be approached. Style mattered, and Clough fell into the category of high-minded aesthetician. It wasn't enough to win – he wanted to win playing beautiful football. He wanted the ball passed elegantly, as if it were on a thread, from player to player, preferring creative intuition to brute force. He demanded style as well as discipline.

As Clough saw it, teams who played the long ball were horned devils. He said to me: 'Any idiot can coach a group of players to whack the ball as hard and as high as possible, and then gallop after it. Give me time, and I could train a monkey to do that and stick it in the circus. What pleasure does anyone get watching a side like that? You may as well go plane spotting at Heathrow – 'cos you'd find yourself staring at the sky all the time, and then you'd go home with a stiff neck.' When he talked that way, his eyes became flinty, and the skin around his mouth tightened into a snarl. He would jab out his right hand, like a southpaw sparring in the gym.

The game, Clough argued idealistically, was simple. He would lay a towel on the floor of the dressing room and place a ball at the centre of it, striving to make a mental symbol of it take hold in a player's mind. 'This ball is your best friend,' he would say. 'Love it, caress it.' He preached the simplicity of football with the passion of a TV evangelist. The game, he said, is 'the most straightforward on God's earth – beautiful grass, a ball, a defined space in which to play it.'

Clough believed that everything in life was overcomplicated and that most coaches were guilty of overcomplicating football, as if it were 'something like nuclear physics and Einstein had written a book about it'. A pained expression crossed his face whenever he heard coaches talk about 'systems' or saw chalk lines scratched on the blackboard. He looked at 'Subutteo men being pushed around a felt pitch' with disgust. 'Get the ball,' he said. 'Give it to your mate or try to go past someone. Score a goal. Make the people watching you feel as if there's been some skill, some flair in what you've done.'

Near the end of what was to become his penultimate season in 1992, I was walking back from the training ground with him. We talked about football as entertainment. 'You know why so many people queue up for hours to look at the *Mona Lisa*?' he asked, all ready to roll out his own answer. "Cos it's an attractive piece of work. It moves them. They feel the same way about a beautiful woman, like Marilyn Monroe. They feel the same way about a statue or a building. They even feel the same way about a sunrise. Now if we're half as good-looking as a football team as Mona, Marilyn or a sunrise, then we might get one or two people prepared to come and see us every Saturday – even if it's pissing down.'

No team, Clough believed, could claim to be ascetically superior if a streak of ill-discipline or a tendency to wantonly bend the rules ran through it. That, he said, is why he so 'hated' Revie's Leeds.

On a Friday he had a habit of writing out his team sheet to the accompaniment of a Frank Sinatra record. A 'gramophone player' (he never referred to a 'record' or 'tape deck') sat on the low glass-fronted bookcase in his office. A drawing of Sinatra hung on the wall. He would sometimes spend a long time hunting for his reading glasses before beginning the painstaking process of putting down each name in large capital letters.

'You know,' he said one day, handing me the team sheet, 'I'd love all of us to play football the way Frank Sinatra sings . . . all that richness in the sound, and every word perfect. How gorgeous would that be?' His face glowed like a fire, and he began to sing along with Sinatra, always a word ahead of him, as if he needed to prove that he knew the lyrics. *'I've got you . . . under my skin . . .'* He rose from his chair, still singing, and began to pretend he was dancing with his wife. When the song finished, he laughed until tears ran down his cheeks. He fell back into his chair, arms and legs splayed.

The smile looked as if it might stay on his face for ever. 'Oh, that was good,' he said. 'Blow me, if only football could be *that* much fun . . .'

CHAPTER ONE

Who the fuck are you?

The first words Brian Clough ever said to me were: 'So who the fuck are you then?'

He asked the question in a perplexed rather than an aggressive way, breaking the cold silence of a late winter afternoon. I was sitting in the corridor outside his office, the grey carpeted floor dull and dirty, the cream-coloured walls in need of paint. A queasy apprehension filled my stomach. Clough lowered his head and peered at me, as if looking over the frames of a pair of horn-rimmed spectacles.

'I'm here,' I said slowly, and managing not to stammer, 'for the interview you promised me. I've brought my letter.'

I took the folded letter from my inside pocket and offered it to him as if it was an engraved invitation, my outstretched arm hanging stiffly in the air. Clough was wearing a sun-bright rugby shirt. His eyes narrowed, his brow creasing slightly.

'Which paper?' he asked, this time making the question sound like part of an interrogation.

'*Nottingham S-s-s-sport*,' I replied, betraying the stammer. The 'S' sound came out in a low hiss, like air from a bicycle tyre.

'Then you'd better come in,' he said. He took a pace towards the pearl-glass door that led to his office, and then turned back to face me. 'If you were a bit older, you could've had a Scotch with me.'

I stood up and smoothed down the front of my jacket, trying to look nonchalant.

I was eighteen years old, wearing the only suit that belonged to me – a pale grey check with matching waistcoat and lapels as wide as angel's wings. That morning I had put on a white Panda collar shirt and a tie, carefully chosen from Burton's the previous Christmas. I had carefully trimmed my beard, which I'd grown a year earlier to make myself look older. The beard seemed to confuse him – he kept staring at it. Did he think it was stuck to my chin with glue? I must have looked like a short, smartened-up version of Shaggy from *Scooby-Doo*.

I was carrying a large black briefcase in which the night before I'd put a new spiral-bound notebook ('The Reporter's Notebook'), three ballpoints (in case two failed) and a page of typed questions I intended to ask. I had made the list a week before, sitting at the kitchen table in my parents' council house, typing on the grey Imperial my mother had bought for me on weekly hire purchase from the *Empire Stores* catalogue. I kept making mistakes, and soon the floor was littered with screwed-up balls of discarded paper. I wrote in capitals so I didn't have to press the shift key. The ribbon needed changing so some of the letters were faint. In the next room my father, soon to start the night shift at the coal mine, was listening to the six o'clock news: more gloom for the Callaghan government.

It was February 1977. Of course, football was very different then: unpolished and unpackaged, like the decade itself. There were no all-seater stadiums, no executive boxes serving canapés and chablis, few slick agents with sharp suits and blunt jaws. 'Hey,' Cloughie said years later, when we reflected on how even nondescript players now carried an agent around with them like a handbag. 'The only agent back then was 007 – and he just shagged women, not entire football clubs.'

Watching football on TV was rationed: *Match of the Day* on Saturday night, *Star Soccer* or *The Big Match* Sunday lunchtime. Often a grim goalless draw was padded out to fill an hour. Newspapers were thinner and uniformly black and white. There were no dedicated pull-outs carrying the statistical minutiae, or gossip and quotes and graphics to record what had happened the previous Saturday when, observing strict tradition, almost every game had kicked off at three o'clock rather than being spread across a long weekend for the benefit of television. Most matches outside the First Division were hardly covered at all – except in the inky pages of countless Pink 'Uns, Green 'Uns and Buffs available in provincial towns and cities and in the late Saturday edition of London's *Evening News*.

No national newspaper had properly cottoned on to football's potential to sell copies for them. Sport was just a buffer to stop the advertisements tipping out of the back of the paper. In many papers, match reports were squeezed onto three, perhaps four, typographically unappealing pages – blocks of smudgy words set in hot metal type, indistinct black and white photographs and a headline font as out of fashion today as men's platform shoes.

The newspaper I eventually joined, the *Nottingham Evening Post*, was a broadsheet. A red seal, in the shape of the city's landmark, the Council House dome, sat alongside the masthead to denote the various editions of the paper printed throughout the day. The stop press column was full of the late racing results and, in summer, the cricket scores at lunch and tea.

The average weekly wage for a footballer was around £135. The average wage of the ordinary working man was less than £70. You could sit at a First Division match for £2.20 or go on the terraces, thick with cigarette smoke, for a pound or less. (If you did stand, there was always a risk, in such a very cramped space, that the man behind you might piss his lunch-time beer down the back of your legs). Forest's matchday programme, like most others, cost 12p, and the back-page advertisement was usually for a cigarette company. 'It's Still the Tobacco that Counts', claimed John Player.

That season, 1976/77, Chelsea's future was clouded by precarious finances. The Greater London Council was urged to put together a rescue package for them. Sir Harold Thompson was elected as the new chairman of the Football Association, a decision that would have implications for Clough less than eighteen months later. Tommy Docherty called for hooligans to be birched. Don Revie, the England manager, appealed for more sponsorship in football. Laurie Cunningham became the first black player to be chosen for an England squad – in his case, the Under-21s. Arsenal paid £333,000 to bring Malcolm Macdonald to London from Newcastle.

By the end of that season, Liverpool had completed an exhausting but ultimately failed attempt to win a treble. The League and the European Cup were captured, but in between Liverpool lost the FA Cup final (when that competition was taken more seriously) to the club that was to achieve all three trophies in one season twenty-two years later, Manchester United.

Matches were played in ageing, dilapidated stadiums, and clubs thought silver service hospitality meant providing a clean gents toilet. The terraces were rough and uncovered. Other facilities – if you could find any – were appallingly primitive.

The football itself was, by today's standards, slower and intensely more physical: tackling back then was a legitimate form of grievous bodily harm. It was a miracle that the number of serious injuries wasn't greater than it was.

But the games themselves were just as compelling, and the players remained part of, rather than apart from, the localised community of supporters who watched them. I'd see players supping pints in the same pubs and clubs as fans on Thursday and Saturday nights. Thursday was particularly popular for a beery midweek session because there was only a light day of training on Friday. Some players, especially in the lower divisions, travelled to home games on the bus.

Long before pasta became a culinary staple of the professional's diet, footballers stuffed themselves on chips and well done steak for a pre-match meal and then gathered around the TV to watch *On The Ball* or *Football Focus* at lunchtime. Managers sat in dugouts wrapped in sheepskin coats and took training sessions wearing tightly fitting Umbro tracksuits. A few still smoked pipes.

Players didn't look like advertising billboards. They wore shirts with nothing but a number and the club badge stitched to them: no sponsor's name emblazoned on the front, no name decorating the back, no logo on the sleeve. Footballers' wives were likely to be found in part-time jobs to bolster the household income. You might occasionally see a wife photographed, not in a glossy magazine or on the fashion or 'celebrity' pages of the Sunday tabloids, but in a football weekly. These dreadfully cheesy 'at home' shots usually captured the husband in the kitchen pretending to wash up or cook while his wife stood decoratively behind him. The player looked distinctly out of place, as if he'd needed a map and a compass to find his way to the kitchen.

Like workers on the factory floor, or down the pit, the players deferred to managers. In the best cap-doffing tradition, the manager was always the 'boss' or the 'gaffer', as if he was running a building site. I addressed Clough as 'Mr', as if he was the headmaster of my comprehensive school.

Inside Clough's office, he sat me down in front of his vast desk, which was covered with mountains of paper. I laid my briefcase carefully on the floor. His glass-fronted bookcase held old copies of the *Rothmans Football Yearbook*, a black-spined history of mining and a picture atlas of the North-East. There was an empty kitbag in the corner of the room, a heap of training shoes and three squash rackets. An orange football lay behind the door next to a coat stand, on which Clough had hung a dark blazer. The only natural light came from a narrow window that ran the full length of the wall behind him and overlooked the back of the Main Stand.

'I'll get you a drink,' he said, disappearing along the corridor and reappearing a minute later with two goblets filled with orange juice. Of course, I didn't suspect then that his own might be spiked with alcohol. He closed the door, and then sat down and picked up one of the squash rackets and a ball that lay beside it. He began bouncing the ball on the strings of the racket.

'Now then, tell me again. Which paper do you work for, young man . . . ?'

I told him that I was writing for the *Nottingham Sport*. It was a weekly A4-sized newspaper (now long deceased), cheaply produced and so impecunious that it was unable to pay most of its contributors. I was working voluntarily, I explained. I had ambitions to become a newspaperman. I added that for the previous six months I'd telephoned the scores through to *Grandstand* and *World of Sport* on behalf of the local freelance agency and listened as professional writers dictated copy at the final whistle.

'So you want to be a journalist?' he asked, still bouncing the ball on the head of the racket, and then not waiting for an answer. 'I thought about being a journalist once – well, for about thirty seconds. Would have been brilliant at it too. Can't type, though. Can't spell either. Can you spell?'

I nodded. 'Yes,' I lied.

He plucked the squash ball out of the air. 'And what does your dad do? Is he a journalist?'

'He's a miner,' I replied.

'Votes Labour?' he asked.

'Always,' I said.

'What about your mam?'

'Works part-time.'

'Any brothers or sisters?'

'Just me.'

'Where were you born?'

'Newcastle.'

'Do you like any other sport.'

'Cricket.'

I wondered where all this was leading. Wasn't I supposed to be asking the questions? My palms began to sweat. I dragged them across the knees of my trousers, praying he wouldn't notice.

Clough dropped the squash racket and the ball and leaned forward, as if trying to get a closer look at me. The ball rolled off the edge of the desk and began to bounce towards the door. He pretended not to be bothered.

'Ooh,' he said, wagging his finger. 'Now that's a very good start with me young man . . . North-East, working background, cricket. I bet your mam has dinner on the table when you get back home. And I bet she cleans your shoes and makes sure you have an ironed shirt every morning.'

I nodded in agreement, ignorant then of how powerfully influential his own mother had been, how much his upbringing in part mirrored my own.

'Go on then,' he said, 'ask me a question. You've got twenty minutes. And we've just wasted two of them.' Clough leant back in the chair, plonked his feet on the corner of the desk and tucked his hands behind his head, as if he was settling down for a siesta.

I looked at him for a moment, half-expecting him to change his mind about speaking to me. He was just a few weeks short of his forty-second birthday, fit and vigorous. His hair was healthily thick and swept back, his face lean and virtually unlined, the eyes challenging and alive. That familiar piercing, nasal voice was an octave or two higher than it finally became; the result, of course, of being soaked in alcohol.

I put down my orange juice, fiddled inside my briefcase and brought out the thick new notebook. Staring at it, he said: 'I'm not filling all that for you!'

What struck me most back then was Clough's supreme confidence, as if he could actually see what lay ahead of him: the League championship and the European Cups and vindication. He had been through three and a half years of violent turbulence – a stupidly impetuous resignation at Derby, an ill-judged decision to manage Third Division Brighton, the forty-four days he spent nursing Don Revie's dubious inheritance at Leeds and the early traumas at struggling Forest – but he was well over the worst of it when I met him. He was swimming with the current again, and back with Peter Taylor. Forest were fifth in the Second Division. Promotion was seventeen matches away.

The wilderness period changed him, he told me many times later. Each embarrassed step through it taught him career-altering lessons. After Derby he learnt that resigning on a whim led to remorse and regret. After Brighton he learnt to be more careful about his career choices, for going there had been as grievous a mistake as leaving Derby. But it was at Leeds that his most profound transformation took place. He learnt that he needed Taylor beside him, that his abrasive approach had to be tempered, and, crucially, that personal wealth – and a lot of it – was more important than ever. He made a financially jewelled exit, which he repeatedly claimed to me was worth almost £100,000 (the equivalent today of around £850,000). However much he got, the money was critical to the way he managed his career later on.

Whenever Leeds came up in conversation – even in the season before he retired from Forest – Clough never tired of talking about both the raw anger he felt towards them, for what he regarded as the spineless collapse of the board at the first sign of player revolt, and the size of the pay-off he had been given.

Why Clough accepted the offer to manage Leeds isn't difficult to fathom. Brighton had high ambitions but low resources. The club was going nowhere. Achieving success for them, he said to me on more than one occasion, was 'like asking Lester Piggott to win the Derby on a Skegness donkey'. The nadir was Brighton's 4–0 defeat to the part-timers of Walton & Hersham in an FA Cup replay. 'I lost to a team that sounded like a firm of solicitors,' he moaned.

Clough had panicked after leaving Derby: 'I had too much time to think – and not enough brain to think with' was the line he always used. He missed the glitz of the First Division. When Leeds rang him after Revie's predictable appointment as England manager, it was like dropping a rope ladder to a man adrift at sea. Of course, Clough snatched at it.

He abhorred Revie and regarded Leeds, then League champions, as insular and rotten. But there was a perverse attraction in managing the club he had remorselessly criticised for half a dozen years or more. He accused them of being cheats and charlatans, cursed them for their gamesmanship. But now he would teach them how football ought to be played. He would do what Revie could not, and in the process, gain his revenge over the club.

Why Leeds picked Clough is beyond comprehension. His rapid sacking confirmed their gross error in appointing him in the first place. It was possibly the most ludicrously misguided hiring of a manager ever made by a football club's board of directors. Revie managed methodically. He compiled dossiers and thought intently about the intricacies of the opposition. Clough managed through gut instinct. He dismissed dossiers as frippery and did not think, let alone talk, about opposition strengths or weaknesses. Revie prepared everything for Leeds, from travel to pre-match meals. Clough prepared almost nothing at all. He liked to 'wing it', as he told me.

For Revie, the matter of his succession was as straightforward as ABC: *Anyone But Clough*. He suggested either Bobby Robson as an external candidate, or Johnny Giles from within the existing staff. In appointing Clough, the Leeds board voted for seismic upheaval rather than calm continuity. The new manager did everything wrong. The very worst traits of Clough's personality – the arrogant swagger, the confrontational manner, the insouciant impatience – all came to the surface.

Clough was still on holiday in Majorca when the team reported back for pre-season training – his first mistake. He found the dressing room wildly suspicious of him and almost uniformly hostile. His meagre placatory efforts, such as a telegram to the captain Billy Bremner, were viewed as patronising. It got worse too: a Charity Shield sending off for Bremner, just four points from six League matches, a rushed decision to try to sell players – Terry Cooper, David Harvey and Trevor Cherry among them – and, at the end, what amounted to a vote of no confidence in him. 'The players,' he complained, 'have more meetings than the union at Ford.'

The vote was hardly any wonder. At his first team meeting, he told the players to 'chuck your medals on the table – 'cos you won 'em by cheating.' When I asked him about it, he was unrepentant: 'Well, I meant it.' Clough had to go, and go he did – with his pride punctured but with his wallet bulging.

Shortly after his sacking, I remember watching Clough being interviewed on TV alongside Revie. The hostility between them was lightning in the air; a decade of stored-up grievances added to the tension within the studio: Clough hated Revie, and Revie was appalled at what Clough had done in his brief tenure at Leeds.

Clough told me that he began to 'hate' Revie when he discovered him colluding with a referee after a match. Clough was convinced that Revie had 'nobbled' the referee. He had gone to watch Leeds and visited Revie in his office afterwards. He was standing behind the door, out of sight, when the referee tapped on it. Clough recalled: 'I heard the ref say to Revie, "Was that all right for you, Mr Revie?"' Revie, Clough added, said a nervous 'marvellous' in reply and waved him away, like a lord dismissing his butler. He carried on talking to Clough as if nothing had happened. 'There was something about it that told me the ref had been given something – and given Revie something in return,' said Clough. 'I knew Revie was bent.'

Clough won the TV contest comfortably on points, his mind too nimble for the ponderous Revie, who had neither the speed nor the wit to defend himself. He merely sounded ridiculous, and so protective of Leeds that you wondered why he had ever left them.

REVIE: Why did you come from Brighton to Leeds to take over when you criticised us so much and said we should be in the Second Division, and that we should do this and we should do that. Why did you take the job?

CLOUGH: Because I thought it was the best job in the country ... I wanted to do something you hadn't done ... I want[ed] to win the League but I want[ed] to win it better than you.

REVIE: There is no way to win it better ... We only lost four matches.

CLOUGH: Well, I could only lose three.

At that moment a question mark appeared across the folds of Revie's face. He struggled to absorb the basic logic of what Clough had just said. A whole minute seemed to pass before the ordinary common sense of it dropped into Revie's brain. He groped blindly for a half-adequate reply. The best he could offer was a tame smile and then: 'No, no, no.'

The surge of relief Clough experienced when he banked Leeds' money, and had recovered from what he regarded as the 'trauma' of his brutal treatment there, carried him through his first, bleakly depressing months at Forest. It was the seminal moment of his managerial career, which I always split into two: before the cheque from Leeds and after it.

I believe Leeds' cash was more critical to his development than what happened to him on a frosty Boxing Day 1962 at Roker Park, when his playing career was abruptly ended in the last stride of a chase for a fifty-fifty ball. Clough slipped on the rock-hard pitch and slid into the Bury goalkeeper Chris Harker. Bone collided with bone. Clough broke his leg and snapped his cruciate ligaments. With twenty-four goals for Sunderland, he was then the leading scorer in all four Divisions.

In psychological terms, his forced retirement as a player – he was approaching twenty-seven when the injury occurred – is often cited simplistically as Clough's turning point. It's as if a player died and a manager was born in that moment, a career reignited by the rocket fuel of rage and injustice, a belief that he had something else to prove and needed to do it urgently. Irrespective of his injury, I'm sure Clough would have become a manager, and cast himself in the same opinionated, single-minded mould. That black Christmas merely sped up the process. But what management could never do was alleviate the crushing disappointment of unfulfilled potential.

One sunlit morning on a pre-season tour of Holland, I was standing with Clough as he watched a Forest training session. The players had finished their preliminary jogging exercises and had begun shooting at goal, the net billowing like a sail.

He began to reflect wistfully. 'I'd give anything for one more season as a player, you know. If I could turn the clock back, that's what I'd do. You never, ever lose the thrill of watching your own shot go past the goalkeeper, of putting on your boots and tying the laces, of feeling the studs press into the turf or hearing the sound of the ball as you hit it and watch it fly, like a golf shot. I try to tell 'em – every player I get – to enjoy every single minute of their career. 'Cos you never know when it might end, in less than a second. You only have to be unlucky once. Like me.'

I became convinced that Clough had a phobia about looking at players in plaster casts and on crutches. I could see him physically recoil from them, as if remembering his own experience. I asked him about it when we were drinking in a hotel one Friday evening. I'd drunk too much so I didn't care. 'I spent enough time on crutches to know that I never want to see a pair of them again,' he replied, and ended the conversation as if he was shutting the lid of a box. I didn't broach the issue again.

With Leeds' cash, Clough became one of the first – and certainly the youngest – of any generation of managers to achieve, at a stroke, financial independence. He described it to me (though not on that first afternoon) as 'fuck you' money. 'For the first time in my life, if I didn't like anything that was going on I could turn around and say "Fuck you, I'm off".'

Clough played in the days of club houses. These were residential properites owned by the clubs and rented to a player for a paltry amount. The house was handed back when the player moved on, retired, or, often calamitously, was released at the end of a season into an uncertain future. He played in the days of the maximum wage, not broken until 1961, when most players needed a trade as well, perhaps plastering or plumbing, and could hardly afford to run a car let alone buy one (Clough's first weekly wage packet was £2.50; when he signed full-time he got £7.00). He played in the days when most of those who moved into management were almost as impecunious as their players, and lived as modestly as other working-class people.

I quickly discovered that he was obsessed with money, as if he feared he might wake up one morning and find himself a pauper again. He was always, I felt, trying to protect himself against the possibility of it happening. That's why he took on so much media and advertising work. He would read out to me the salaries of other people – players, managers, pop and film stars, politicians – if he came across them in a newspaper. And he was constantly pushing for increases to his basic pay. I'm also certain that his fear of future poverty explains why he became embroiled in backhanders, or 'bungs'. It wasn't purely greed, but a form of self-protection against the dreadful insecurity he felt. Money was his armour-plating against life's hardships.

I am sure it all stemmed from the 'make do and mend' of his upbringing. He came from a big family, with a lot of mouths to feed and a lot of clothes to wash. He was poor, working-class. You got an orange and a shiny new penny in your stocking at Christmas, and were grateful for it. 'When you're brought up like that, always fretting about paying the bills, it colours how you feel about life, the way you regard money, and how you view the importance of it as security,' he said. 'I found that the only people who aren't obsessed with money are those who have got more than enough of it.'

But once he had 'enough', he gave a lot away, and did so without ever being showy about it. Sometimes he carried a fat wad of notes in the pocket of his tracksuit trousers. One lunch-time I was walking back with him from the Italian restaurant on Trent Bridge. In the City Ground's car park we came across a father and son walking away from the ticket office. The son was about eleven years old. The knees of his black trousers were shiny, the shirt cuffs threadbare, and the toes of his shoes were scuffed from kicking a ball around the streets. His father, a tall, balding man in a worn grey suit, politely approached Clough for an autograph. His son, he explained, was desperate to watch a match. He'd saved his own pocket money from a newspaper round and odd jobs so he could buy the ticket himself. Clough shook him by the hand and then reached into his pocket. He drew out two £20 notes. 'Son,' he said, 'stick these in your piggy bank.' The boy could barely speak with gratitude. 'Enjoy yourself,' said Clough, and strolled off.

Even though, with Taylor, Clough had won the title at Derby in 1972, and made money from a considerable amount of TV work – also turning down an offer of £18,000 a year to work full-time for London Weekend Television in the early 1970s – he was never financially secure until Leeds' six-figure gift. After that, he said, he was the 'richest bloke in the dole queue.' He felt as if he had won the football pools without filling in the coupon. 'It was champagne instead of Tizer.'

All this came at a personal cost. At Leeds his ego took a battering. There were mornings when he woke up and thought, 'Will I ever win another title, or get the chance to win one?' and nights when he couldn't sleep because he was turning over in his mind what had happened to him, what had gone wrong in a footballing sense and whether he could have changed anything.

So what Forest got in January 1975 was a chastened but maturely reflective Clough; less strident, and in not so much of a hurry.

Having thought about recruiting Clough after his resignation from Derby, Forest's pusillanimous dithering two years earlier worked in his favour. 'Everyone thought Taylor and I would go to Forest then – 'cos it was on our doorstep, 'cos the club was in the shit and 'cos we were out of work. But they were too scared of us to do anything. Good thing too. I might have said yes, and then I'd never have had a cheque the size of a stately home from Leeds,' he said, laughing loudly when I sat with him to write a piece about his tenth anniversary at Forest.

Apart from the geographical advantages the job offered, Nottingham being roughly twenty miles from Clough's home in Derby, Forest were unappealing: a rusting tugboat of a club with leaks everywhere – thirteenth in the Second Division, with plenty of seats that hadn't regularly seen a backside for years. The average gate was around 12,000, and Forest were sinking slowly under the unimaginative Allan Brown, who left sourly: 'The board want Clough – good luck to them,' were his parting words.

Brown was wrong. Not every member of the board hung out the bunting. The chairman, Jim Wilmer, was unconvinced, chiefly because he was so worried about the new manager's temper. With deliberate care, like someone wary that his own words might come back to bite him, Wilmer called Clough 'an energetic young man with an exciting background'. There is a photograph of Wilmer shaking Clough's hand on his arrival. A lopsided smile is fixed rigidly on the chairman's face, as if drawn by an apprentice make-up artist.

Forest, like Clough, were terribly out of fashion. The club had won the FA Cup in 1959 under the avuncular Billy Walker, manager for twenty-one years. Jimmy Carey's 'fizz it about' side – Ian Storey-Moore, Henry Newton, Terry Hennessey – narrowly lost out on the Championship in 1967 and were beaten in the FA Cup semi-final that same year. What followed was a downhill slither: relegation, disillusion, despair, and five managers in just over seven years – striking for a club which, priding itself on stability, had only employed three managers between 1939 and 1968. Apathy set in, and with it a tacit acceptance that each season was to be endured, and that Forest would again never compete successfully with Derby.

Clough at last brought light to the City Ground's dark corners; a feeling that something good was on the way. I saved a cartoon that appeared in the *Daily Express* on the day of his appointment. It showed Clough walking on water. He is jauntily crossing the river beside the City Ground, his feet throwing up fingers of spray. The caption reads: 'It's ideal from where I live, it's just down the River Trent and I'm at the Forest ground.'

He arrived, more prosaically, in another of Leeds' generous parting gifts: a Mercedes. 'I've left the human race and rejoined the rat race,' he said provocatively, a smart line which also implied that signing his contract at Forest was an act of self-sacrifice rather than an escape from the stark isolation of unemployment. There was, very briefly, a mutual dependence between club and manager. For all his bullishness, Clough had to prove himself again and Forest risked falling through three Divisions if he failed.

The City Ground was just like the rest of football's dilapidated architecture in the mid-1970s: a bank of unwelcoming, uncovered terracing at one end, a low, rattling tin roof for protection at the other. The East Stand had hard, wooden flat boards for seats, and the wind came off the Trent and swept through it like a scythe. Only the Main Stand, rebuilt after a fire in 1968, gave a slight nod to modernity.

Nottingham was a coal-mining county, slag heaps and skeletal headgears rising out of the clay earth to the north and south. The nearest coal mine was less than five miles from the

City Ground (today it is mostly acres of empty grass), and my father worked in it. The National Coal Board advertisement in the Forest programme proclaimed: 'Mining means business'. Raleigh still turned out bikes at its factory in Triumph Road, and Nottingham's filigree lace was still among the finest in the world. The Thatcherite revolution, like Clough's own, lay in the future. The daily news was dominated by stories about strikes and industrial action.

I bought every newspaper that I could afford. In the Daily Express, I read that Forest had sold £4,000 worth of season tickets in the first twelve days after Clough's appointment. I read a piece in which he said 'Hope is all I can offer,' and meant it. I read the list of the players who had been sold, scattering Carey's side across the First Division, and Clough's response to it: 'Forest collected £1m in transfer fees for them. But it's been the £1m failure. There is only one thing in the club's favour now. It's got me.'

His first signing wasn't a player. He sold a ghosted article to a national newspaper and bought a cooker with the money. 'Well,' he said, explaining himself, 'the one the club had was knackered. But, frankly, I nearly picked it for the team 'cos it was better than most of the squad.'

I went to his first home League game, a 2–2 draw against Orient, wrapped in a parka. I didn't support Forest. My father was obsessive about Newcastle, where I was born and then lived until we moved to Nottingham after his pit closed in the early 1960s. I was brought up on Milburn and Mitchell, and later, on Moncur and Macdonald. But Clough's story was irresistible to me. I went to see the man rather than the team. I was just 16 years old, and squeezed myself in behind the goal at the old Bridgford End. In the crush of bodies, I could barely see over the top of the white perimeter wall. I heard the crowd's reaction to Clough well before I spotted him, a pencil dot in the distance, as he waved like royalty to them.

Clough came to Forest alone. Taylor, who was born less than mile from the City Ground, was still in Brighton, uninterested in contributing towards the rehabilitation both of Forest and his former partner.

'I knew it would be bad at Forest. I just didn't know how awful,' Clough admitted to me well after the Championship and two European Cups had been won. 'Our training ground was about as attractive as Siberia in midwinter without your coat on, our training kit looked like something you got from the Oxfam shop. We barely had a player in the first team who I thought could play – or, at least, take us on a stage. I even had to teach one of them how to take a throw-in. I also had to teach them to dress smartly, take their hands out of their pockets and stop slouching. Early on, I thought I'd dropped a right bollock. To cap it all, I got pneumonia and spent a week or so in bed. I'm telling you, we could have been relegated in my first season. We were that close to it.' He picked up a white sheet of paper and ran his finger along its edge. 'We'd have almost deserved it too. We were useless.'

What saved Forest was Clough's belief in himself, and the knowledge that failure again – while it would be personally and critically damaging – was never going to lead to the poorhouse. The money from Leeds enabled him to look at things with a surgeon's exacting eye.

'I was – though probably only Jimmy Gordon (Forest's trainer, lured out of retirement) noticed it on a daily basis – more relaxed. I was a wee bit more subdued for a while – just a while, mind you – in what I said publicly.'

Clough said that when he got home at night after a 'rotten' day, he just had to look at his bank book to realise that he was fireproof. For the first time in management, he told me he actually showed a bit of patience. 'I knew, if we just rolled up our sleeves and bought the right players, we'd be fine eventually.'

My first interview with Clough didn't yield much. In fact, it was awful. Those questions I had so painstakingly typed out were just too predictable and naive.

As I spoke, he went to retrieve the squash ball and began bouncing it on the racquet again. When he got bored, he put the racquet down and began shuffling the papers on his desk. I wondered why he had agreed to do an interview with a teenager he had never met and for a newspaper he'd apparently never read.

I dutifully took down notes in my improvised shorthand and wrote up the piece back at the kitchen table among the scents and steam of a Sunday lunch. I retyped it a dozen times.

Clough declared he wanted to play entertainingly, called Peter Taylor 'the best spotter of talent' he had ever seen, and lamented Forest's meagre gates because, he argued, 'the people of Nottingham wanted [success] handed to them on a plate.'

As I left, he said: 'Come back and see me soon, son. Have a Scotch next time. You'll enjoy it.'

CHAPTER TWO

The shop window ... and the goods at the back

Brian Clough and Peter Taylor were locked into a marriage and behaved like an eccentric married couple. That is a glib but accurate analogy for a relationship which, by the time of its slow collapse, had grown complex, bitter roots. From the moment the two of them met as players at Middlesbrough in the mid-1950s until their eventual divorce, their relationship would experience the ups and downs of any real marriage.

At first there was the cupid's arrow of courtship: Taylor, older by almost seven years, let it be known around Middlesbrough's training ground that Clough was in his eyes the best player at the club. He described him, in a voice loud enough for Clough to hear, as underrated and unappreciated.

Clough was the fourth-choice (sometimes fifth) centre forward in 1955. He was a young man with a crew cut and a sharp tongue, ostensibly self-assured, who rubbed up Middlesbrough's management and dressing room the wrong way with his brazen and conceited approach. In Taylor, Clough found what he had been lacking: an ally, a kindred spirit and a teacher-cum-father-figure. Taylor found what he had been lacking too: Clough was a disciple to preach to, a one-man congregation prepared to listen to Taylor's sermons on football.

Second came the 'dating', as Taylor broadened Clough's foot-balling, social and even political education. Politics and social welfare were important subjects for Taylor. He was particularly conscious of the pay and conditions of the average working man, the distribution of wealth and a rigid class system that, amid the conformity of the 1950s, looked unbreakable to him unless a party of the left (not necessarily Labour) became cap-able of winning elections consistently. Taylor laid down his political credo to Clough. 'He was slightly to the left of Labour in those days,' said Clough. 'Even Clem Attlee hadn't been rad-ical enough for him. He wanted the ship-builders to earn as much as the ship-owners. He thought the miners were treated like skivvies. He felt the steel-workers got a rough deal. He wanted the Tories out. The only thing we ever talked about, aside from football, was politics 'cos we agreed on it.' One Sunday afternoon Taylor took Clough to listen to the then Shadow Chancellor Harold Wilson speak at a working man's club in Middlesbrough. 'You could hear the passion for change in what he said,' Clough remembered. 'We went back to Taylor's house burning with it ourselves.'

Taylor and Clough – for at this stage Taylor was, very briefly, the senior partner – were united by four things: a working-class background, a passion for the game and an unshakeable convic-tion about the style in which it ought to be played, a dislike of authority and obsequious behaviour (except towards them) and, most significantly, the shared belief that Clough was supremely talented.

Taylor saw in Clough much more than the predatory instincts required of a goalscorer. He instantly registered, in that com-puter-like brain of his, Clough's good positioning, his skill both on and off the ball, and his ability to strike it exceptionally hard

43

with a minimum of backlift. Scoring unexpectedly with shots from the edge of the box and beyond came to him so easily. 'He could launch rockets,' Taylor told me.

Clough went through his footballing adolescence at Middlesbrough, where life was plotted on a graph of struggle versus hardship. Looking back, Clough saw that period in soft focus, and, after his dreadful falling-out with Taylor, in a forgiving light.

More than a year after the sadness of Taylor's abrupt death in October 1990, but with the shock of it still evident in his voice, Clough sat in the chairman's room at the City Ground and reminisced about what life had been like for both of them in a tough town in the North-East. He was drinking a pot of tea and had ordered a round of sandwiches. There were only the two of us in the room, which had low, orange leather seating on opposite walls and a drinks cabinet. The furniture design belonged to the 1960s. Outside, I could hear fans talking to one another in the car park as the autumn skies darkened. When the sandwiches arrived, cellophane-wrapped on a silver tray, there were enough for six people.

'Bloody hell,' said Clough. 'We could have fed Middlesbrough in the 1950s on that lot.' It was if the phrase 'Middlesbrough in the 1950s' was enough to transport him back there. Clough removed the cellophane, took a sandwich in each hand and gestured to me to do the same. He perched himself on the edge of his seat, and began to talk. Although I was sitting directly across from him, he didn't look at me.

'We had nowt back then – except a belief in ourselves,' he said. 'No money, no car. A trip to the pictures was the social event of the week. A new coat was a major investment. I could barely scrape together the money for one.'

He saw men who had slaved for decades at the same factory become bent and worn down by the daily grind of work. He appreciated how fortunate he was to be a footballer and not trapped in a numbing and mundane occupation. He appreciated as well how much football meant to the people who came to watch him – 'all of 'em wanting to be you'.

On Saturdays, he said, the same men would go to the match, then head for 'the boozer', and afterwards pick up fish and chips on the way home. 'If they could manage it, there was probably a bit of rolling around on the bed with the wife and then snoring for ten hours,' he added.

Middlesbrough in the 1950s was the archetypal working-class town. But as nostalgia gripped him, Clough began to call it 'our golden time', the years in which everything and anything seemed possible for him and Taylor.

'When you're young and daft and big-headed like I was,' he said, 'you don't mind going through a few tough times because you know, deep inside yourself, that you're going to make it. That's how I felt – and then I found that Pete thought so too. You didn't normally find pearls in Middlesbrough. I did, the day when I met Pete for the first time.'

Clough and I kept eating, but the heap of sandwiches didn't shrink much. As he poured both of us a beer in long glasses, he described Taylor's unflinching support after many of Middlesbrough's first team had signed a petition against the decision to make Clough captain at twenty-three. He remembered Taylor's strength and resolve on his behalf during the rebellion when there was 'nowt in it for him – except friendship'. He also remembered going regularly to Taylor's home, which he used as a refuge cum safe haven. He told me he felt comfortable there. 'It was one of the few places I could totally relax – away from absolutely everything. I could say what I liked. At home (Clough was still living with his parents) you still minded your p's and q's.'

Clough began to shake his head, as if trying to stir a memory he had long ago forgotten. After a pause, he said that he was thinking whether anything, such as winning the Championship or the European Cup, had ever come close to the exhilaration he had felt at making his way in the world, and the sense of expectation he and Taylor experienced at Middlesbrough. 'If only we could go back,' he mused, 'relive it . . . see the way things used to be, we'd be more grateful for what we've got now. I know one thing: we'd never have fallen out.'

I believe that Clough was drawn back into the past because the present was getting too uncomfortable for him to contemplate – Forest were now sinking towards relegation. Having spent a decade forcefully pointing out that he could survive and prosper on his own, and arguing that Taylor, a racing buff, wasted too much of his time studying form in the *Sporting Life*, Clough began to recant. The man he had regularly referred to tersely as 'Taylor', as though the word itself might choke him unless he spat it out quickly, was now always 'Pete'. No longer was Taylor a 'lazy bugger' who 'didn't pull his weight' and sloped off home early or went to the races rather than scouting for talent or watching the opposition. Instead of talking purely about himself, he began to use phrases such as 'the two of us' and 'what we did together' and 'our teamwork'.

By this time, of course, Clough's managerial career was beginning to slip away from him, and just as it had when Taylor died, the important role his former partner played now assumed a greater significance. Clough was always bluntly honest with me about what attracted him to Taylor: hardly anyone else believed in him. 'At first Middlesbrough thought I was crap – too mouthy, too awkward. The club used that as an excuse not to see what I could do on the pitch. I was too much bother for them. When you're being ignored or dismissed, and then you hear someone singing a song about you somewhere in the far distance, the way Pete did about me, you want to hear it.'

Clough and Taylor became inseparable, and the talk between them was constantly about football: tactics, teams, players, coaching methods. As a management duo they tolerated various barbed sobriquets: The Kray Twins, The Blood Brothers, The Brothers Grim. But at Middlesbrough, Clough and Taylor were just friends obsessed with football. Taylor told Clough that there were things he had to learn about the game, and about life. 'Nothing separated us in those early days – it was the closest we ever came as friends,' said Clough.

Like a professor escorting a student on a field trip, Taylor led him to matches where the two of them stood behind one of the goals to study tactics and pass judgement on other players, deciding who could play and who couldn't. When other professionals might be out 'boozing it or birding it', as Clough put it, or sitting in card schools to make a 'few bob', Clough and Taylor would be 'sitting in Pete's front room or in a café, pushing the salt and pepper round the table and talking about tactics.'

'Hey, you'd be staggered at how many footballers aren't interested in football,' Clough told me. 'You'd see them nip off to the snooker hall or to the bookies or just go home and lie on the sofa. That was never, ever our way. We were preparing ourselves for management even then.'

And that is why the third stage in their relationship, the marriage, took place. Like a lot of other marriages, there were long periods of happy-ever-after bliss and doting, loving respect; later came arguments, jealousy, envy and pernickety point-scoring, which led to separations and cold silences. Finally, there was the acrimonious divorce, an undignified squabble over what – among their trophy-winning legacy – belonged to whom, and the mutual feeling of hurt, damaged egos.

This was never a marriage of equals, and Taylor knew it. Clough was soon the dominant partner. Far more articulate, far more adept at promoting himself and far more comfortable in his own skin, he was consistently the more popular of the two of them – for journalists demanding quotes, for supporters wanting an idol, for other clubs in search of a coach or manager. In management it was always 'Clough and Taylor', never the other way round. Once Clough had begun his prolific goalscoring – he claimed 197 League goals in 213 matches for Middlesbrough, and another 54 in 61 for Sunderland – Taylor was locked into his crucial supportive and advisory role, and his salary never matched his partner's.

However much Clough referred to him as 'my mate' and 'my blood brother', however much he described him in generous terms such as 'I'm the shop window – he's the goods at the back', or 'Pete's the brains', much of it, especially towards the end, was no more than an attempt to placate Taylor. Clough viewed himself as the head of the firm, and he wanted everyone else to recognise it.

While Clough was regularly the subject of newspaper and magazine profiles, and appeared on TV, Taylor stayed mostly in the background. On one occasion I was sitting with Taylor high in the stand watching a reserves match on a bitterly cold night when the was wind so strong that the roof shook. Taylor was wearing his scarf and flat cap, his raincoat collar pulled up round his neck. His alert eyes darted across the pitch. After every player had touched the ball at least once, Taylor delivered his clinical assessment of each of them: speed, positioning, best foot, weaknesses. It was a fascinating experience being with him and watching just how expertly he read the game.

Taylor didn't want to live his life, like Clough's, in a blaze of neon headlines. It discomforted him. He was all tics and facial expressions: a twist of the mouth, a widening of the eyes, an expansive hand gesture. When he was nervous or ill at ease, or just thoughtful, he would push his tongue into his cheek. He avoided crowds and was constantly nervous about being recognised. He didn't like going into restaurants or pubs in case he was pestered. Sometimes I had to go inside first to discover how many tables were occupied.

I know he didn't particularly enjoy confronting the knot of back-slapping supporters who waited for autographs outside the City Ground after matches. I saw him do anything to avoid it. Whereas Clough was fluent in small talk, Taylor found it difficult to communicate with strangers. I would listen to him struggle to find a casual line to begin a conversation.

The narcissistic streak in Clough was buttressed by his actorly expertise. He didn't mind being gawped at or pointed out – in fact, he wanted it that way. Taylor preferred the company of his family and the people he knew. He liked solitary walks with his dog or a quiet day at the races. He did, however, expect credit when and where it was due.

Sometimes I think I grossly underestimated Taylor's sensitivities. As a journalist, I knew that one quote from Clough was worth two of Taylor's. I would often interview Taylor first, as insurance, and then hang around for Clough to garnish the story. Taylor once asked me, 'Are my words not good enough

49

for you?' in a tone that suggested he knew the answer. He walked away shaking his head.

To see Clough and Taylor together, however, especially when both were in their pomp, was to witness two people of one mind. One would begin a sentence, the other finished it; one would espouse a theory, the other affirm it. One would attack or praise someone and the other took up the argument, splicing his thoughts into the narrative so seamlessly that it became impossible to disentangle their words.

At their most convivial, I imagined them as a polished comedy double act. But I could also picture them as good cop and bad cop, sharing a conspiratorial smile and interrogating their victim in a claustrophobic box of a room with a naked light bulb hanging from the ceiling.

To look back over the partnership is to appreciate how the foundations of their management philosophy were laid in the bleakness of Middlesbrough and Hartlepool, built up at Derby, and topped out at Nottingham Forest. An unmistakable pattern emerges of the way teams and players were assessed, a stranglehold gained over the board of directors and publicity ingeniously garnered. In style and method, the Clough and Taylor at Hartlepool in 1965 were much the same as the Clough and Taylor who sat pitch-side at Munich's Olympic Stadium fourteen years later watching Forest win the European Cup.

Simplicity was the heart of it, because the game itself was simpler then, far less sophisticated tactically. That is why Hartlepool, down in the Fourth Division, were managed exactly like Derby's or Forest's Championship winners.

Clough outlined to me how the two of them approached the job. Team talks were brief and uncomplicated. There were no thick dossiers on the opposition, no blackboards (or 'black-bores', as Clough called them), no diagrams to follow, no fret-ting about what tactics the other side might use. Those who could tackle were told to win the ball and pass it to 'someone who can play – 'cos that's yer job'. Everything was explained as if Clough and Taylor were teaching the rudiments of the alpha-bet. A 'spine' ran down the team – the best goalkeeper, centre half and centre forward the partnership could afford. The ball always had to be passed, never indiscriminately hoofed, and done without fuss – 'linear' and pure. There was an obsession with clean sheets, the words chanted like a religious mantra. The team had to be disciplined. 'If you get booked, you'll get a kick straight up the arse the second you're within range of me,' was Clough's threat. He didn't want crude cloggers, he wanted tacklers who won the ball so fiercely that no one would come near them for ninety minutes.

With Hartlepool, and later at Derby, Clough and Taylor methodically set about the task of rebuilding. Clough's mega-phone approach to publicity went alongside Taylor's unobtrus-ive gathering of knowledge – observing the quirks and habits of players, scouting, and promptly recommending who might be bought, who should be sold. For Taylor it was a question of combining common sense with psychology to judge the mood of an individual or a specific situation and predict what would happen next. Players were psyched up or psyched out depending on the circumstances. 'We goaded some, we built up others – everything was done to an instinctive plan,' Clough told me. But mostly Clough would do what was least expec-ted of him. If a player thought he was going to be praised, he would get a bollocking. If he thought he was going to get a bollocking, Clough would send his wife chocolates and flowers.

The partnership was based on need and faith. The keystone was that Taylor could – and regularly did – tell Clough when he was in the wrong, when he was close to overstepping the mark, or when he was in danger of making a horrendous spectacle of himself. Had Taylor been at Leeds to take the temperature of the club, I know Clough wouldn't have blundered around like a novice, falling into traps of his own making. Had Taylor been around in Forest's final season, when Clough was ruined by drink, his judgement shot, I'm convinced he would have ushered him into early retirement well before it became inevitable.

'Pete', said Clough, 'was the only bloke who could stick an arm around my shoulder and tell me – straightforwardly, mate to mate – that I was wrong, or right, or to shut up and just get on with my job. When I rang him to say I'd got Hartlepool, and did he fancy it, we'd barely spoken for four years. We'd gone our different ways, taken separate paths out of necessity. We were football people, and, like the circus, sometimes you have to travel to scrape a living. But I knew I needed him. I knew we were right together.'

Clough and Taylor were not the first management team in the Football League. Matt Busby leant on Jimmy Murphy, Don Revie used Syd Owen as a sounding board, and Liverpool's bootroom staff were the cabinet to Bill Shankly's Prime Minister. But Clough and Taylor were the first to publicly formalise the arrangement and to make it clear, whatever the respective titles of manager and coach/assistant/trainer, that two men, not one, were running the club.

Taylor was like a protective skin for Clough. When Hartlepool recruited Clough, his playing career was over, and Sunderland –

citing spurious financial difficulties – had already released him as youth coach. 'I wasn't at my best,' he was frank enough to admit. He was 'down', and 'there wasn't much confidence left in the tank'.

Clough was afraid of a lot of things back then: 'mostly', he told me, 'of failing, and of being labelled a failure, and of wondering how I would cope with it'. We were talking about a fear we shared. We were at Nottingham's East Midlands Airport, waiting for a flight to be called, and he caught me taking a drink from a miniature gin bottle.

'I don't like flying,' I confessed. 'I'm petrified of it.'

'I know how you feel, pal,' he said, pointing at the bottle. 'Let me have a swig.' I was well aware of Clough's anxiety about flying. He was always fidgety and nervous before boarding a plane.

He sat down beside me. 'It's not the most scary thing, though, is it? It's whether you've got enough money to live on to feed your wife and bairns. Now that is scary . . . and I remember when . . .' That's when Clough's time between Sunderland and Hartlepool flickered into the conversation. It deflected our thoughts away from the flight we were about to take. Witnessing my agitation over flying seemed to lessen Clough's own apprehension about the journey. In trying to calm me down, he calmed himself down too, and we both felt better for it. Mind you, the gin helped.

I think about that now because, in much the same way, Taylor calmed Clough with his presence. Clough was asked in 1983 to name the chief influence on his career. 'Me,' he said, without hesitation. It was a flip answer to a searching question.

In reality, he borrowed heavily from two men: Alan Brown (not to be confused with Clough's predecessor at Forest, who spelt his name with a double l) and Harry Storer.

Storer had been manager at Coventry when Taylor played there as a goalkeeper. Under Taylor's influence, Clough became Storer-like. There are two vignettes, which I heard recited time and again by Clough, which perfectly demonstrate the manner Storer adopted and why his players learned to expect the unexpected, the one-liner that might demolish them like a slap in the face.

After one game Storer had hauled a player back on to the pitch and shot him a question:

'Where is it?'

'Where's what?' the player asked, bemused.

'The hole you disappeared into for ninety minutes,' snapped Storer. 'It has to be here somewhere.'

Storer once gave a trial to a trainee hairdresser. He pulled him aside afterwards and told him to sell his boots and buy another pair of scissors.

Clough gleaned from Storer nuggets of wisdom and followed them like commandments from the Old Testament:

- Directors know nothing about football.
- Directors never say thank you (no matter what you do for them).
- Directors are essentially untrustworthy, so don't make them your friends.
- Buy players who show courage.

Taylor also took away a rich inheritance from Storer. Like Storer, Taylor's antennae learnt to pick up tell-tale psychological signs about players. He would notice the way someone

54

walked or carried his bag, or sat on the bench beneath his kit-peg, or offered a throwaway, apparently trivial comment as he came in. Nothing, Clough maintained, was innocent or meaningless to Taylor. The nuance of everything mattered. It was as if, he added, the man had X-ray vision. 'He was brilliant at it,' said Clough. 'It was almost as if he could read minds. He'd nudge me and say, 'So and so needs picking up – can't you see the droop of his shoulders?' Or, 'That bloke is too cocky by half. He needs yanking down a peg or two.' Or even, 'I think it's time we gave the lad over there a day off.' He could twig a group of players at fifty paces, who had guts and who didn't, just by looking at them.

In Storer and Alan Brown, the manager who bought him for Sunderland, Clough saw managers who circumnavigated directors by running the club themselves as much as possible, and he imitated them. Brown's influence on Clough was particularly deep. Brown was tough and implacably strict. He created his own set of uncompromising rules governing conduct off and on the pitch, and the squad obeyed or suffered; in just the same way, Clough made his players meekly comply to his own rules. Players had to be smart, polite and obedient. Hair had to be short, preferably like an army crew cut.

There were times throughout his management career, said Clough, when he 'wished Alan Brown was beside me ... I'd have got a straight answer to any question – and it would have been the right one too. I know a lot of managers who have been kind enough to say I influenced them. Well, Alan Brown influenced me because I respected him so much. And he scared me half to death. You didn't want to be on the end of one of his bollockings. The first thing he ever said to me was, "You may have heard that I'm a bastard ... well, they're right." And yes, he could be. But he was a brilliant one.'

There is no secret to running a club, argued Clough, as though it was obvious to anyone. Brown had shown him the way. It was Brown who forced the Sunderland first team to act as ball boys for the youth side. It was Brown who yanked Clough, on his first day at Sunderland, off the touchline of the training pitch for talking to a friend and publicly dressed him down for it, like a schoolboy caught with matches in his pocket. It was Brown who made him brew the tea. What Brown did at Sunderland, Clough incorporated into own his management style. For him, Brown was the coaching book, the manager's 'how to' manual, and each page glittered with good sense. In essence, he made things simple.

At Hartlepool, 'the cupboard was financially bare', with 'not a scrag end in it'. So parlous was the club's financial state that Brown, who had moved on to manage Sheffield Wednesday, gave Clough his squad's cast-off training kit. Clough and Taylor had no option but to work on the very fabric of the club: painting and repairing the stands and doing odd jobs themselves. Clough got a licence to drive the team coach: a practical necessity, but also a valuable piece of publicity. He knew that headlines would lead to increased gates, and Clough's natural bent was excess. There were other gimmicks. He worked for two months without pay (Taylor politely declined to match this act of self-sacrifice). He even loaned the club money from his own testimonial fund on the proviso that the identity of Hartlepool's 'mystery benefactor' remained secret. It created yet another headline for the club.

The value of a proper, shared partnership became apparent, if only on a practical level. 'Without Pete, the job would have been impossible,' said Clough. 'It would have been too much for one bloke. Blow me, I'd have been a wreck – just through the sheer exhaustion of what we had to do every day, covering leaks in the roof, covering leaks in the team, rattling the begging bowl wherever we went. We didn't have time to stop for a piss . . .'

Their reward for driving themselves so relentlessly came in 1967: a job at Derby. Hartlepool were already on the brink of promotion, which was sufficient to back up Len Shackleton's generous recommendation of Clough – the equivalent of a papal blessing – to Derby's sceptical board. Shackleton, an ex-Sunderland and England player, had become a journalist with the *Sunday People*. He was revered not only as a player but also as an acute observer of the game. If Shackleton said something, you knew it was true. Almost as if he was Clough's agent, Shackleton had been responsible for tipping off Hartlepool about him too. Clough was persuasive enough to impress Derby and, typically, he arm-twisted them to take on Taylor as well, albeit for much less money. Clough's status was amply reflected in his salary of £5,000 compared with Taylor's £2,500.

Derby *made* Clough and Taylor. What happened there – the renaissance of a small, inconsequential provincial club who went on to become League champions – was a lavish dress rehearsal for what was to follow at Nottingham Forest. Powered by the force of Clough's charismatic will and Taylor's shrewdness, success at Derby hardened the partnership's intransigent attitudes. There was no other way to approach football or to run a club – just the Clough and Taylor way. You were either with them or you were frozen out.

At Derby, Clough and Taylor showed their ability to buy players: the unknown Roy McFarland, plus John O'Hare, John McGovern, Alan Hinton and Archie Gemmill. Clough and Taylor took on board Storer's insistence that courage was as important as ability, and the signing of Dave Mackay became as critical to Derby's development as Clough and Taylor's own arrival. Mackay was a totem, a venerated figure at Spurs in the 1960s. Clough knew that if Mackay could be persuaded to come to the Baseball Ground (Derby's home before Pride Park) the entire balance of the team would change. Clough likened it to a veteran composer rewriting a symphony, and creating for it a wholly different sound and rhythm.

Mackay brought credence to Clough and Taylor's claim to be regarded as serious coaches, unafraid of reputations and able to do more than mould young players. Clough admitted to me that he was, just briefly, intimidated by Mackay's reputation. He was the granite figure Derby needed to build a team around. He was almost thirty-four, but there were others who would do the graft and hard running on his behalf. What Clough and Taylor wanted most of all was Mackay's brain, his imposing personality. On the pitch, he was Clough and Taylor's eyes and lungs – bellowing, ordering, cajoling. He cost them £5,000 – 'a bit like getting Laurence Olivier down to the village hall to act for thirty bob' was how Clough put it. In buying him, Clough and Taylor were again doing the unexpected. 'We were seeing', said Clough, 'what no one else could see. Most people thought Mackay's days at the top were over. We thought his best contribution was still to come. In relative terms, we were right.'

By 1972 Clough and Taylor seemed indestructible. Derby County won the title that year by a solitary point, ahead of Don Revie's Leeds, Liverpool and Manchester City. The title – and the double – ought to have been Revie's. Leeds, having beaten Arsenal in the FA Cup final, lost abysmally at Wolves forty-eight hours later in the final match of the season. But even victors are by victories undone, and so it proved with Clough and Taylor.

When Clough spoke about Derby, as he did frequently, he did so with a sense of unfinished business. I could almost see him replaying in his mind the week in which the heart of the club became the prize in a tug of war, with Clough and Taylor at one end of the rope and Sam Longston, the chairman, at the other.

The higher profile Derby afforded Clough led to more TV appearances and ghosted newspaper articles, which were turned out at an industrial rate. Success lent greater weight to his outrageously candid opinions. It also sealed his departure. With the League championship trophy decorating his club's trophy cabinet, Longston described Clough as his 'pin-up boy'. Within eighteen months he was sticking pins into him. Longston's move to curb Clough's media work was as pointless as asking a hungry fox not to bite the head off a chicken.

Tempers frayed and finally broke, and Clough and Taylor resigned, each man wholly supporting the other. It turned into a costly demonstration of pride that continued to damage them long after Forest had won two European Cups. Had the split from the Baseball Ground been less acrimonious, Taylor might not have spent so much of the late seventies and early eighties day-dreaming about going back there. Clough might not have treated so many of the directors at Forest with such obvious disgust, fearing another Longston in the boardroom just waiting to 'betray' him.

I used to watch Clough's face whenever the subject of Derby came up. Any mention of them, and especially of Longston, made him wince as though he had been punched in the gut. As the years passed, Clough's anger was only with himself, not just for slamming the door behind him but also for ignoring one of the rules Storer had instilled in him: Do not stroke the ego of a director. He'd done so with Longston and suffered as a consequence.

In walking out of Derby, Clough dropped the worst 'clanger' of his career. He knew that he and Taylor ought to have stayed, hammered out a compromise, however unsatisfactory to them in the short term, and then worked to rid themselves of Longston. Instead, Clough tore up a four-year contract, handed back his office and car keys, and 'chucked away the chance of a lifetime'.

He often indulged in a game of what might have been. Derby, not Liverpool, should have been the dominant force of the mid-seventies at home and abroad. He thought the best was yet to come from players such as McFarland, Gemmill, Kevin Hector, Colin Todd, David Nish and Henry Newton, all of them well short of their peak. The problem, Clough added wryly, was Taylor. Taylor repeatedly said that the team was so good he thought Longston could manage it. The joke backfired – Longston began to believe him.

What was torn down so needlessly at Derby was rebuilt, bigger and better, at Forest. In the afterglow of Madrid in 1980, after Forest had collected their second European Cup – John Roberton's low drive from outside the box beating Hamburg 1–0 – it seemed as if the decade itself might belong to them. Just ten minutes or so after the final whistle I had somehow managed to get from the press box down to the dressing rooms, past a line of armed guards. Taylor came down the tunnel and stood outside the door, leaning against the wall. Clough was already inside the dressing room, the door ajar and the players inside strangely quiet.

Taylor's face was inscrutable, and his gaze seemed far away – perhaps he was trying to work out how he had come to be standing there. He stroked his chin, ran his fingers through his hair and began talking about the match and its critical stages, and the importance of retaining the Cup. As a way of closing the conversation, so he could slide into the safety of the dressing room, he said: 'We haven't finished yet. There's more to come. We've hardly started. This club is really going places, you wait and see. We haven't done ourselves justice in the FA Cup yet.'

I can still hear Taylor speaking those words, and the moment makes me think, incongruously, of the final passages of Fitzgerald's *The Great Gatsby*, of the dream so close that Gatsby could hardly fail to grasp it. Like Gatsby, what Taylor didn't know was that the dream was already behind him: the pinnacle of his career had been reached at that very hour.

In the late 1980s, when the bitterness between them had calcified into a high, insurmountable wall that neither could scale, Clough insisted that he hadn't seen or didn't care what Taylor had said in one of his frequent ghosted columns in a tabloid newspaper. In them, he often urged Clough to retire before he was pushed out by ungrateful directors or, very presciently, warned that ill-health brought on by the stresses of the job would force him to quit prematurely.

I have a memory of Clough reading one of these pieces to me as he sat in his office. When he had finished, he screwed the paper up in his hands, as if he was strangling a chicken. He tossed the paper to one side, letting it fall on the floor. 'Not fit for the fish and chips we ate in Middlesbrough,' he said.

He wasn't mollified when Taylor began to write expansively about Nigel Clough, an unsubtle attempt to heal the feud between them. 'It doesn't matter what he says about our Nige,' said Clough. 'I'm not picking up that phone. I'm not talking to him. We used to be friends once – but we never will be again. And that's final.'

CHAPTER THREE

What a waste

Like a blind man feeling for a line of Braille, Peter Taylor ran his thick fingers along the underside of his desk. Silently, he got down on his knees and twisted his neck so he could see beneath it. He stood up stiffly and examined the phone on the desk, shaking it and staring blankly into the receiver, then placing it against his ear as if listening for something other than the low, persistent burr of the dialling tone. Slowly, he put the phone back on its cradle and, hands on hips, stood statue-still, the only movement a swivelling of the eyes across the length of his shadowy office.

'Can't be too careful at the moment,' he said at last, without looking at me. 'There's lots of listening going on, strange things happening. Some of what I've said has been repeated to me by people who couldn't have heard it. I've seen quotes from phone conversations I've had published in newspapers.' His voice sounded agitated. He turned and tapped the wall behind him with his knuckles, as though he might find a secret passage there.

It was a late afternoon in January 1982, and the light was beginning to fade quickly. Taylor had rung me at the office and asked me to come and see him without delay because of 'something I want to discuss with you – and I don't want to do it on the phone'. He had spoken with an impatient briskness. I put the phone down and tried to think about what I'd written over the previous few days that might have upset him. I went to the untidy heap of back issues that lay in the corner of the sports department and began flicking through them. There wasn't any piece with my by-line that I couldn't legitimately defend: nothing I'd written seemed unfair or harsh. I nevertheless expected to be met with a hailstorm of criticism, and I steeled myself for it. Taylor had been particularly touchy of late, as if he had a permanent headache. In some ways, I suppose he had.

It had been a season of personal torment and, as it transpired, Taylor was then less than four months away from admitting that stress, the cumulative pressures of striving to maintain Nottingham Forest's handsome record, both domestically and in Europe, had shredded his nerves to such an extent that he could no longer function. Everything that season had gone wrong, for him and for Forest.

When he ushered me into his office and began his strange routine, I began to wonder whether I was being teased or set up for an elaborate practical joke. But when I looked into Taylor's vacant eyes, I realised he was serious. He was genuinely distressed about something.

Forest were on their way to finishing a miserable twelfth in the League and had been abjectly knocked out of the FA Cup by Wrexham, a Third Division side. There was creeping unease at the casual way in which the European Cup winning side of 1979 and 1980 was being slowly but steadily dismantled. And Forest had bought Justin Fashanu from Norwich for £1 million – the worst deal of Clough and Taylor's managerial career. Trevor Francis was sold to pay for him.

Taylor had once been the Midas of football's transfer market, and now, unfathomably, whatever he touched turned to lead. Forest were in acute financial difficulties. The club was guilty of overambition in grandly rebuilding the East Stand at the very time it needed to reconstruct and strengthen its team.

Worse, Clough fell ill over Christmas – a suspected heart attack – and found himself in the coronary unit of Derby Royal Infirmary. For just over three weeks, Taylor took on the entire management burden, and began to collapse under it.

During that bleak season, and the one before it, the atmosphere between manager and assistant had turned sulphurous. The relationship became a feud, a perpetual arm-wrestling competition over pride and principles. At the very beginning of the last nine months of the partnership, Taylor developed a curious but helpful habit of phoning me at home after matches. The call would come either as soon as *Match of Day*'s closing music began on Saturday night or sometime on Sunday morning. If it was Sunday morning, he would ring from a phone box – I could hear the coins jingling in his hands. Sometimes the pips went in mid-flow; he didn't call back.

Taylor didn't necessarily want to be quoted. 'I'm just marking your card,' he would say. His motive soon became evident: he was keen to promote the players he had been chiefly responsible for buying – Fashanu, Ian Wallace (again for £1 million, from Coventry) and Peter Ward (who cost £450,000 from Brighton) – and to justify his purchases. 'He can play, he'll come good,' was Taylor's optimistic verdict on Fashanu.

Fashanu made his reputation on the basis of a solitary goal against Liverpool in February 1980, a volley struck from the edge of the box which *Match of the Day* replayed so often that I was surprised the videotape didn't split or wear out. The ball rose into the net with stinging pace. Pele would have been proud to have scored that goal.

When Forest bought him in August 1981, Fashanu was six months short of his twenty-first birthday. The pressure of such a fee was too much for such a slender talent. It was October before he got off the mark in the League for Forest – one of just three goals in thirty-one appearances that season. His form was abysmal, the confidence ripped out of him by a depressing succession of stumbling performances. The striker was so hopelessly disoriented in one reserve match that he nearly put the ball into his own net with a back pass from the halfway line. The ball mercifully dropped over the bar. The more he tried, the less of a footballer he seemed to become.

Taylor soon gave up trying to pretend that Fashanu would somehow repay the money Forest had paid for him. He did not, however, stop trying to press home his agenda ahead of Clough's. The number of stories I filed about Taylor's opinions made the red mist rise across Clough's eyes. A month or so into the season, I was walking past Clough's office towards Taylor's, and stopped to glance through the open door. Clough saw me and called out, 'Hang on there, shithouse!' From his tone, the word 'shithouse' had been temporarily suspended as a term of endearment.

I waited while he got up and walked over to me. 'What am I at this club?' he asked, pointing to himself, his finger jabbing at his chest.

'Manager,' I said, puzzled.

'Well done, genius. Now don't forget it. Remember that fact when you're off chatting to your mate down there. Remember who really runs this club, who's really responsible for winning a League Championship and two European Cups, and who's going to be responsible for getting us out of the hole we're in now.'

Although I wasn't sure how I would reply, I shaped to speak. He shut the door in my face.

Clough and Taylor's partnership had begun to decay a few months after Forest's second European Cup win. What started the process was words on paper: Taylor's auto-biography.

Clough was livid. It was Taylor's book, but indisputably Clough's story. It began with a chronology of his career, rather than Taylor's. Clough dominated the cover photograph; Taylor was, for symbolic reasons as well as to help sell more copies, caught in the middle distance, ever so slightly out of focus. Above and below the photograph the title was set in stark, blood-red letters: *With Clough By Taylor*. What enraged Clough was that Taylor had struck the deal for the book and written it before Clough found out about its existence – or at least that is what he originally claimed. Taylor's defence, a very weak one, was that Clough had rejected several flattering financial offers to commit his life to paper. Taylor argued that as a consequence he was entitled to accept the publishers' shilling. Clough pointed out the obvious flaw in this line of reasoning.

'I didn't want to write an autobiography or a biography,' he explained when I asked him about it. 'That's why I didn't fucking do it. And when I saw the book . . . well, blow me. He wouldn't have shifted a copy without my mug on the front, my name alongside it and my thoughts on every page. We weren't exactly strangers, Taylor and me. You'd have thought he'd have just dropped what he was doing in conversation at some point.'

Clough stretched credulity when he added: 'I never mind anyone making a few bob out of me. But not when I haven't given them my permission to make it.' Although our conversation took place after Taylor had taken another pot shot at him from the comfort of retirement, Clough protested too much. He did discover Taylor's intentions a month or so before the advance publicity for the book began; though, admittedly, not from Taylor. 'I just kept it to myself,' he told me. 'I wanted to see whether he'd have the guts to tell me.'

For Clough, the principle mattered. Trust had been broken, loyalty taken for granted. He regarded Taylor's behaviour as unforgivable. He viewed the biography as a betrayal, insisting it should not have been written to satisfy 'cravings of worthless curiosity'. I doubt he'd have complained at all, however, if Taylor had offered him a substantial cut of the profits.

'If Taylor wanted to write a book, he should have done a coaching manual or something about tactics, or how to pick the best players – he used to be good at that,' said Clough, still seething about it shortly before Taylor died. After Taylor's death, he never mentioned the book to me again.

In one sense, Taylor's decision to publish was understandable. His was a compelling account of a hard upbringing, misfortune, penury and, finally, unimaginable success against the odds. In football terms, it was an almost Dickens-like rise out of the blacking factory. He was also making some money, 'a bit on the side' as he used to put it. In terms of basic wages, Taylor had always earned less than Clough. In the early days, parsimonious clubs were reluctant to pay out twice for what was erroneously judged to be the same job. Often Taylor had to explain exactly what he did to justify his pay packet. At the time, it wasn't common practice to divide management responsibilities to such an extent that the 'assistant' shared decision-making. Some directors were incapable of under-standing the fact that in this case one man complemented the other.

Taylor was used to watching Clough bolster his earnings from television appearances as a panellist or summariser, or from ghosted articles for any national newspaper willing to give him a contract. Most of the tabloids did. For Taylor, the book was an irresistible opportunity for a pay day of his own. In *With Clough By Taylor* he implied that he was worthy of it, reflecting on Clough's decision to accept a £5,000 rise at Derby without championing an identical deal for him. I rate the book as one of the best ghosted autobiographies ever written: Taylor's voice is evident on the page.

Most wounding for Clough was Taylor's demeaning psycho-logical analysis of him. He said that Clough suffered from insecurity and a lack of self-belief. Clough, he pointed out, never liked being on his own, which according to Taylor was 'the most obvious way that he betrays his lack of confidence'. He delved into his childhood by suggesting that Clough's failing the eleven-plus – the only one in the family not to pass the exam – caused him to develop anxieties about his self-worth, which were disguised beneath surface bombast.

Although Clough had always been keen to stress Taylor's skill in assessing people – indeed, he made it clear that it was one of the reasons why the partnership was so successful – he didn't want a psychological profile compiled of himself and made public, especially when it showed him as nakedly narcissistic and constantly craving approval and support. When I read *With Clough By Taylor* I appreciated the slow burning resentment that had already begun between them.

Taylor revealed a glimpse of his own jealousy, the resent-ment that so much of his work had gone unrewarded. Clough, he said, had never asked Bell's Whisky to pass on a second bottle to him as joint Manager of the Month. The implication was clear: one person in the partnership was, like Orwell's pigs in *Animal Farm*, always more equal than the other. Discussing the reason for his and Clough's success, Taylor ironically cited the basic ingredient as 'togetherness'. There was no togetherness at the Nottingham launch of the book in a city centre hotel – Clough didn't turn up. The snub was publicised as much as the book itself.

I went to collect a review copy. I was flicking through the book when Taylor snatched it out of my hand. 'You're not having that,' he snapped. 'It's coming home with me.'

When, almost a decade later, I told Clough about it, he said: 'He probably wanted to sell it to someone. You know what he's like for making money.'

In the first few months after publication, Clough could barely bring himself to speak to Taylor. The book drove a wedge between them, and a partnership that had endured for seventeen years quickly began to fall apart. Soon the relationship turned into a horrendous collision of egos. Clough and Taylor began to think and act separately, squabbling over minuscule squares of private turf. So distracted did the pair become with their personal animosities that the team suffered ruinous losses. Clough blamed Taylor for bad judgement; Taylor blamed himself for 'losing it'.

For most of the time in public, Clough and Taylor maintained an air of congeniality towards one another. In private it was a different matter – a snarling, spitting hatred fuelled by ridiculous arguments. When the *Nottingham Evening Post* awarded Clough its Citizen of the Month Award for talking a man out of suicide – the man was about to jump off Trent Bridge – and gave him an inscribed radio, Taylor hauled me down to his office. He thrust into my hands a battered radio that must have been made in the mid-1960s. 'You swap this radio for one like his,' he demanded. 'I deserve it as much as he does. From now on what he gets, I want.' As the weeks passed, he kept on asking 'Where's my radio?' I fobbed him off as best I could. Eventually, he let it drop.

Taylor was not happy about the paltry sum the *Nottingham Evening Post* had paid for the second serial rights for *With Clough By Taylor* (Clough was just as displeased because the paper published extracts). He began giving me classified ads to place in the newspaper on his behalf, mostly household items he wanted to sell on behalf of relatives. 'You got the book cheap. I deserve something free.' Taylor would grumble. I was astonished at the pettiness of it.

There was a spat between them over bottles of wine that Taylor carried home from the team bus. 'He treats it as if it were small bottles of shampoo from a hotel bathroom,' said Clough. 'His garage must look like a French vineyard.' After Forest were knocked out of the European Cup in the first round in 1980, it was Clough who arrived for the press conference with champagne and the trophy the following morning. 'We'd better say goodbye to it in style,' he announced to the journalists gathered around him. Taylor was nowhere to be seen.

On occasions Clough didn't want to see Taylor and vice versa. 'Has he gone yet?' asked Taylor after a match. I nodded. 'Good. I'll come out then.'

'What's the bloke down the corridor saying?' asked Clough. 'Nothing yet,' I said. 'Good. I'll start talking then.'

Players were caught in the crossfire. The captain, John McGovern, was put on the transfer list by Taylor and taken off by Clough. The European Cup team managed somehow to finish seventh in the 1980/81 season and reached the last eight of the

FA Cup. But for a club now used to winning trophies, the results were thin gruel.

By the following season, I got the idea that Taylor was worried about being marginalised. He seemed to fret about what people were thinking and saying about him, especially in the news-papers, and began to wonder how he would be judged. The humour slowly seeped out of him. A man who could be marvel-lous company, even when you were the butt of his jokes, had become bad-tempered and snappy. He'd say to me: 'You've got the worst beard I've ever seen. But I suppose if you shaved it off you'd look thirteen.' Or he would criticise my clothes: 'Did you get them from the charity shop?'

He became defensive, irritable and broody. He began to look pale, his expression constantly nervy. He saw conspiracies everywhere, and picked at what any critic of the club said or wrote about him. Melancholia gradually turned to paranoia.

It was evident that January afternoon as I watched Taylor searching his office like a Cold War spy hunting for a listening device. Eventually he sat down in an armchair away from his desk, a solitary blade of light from the narrow window above him, casting his face in heavy shadow. He began to talk in a whisper, as though he was afraid of being overheard.

'You know the score,' he said. I nodded, though I had no idea what he was talking about, and he may not have been able to see me across the growing darkness of the room.

'I've been running this club for a few weeks now, and yet I keep reading – even in your paper – [he leant over, arm out-stretched, and pointed at me] that soon he'll [he couldn't bring himself to call him Brian] be back in charge. That's the phrase.

Back in charge. I don't like it. The suggestion is that I'm not in charge. Well I am, and it's about time you knew it. I have to be very careful what I say, how I say it. It's a very delicate situation. You do understand, don't you?'

He didn't let me answer. 'It's been a difficult season for us, and it's going to get more difficult over the next month or so. But I want to make it absolutely clear that we'll get through it. I'm in charge.' He repeated that last sentence over and over again.

He made little eye contact. His gaze was fixed on a spot on the ceiling above me. He fiddled with the V-neck of his sweater, and kept wiping his hand across his face. Staring at him, I became aware of how swiftly he had aged: at least five years, it seemed, in as many months. After what seemed an endless silence, Taylor was dumb with misery and apprehension, and I was utterly confused. With apologetic softness, he said: 'I don't have anything else for you. You can go.'

I got up to leave, opening the door without a backward glance. I was relieved to have escaped. It was the first time I had experienced, close up, the horrible effects of extreme stress. Taylor was perfectly sober, but he looked and sounded like a rambling alcoholic, disoriented and confused. That day, and for the next few months, he seemed adrift from himself, as if slipping into a breakdown of some kind. Gone was the assertive Taylor who knew with perfect, arrogant certainty that he was good at his job and could make people laugh with him, like a natural comedian.

When Clough, wrapped in a sheepskin coat, returned from his period of convalescence very shortly afterwards, the reports, including my own, did intimate that he was 'back in charge'. Taylor just looked more gloomy. In early May, after a mid-week match against Manchester United that had brought another defeat, he walked casually out of the dressing room, turning to the players as he went and saying, 'See you on Friday.'

Only he and Clough knew it was a white lie: there would be no more business as usual for Taylor – not at Forest, anyway. Clough sorted out the details of Taylor's pay-off and made sure he could keep his club car. The door, Clough said, was ajar; Taylor could reconsider his decision to retire whenever it suited him. In a typical, bemusing flourish, Clough at one point threatened to resign as well and discussed a joint pay-off. 'I wasn't serious,' he said to me years later. 'I was just trying to get him a bit more cash. And I was upset too. You can anticipate things, but when they actually happen you don't know how you'll react. I did react badly.'

In an effort to explain the reasons for his departure, Taylor said it had been a 'season of seasons' and that he was 'mentally and physically drained'. I thought back to our meeting in January, four months earlier.

The news broke late on the afternoon of my day off. At six o'clock I rushed to the City Ground, half-expecting no one to be there. I saw Clough's Mercedes parked in its usual place outside the main doors. The doors were locked. I ran round to a side door, but it too was locked. I pulled at the handle, so hard that it threatened to come off its hinges. Eventually I heard a familiar voice from behind the door. 'What the fuck are you doing? You're going to pull the whole ground down.' Clough had the door opened for me. 'You'd better come in,' he said wearily.

My cheeks were red with embarrassment. He knew I was panicking, afraid of the rebuke I would get if I didn't get a new line for the story. He calmed me down. 'What do you want me to tell you? Don't worry. I'll give you a line to take back. You better have a drink first, though.'

More for Taylor's benefit than his own, Clough claimed that he would 'never again' appoint an assistant manager. Of course, he eventually did. He went over Taylor's final season at Forest. 'Peter came into me and said we'd shot it. I said "No, you've shot it." It was awful. I cried. I cried a day or so later when I thought about him again. After seventeen years, you can't just lose someone and not feel it in your heart.'

What Clough felt not too long afterwards was anger. Only 186 days later, a 'refreshed' Taylor was back in football, at Second Division Derby. He rang Clough to try to persuade him to return there with him.

Clough pretended that Forest's supporters, significantly the 'foul mouthed' Trent End, kept him from accepting. In reality, the claim was a brutal dig at a handful of directors who he thought had begun to question his competence. When Taylor's offer came, Clough had still not signed a contract with Forest which he had agreed at the end of the previous season. He saw Taylor's invitation as a glorious chance to get himself a better deal. First making sure that the supporters were on his side, he laid into the Forest board for treating him shabbily, showing him no respect. It was an expert piece of manipulative play-acting. He got his improved offer.

'The truth is that he [Taylor] was obsessed by Derby,' said Clough. 'He thought we could go back and recreate the past, make the club the way it had been before we left it. Relive the good old days. Well, I knew that wouldn't happen. Once a moment like that is gone, it's never coming back – and neither was I. Derby was ancient history to me. And I was also resentful. He'd told me he was quitting the game. I'd done everything to help him with his financial package and there he was, smiling broadly, sixteen miles down the road as soon as I'd turned my back.'

His private seething contrasted with the public bonhomie. Clough made excuses for Taylor, talking about 'pride' that prevented Taylor from returning to Forest. There was only the slightest jibe: 'To have come back into football after what he originally said was more than a U-turn. It was a double somersault.'

Taylor's decision to go to Derby impacted on Clough immediately. He became convinced that if he didn't win a trophy on his own, history would exaggerate Taylor's contribution to their partnership. Everything was vanity. He very badly wanted to lift something that he and Taylor had not managed to win together: the FA Cup. And then fate intervened.

When the draw for the third round of the competition in January 1983 pitched Derby against Forest, Taylor against Clough, it was dubbed 'The Cup of Hate' or 'The Cup of Poison', depending on which tabloid newspaper you read. Derby won, improbably, 2–0 on a muddy pitch, and Clough was 'slaughtered' (as he saw it) for failing to shake Taylor's hand or share a drink in his office afterwards. The slur was unjust.

I had followed Clough along the narrow corridors of the ramshackle Baseball Ground, saw him knock quietly on Taylor's office door and watched as he pushed it ajar to discover that his ex-partner was not there. He strode off, stony-faced. I hurried to catch him up. 'Is there anything you want to say about the match?' I asked. 'No, fuck off,' he replied.

The following week I couldn't get him to talk much about the match. A few months later, after Forest had finished fifth in the First Division and qualified for Europe, he admitted to me that the defeat had 'crushed him. I couldn't stand to pick up a paper and read about it.'

The FA Cup tie became another reason for Clough and Taylor not to speak to each other. Partly, however, the defeat was Clough's fault. He left out a perfectly fit Colin Todd for no other reason, or so he claimed, than he thought Todd's time with Derby might prove a psychological burden for him in such a pressurised situation. Playing against your old club can nevertheless work both ways. The first goal was scored by Archie Gemmill, who Clough had sold and then unsuccessfully tried to buy back. Clough, nonetheless, just wouldn't accept his share of blame for Forest's inadequacies.

The split with Taylor became really acrimonious on FA Cup final day, four months later. Manchester United were drawing with Brighton at Wembley. Clough was on the 100-mile Yorkshire Dales Centurion Walk to raise money for charity. Taylor was signing John Robertson for Derby.

Robertson, then thirty, wanted a three year-contract at Forest, and Clough had been haggling with him. Taylor was able to tempt Robertson with the security he craved. The outcome was a degrading mud-slinging contest in which Clough and Taylor matched each other clod for clod.

It was no ordinary transfer. Robertson was symbolic of Forest's Championship and European Cup success because his own astonishing rise tallied exactly with the club's. He'd been mooching around in the reserves when Clough arrived in 1975, overweight and underrated. When Taylor joined Forest, Robertson's skill on the ball convinced him he had found buried treasure. But Robertson's attitude was casual, and Taylor regarded him as fat and loafing, and with the dress sense of a tramp.

Taylor put Robertson on a diet, and forced him to train

harder. Within two years he was in Scotland's 1978 World Cup squad in Argentina. In 1980, his edge-of-the-box shot in Madrid brought the goal that retained the European Cup against Hamburg.

By the time Taylor poached Robertson for Derby, Forest were in transition: no Trevor Francis (sold to Manchester City), no Peter Shilton (sold to Southampton) and no Tony Woodcock (sold to FC Cologne). No Gemmill, no Burns and no Lloyd either. The side Clough and Taylor had created together had now been stripped down and shipped out so that it could be replaced. Clough wanted Robertson to be the bridge between the two eras.

When Taylor originally went back to Derby, Clough said he would give him a lift there. After the Robertson signing, he threatened to run Taylor over on the A52 and described him as a 'rattlesnake.' Taylor snapped back, threatening to sue, condemning Clough's outburst as 'poisonous, vicious, disgraceful . . . unfortunately, it is the sort of thing I have come to expect from a person I now regard with great distaste'.

Less than two months later, Clough and Taylor sat ignoring one another on opposite sides in the foyer of the Great Western Hotel in Paddington. Not a word was spoken between them. I had travelled to the Football League's transfer tribunal with Clough and spoke at the hotel to Taylor. He was polite and helpful, but kept looking apprehensively over my shoulder to check whatever Clough was doing. Derby were told by the tribunal to pay Forest £135,000, and Clough and Taylor exited separately.

Clough wailed that the negotiations for the Robertson deal had gone on 'behind my back when it only needed a five-second phone call to let me know what was happening'. He maintained that line stubbornly. According to those who witnessed him receiving the news of the transfer – in a phone call from his wife, the wild temper it whipped up in him suggested he was genuinely ignorant of the preliminary discussions between Robertson and Taylor. After his own retirement, however, Clough admitted to me that he'd had an 'inkling' beforehand of 'the way the wind was blowing'. He boiled over at what he still saw as Taylor's calculated dishonesty in not telling him about his interest in Robertson – even though Taylor was perfectly entitled not to disclose it. His public expression of sudden outrage was merely gamesmanship. Already knowing the Robertson deal was effectively in ink, Clough decided to use it to his advantage and employ reverse psychology.

Just days before the move was revealed, Clough deliberately upped the ante. He said he would consider resigning if Robertson failed to agree another contract. The transfer would became an excuse to beat Taylor hard and regularly with what he believed was, and would be perceived by others as, an insult to a friendship and an act of back-stabbing disloyalty, rather than a sharp but strictly legal piece of business. More level-headedly, Clough reckoned that the Football League was hardly likely to favour Forest at the tribunal if he reacted meekly to the loss of Robertson, so he decided to make as much fuss as possible. He lost the skirmish over Robertson's signing, though he did get a fair price (£130,000) and won the propaganda war.

Taylor was honest enough to admit that he had left Forest because of 'mistakes I was making'. But his real mistake was to go to Derby, a club with a mountain of financial debt. The following season Derby won only eleven League matches and were relegated, having finished in twentieth place, five points adrift of safety. Clough toasted their failure with a double whisky. 'Something to celebrate,' he said, as we sat in his office.

Taylor had retired for the second time a month earlier,

accepting once more his misjudgements. He surfaced now and again to snipe at Clough, mostly in lucrative newspaper articles. He was publicly critical of Clough's decision to appoint Ron Fenton as his assistant. The implication, an unfair one, was that Fenton wasn't strong enough to stand up to Clough and would not tell him, as Taylor said he had done, to 'shut up' when he talked nonsense. Every time Taylor spoke out, Clough recoiled still further from him. Reconciliation might have been possible, but not as long as Taylor was dispensing his thoughts so freely.

'Every time I pick up a paper, he's shooting his mouth off,' Clough complained. 'Can't he just be quiet for five minutes? After all his years with me, you'd think he'd learnt the lesson we used to preach together – the hardest thing is to say nowt, but sometimes it's the best thing you can do.'

Clough came to regret his intransigence. When Taylor died, aged sixty-two, while on holiday in his beloved Majorca, the pair hadn't spoken to one another for seven years. Fenton rang Clough at home to tell him what had happened, and the news was met by a grief-filled silence. Clough, I'm told, put the phone down without speaking. I was standing in the corridor outside Clough's office. When Fenton at last emerged, I asked whether there was a quote I could use. He shook his head sadly.

Death brings to the living a fresh perspective: a reflection on chances used or misused, a reminiscence of times past, a belated appreciation of what has been lost. With Clough, it also brought out the anger in him, and perhaps an underlying guilt. He began to reanalyse his relationship with Taylor, and blamed himself for being unforgivingly harsh on his former partner, and for not making a magnanimous gesture that would have repaired the friendship and brought them together again. 'I should have picked up the phone. Just one phone call would have done it. In five minutes we'd have forgotten all the harsh words, all the bitterness,' he said when we talked about it.

He wasn't satisfied with the eulogies written about Taylor. Not because each one did not describe him generously, but because in Clough's eyes none did Taylor sufficient justice or apportioned enough credit for the work he had done in the partnership. It was as if he'd become the guardian of Taylor's posthumous reputation.

'Your obit on my mate was crap, utter crap,' he yelled at me, his face flushed, the voice rising in protest. 'You're all the same, you journalists – crap. Every paper missed the point, the real story. No one showed him the way he was. No one managed to give him the send-off he deserved. He was funny – you know that. He was intelligent – you know that too. He had a football brain – everybody could see it. And he was my mate. And we had some great times. And now . . .'

Clough slumped into a chair. He seemed to be stringing together in his mind all the bright days he had shared with Taylor.

'What a waste,' he said after a long pause. 'All those years when we could have been sitting together having a beer. All those years when he could have come, as an honoured guest, to watch us play. All those years without the laughter he was capable of providing. No one – absolutely no one – has made me laugh like him. I always missed that, and now . . . he's gone. I can hear his voice . . . telling joke after joke. But all we did at the end was slag one another off. Oh, fuck.' He shook his head slowly, his eyes staring at the floor.

Just weeks before his own retirement, at the end of his most wretched season in management, Clough had conferred upon him the Freedom of the City of Nottingham. After spending the morning and early afternoon touring the city, and before the formal presentation in the evening, he went back to the City Ground and sat in his office. I was alone with him for most of the time.

As he got ready to leave and prepare for more smiling and hand-shaking, he turned to me and said, 'There's just one regret today. I wish me mate had been here with me . . .'

I didn't need to ask who he meant.

CHAPTER FOUR

Striking gold in Mansfield

Of all the quotable sayings that left Brian Clough's lips, I thought one of the most insightful was this: 'Sometimes you win matches in unusual places – often before you put a foot on the field.'

After he died, and newspapers printed columns of the most famous of his quotations, I didn't see that line included anywhere. But it was a piece of advice he frequently passed on to other managers in an offhand way. Some of them, I sensed, dismissed it as a typical Cloughism or didn't fully understand what he meant. I was there when Tony Barton, who won the European Cup with the team Ron Saunders had built at Aston Villa, received the lecture in Clough's office. Clough, as usual, was dispensing the Scotch and talking at speed. As Barton got a large glass shoved into his hand (though I immediately got the impression he didn't want it), Clough was complaining that England had to think more creatively off the pitch as well as on it, and do so at all levels. The FA, said Clough, didn't yet appreciate that the little things mattered. He launched into his theory. Barton began nodding his head in vigorous agreement. 'Yes, Brian,' he replied. But, as I looked across at him, I thought the bewildered expression on Barton's face revealed that he hadn't grasped what Clough was talking about. It was as if he was listening to someone talking in a foreign language.

The conversation with Barton was Clough's way of explaining that preparation away from the training pitch, and a proper psychological understanding of players, was paramount for success. If the manager with the Scotch in his hand had bothered to ask for evidence, Clough would have provided it.

Nottingham Forest won the League Cup against Southampton in 1979 after he forced the players into a late-night drinking session the night before the Wembley final. He took them into a private room at their hotel, ordered enough champagne to float a longboat and twisted the key loudly in the lock. 'No one leaves until you've drunk that lot,' he ordered, pointing at the stack of bottles. Clough and Taylor then put on a vaudeville act about their experiences at Hartlepool.

A week or so after the final, I spoke to Clough about it. He said that the players had looked tense climbing on to the coach, and were quiet throughout the journey. He decided that he needed to relax them. The only way to do it was booze, and plenty of it. 'We supped a vat of the stuff,' he said, 'and there were lots of bleary eyes at breakfast. But I preferred that to the alternative of players lying awake in their room until the early hours worrying about a Cup final.' Forest beat Southampton 3–2 the following afternoon.

Peter Taylor also believed that a match could be won before a ball was kicked. He believed he had made sure that Forest retained the European Cup in the quarter-finals in 1980 when eyeballing the opposition, Dynamo Berlin, as the side emerged from the dressing room. The players had a bleak, 100-yard walk through a car park before reaching the opening on to the pitch. I remember it was a horribly cold night in East Berlin. Sitting in the press box, I wore four layers of clothes beneath a heavy woollen coat, and a flat cap, a pair of gloves and a scarf. I was still convinced that I would die of hypothermia before the end of the first half. When I exhaled, my breath almost froze into a solid funnel of ice.

Dynamo led 1–0 from the first leg and were favourites to go through. Taylor, however, noticed that the Germans were strangely subdued and apprehensive. During the minute and a half it took for the teams to reach the stadium, he saw them shoot nervous glances at one another and then at Forest's players. He passed the message on. Taylor argued that Forest were so intensely focussed – straight-backed, steely and inscrutable – that Dynamo became scared of them from the moment the dressing room doors opened. The walk on to the pitch, he said, was just too intimidating for them. It was a classic example of one team being mentally tougher than the other. Dynamo saw Forest weren't afraid, and so became afraid themselves.

After the tie, I stood beside Taylor while he gave a press conference underneath the stand, the journalists clustered around him. Clough sensibly stayed in the warmth of the dressing room. Taylor was still reliving the match, on a high after the 3–2 aggregate win. His eyes rolled everywhere, the big hands were expressive. Twice he nearly struck me in the face as he tried to make a point. 'The Germans looked terrified of us,' he kept saying. 'They were so frightened, they looked like zombies. If there'd been a betting shop between our dressing room and the pitch, I'd have dived in and backed us. We won that tie in the car park.'

According to Clough, Forest's League Championship – the only one in the club's history – was sealed on the summer's day when the fixtures for the 1977/78 season were published. Clough let his eyes slip slowly down the list: an opening-day game for

Forest at Everton, the 'private war' against Derby at the City Ground a week later, then a match at Arsenal on the first Saturday in September. He didn't much care. As ever, Clough wasn't too bothered about the opposition. He knew that Forest, freshly promoted, could confound bookmakers who had priced them as 30:1 long shots, just another of the back-of-the-pack nags in a race that Liverpool's thoroughbreds were sure to win at a canter.

Clough's interest was grabbed by the opening-day fixture of another Midlands club – a club even more unfashionable than Forest who had been relegated from the First Division just two months earlier. Stoke City had to face Mansfield Town at Field Mill. Stoke would lose the game 2–1 in front of a crowd of less than 15,000. The match barely troubled the national media; only the local weekly paper took much interest in it. But on the way home from Forest's unexpected 3–1 win at Everton that same afternoon, the first result Clough looked for was Stoke's.

Field Mill was a ground so depressing that it made Forest's modest home look positively palatial. Mansfield was not the place you wanted to start a new season – certainly not if you were the best goalkeeper in Britain.

'When I looked at that fixture list, I nearly choked myself laughing. Peter Shilton at Mansfield? Fuck me! It was like asking Richard Burton if he'd mind doing a few episodes of *Coronation Street*,' said Clough when we spoke about it at the beginning of the season that marked the tenth anniversary of Forest's championship.

Clough had always wanted to buy Shilton, then in his third miserable year at Stoke. The goalkeeper was nearly twenty-eight and had never won a trophy. His only medal had come as an FA Cup runner-up with Leicester City, in 1969. While Liverpool dominated the domestic game in the mid-seventies, and

Shilton laboured in the smoke-filled Potteries, Ray Clemence established himself as England's number one goalkeeper. Shilton won just two caps in almost two and a half years, and in 1976 he asked not to be considered for England selection again because of the perpetual disappointment of being Clemence's deputy. He had been relegated with Leicester, and now he was coming to terms with it once more at Stoke.

For Shilton, the season stretched ahead uninvitingly. There were matches at Notts County, Blackpool, Oldham and, where Clough found him, amid the back-to-backs of Mansfield. Clough reckoned that an afternoon at Mansfield would be like an electric shock for Shilton. If he hadn't already done so, Shilton would look around the terraces of Field Mill and realise how quickly he had to leave Stoke and make a new start in the First Division.

He became the most significant signing of Forest's League Championship season. Without him, Clough and Taylor wouldn't have won the title. The goalkeeper, said Clough, changed the dynamic of his side.

Clough and Taylor had nurtured a team of talents over the previous twelve months and then sprinkled experience over it. Shilton was Britain's premier goalkeeper. Viv Anderson went on to make thirty appearances for England. Larry Lloyd and Kenny Burns meanly locked up the centre of defence. Archie Gemmill was industrious, wily. Up front, Tony Woodcock, thin and mop-haired, was impressive enough to be poached by FC Cologne for Germany's Bundesliga. The harmonious weave of the side included Martin O'Neill, a visionary in midfield, and dependable if unspectacular pros such as John McGovern,

Peter Withe, Ian Bowyer and Frank Clark. And then there was the incomparable John Robertson.

Robertson didn't look like an athlete. He had a slight pot belly, and he often arrived at training unshaven and with his hair uncombed. His skin was the colour of alabaster. He wore desert boots and jeans. After training he would frequently appear in the club bar to have a cigarette and play the fruit or quiz machines. On the pitch, he lacked pace. But none of that mattered.

To watch Robertson was a privilege. He would cling to the touchline, his shoulders hunched like a man huddling in a doorway against the rain. But as soon as the ball was fed to him, he set off with it welded to his left boot. He somehow managed to drag the ball back and then around defenders, a trick he performed with such mesmeric skill that it seemed as if everything else around him – the crowd and the players – had been momentarily frozen, and only he and the ball were moving in exaggerated slow motion. No matter how many times you saw him do it, leaving an embarrassed defender behind him, your eyes never grew tired of it, and you never lost your sense of awe at the way his deftness of touch took him beyond his markers. Nor could you work out exactly how he had managed it.

When Robertson played, I would have paid to sit in the press box. When he trained, on the inhospitable, open pitches Forest used on the banks of the Trent, I regularly stood in the teeming rain for a glimpse of the skill others could see only on match days.

Forest won the admiration of neutrals who cared about good football. It was hard not to respect a team who adhered to such a rigorous code of behaviour. Clough's principles, rooted in Alan Brown and Harry Storer's approach to man-management, barred dissent, and that meant no arguing with the referee or with the manager. He didn't like his players to kick the ball away, waste time, nor indulge in gamesmanship or cruel show-boating.

'All I want is for that ball to brush the grass – just pass it around. We don't want smart-arses. We want players who will do things simply and quickly, and when they're told,' he would say during the Friday press conferences that too often took place in the cramped corridor outside his office. Clough would lean back against the wall, as if the effort of answering questions was tiresome for him. He seemed impatient to be on his way.

Robertson and the creative sparks around him were indebted to the unobtrusive, less glamorous workers who passed the ball to them. As a player, John McGovern was never easy on the eye for spectators, most of whom found it hard to understand why he was on the pitch at all. He was conspicuous by his ungainliness. When he ran, he looked awkwardly spindly and splay-footed, like a duck waddling out of a pond. But to watch again the vivid highlights of Forest's League Championship and European Cup winning seasons is to appreciate his positional sense, the time he created for himself on the ball, his solid distribution, his unselfish work rate and the critical function he fulfilled around more flamboyant figures.

Only later did I come to understand what Clough meant when he signed McGovern and said so provocatively that he had bought him to 'teach the others how to play'. Alongside him, Archie Gemmill was never still, darting everywhere. No blade of grass was a stranger to him. Larry Lloyd and Kenny Burns were about as welcoming to opposition forwards as medieval jailers. A tackle from Burns must have felt like being struck by a chain mail fist. His challenges scooped the ball – and sometimes the player with it – to safety. With his trailing, longish blond hair and a scowl on his face, Burns looked semi-savage to me. I remember interviewing him for the first time and thinking that he might eat me like a rack of ribs. Lloyd had an overpowering strength and, like his partner, jarred bones and bruised muscles.

'I wanted two hard bastards at the centre of that back four – and I got them,' was Clough's succinct tribute. Lloyd and Burns hunted as a pair, choosing together which striker to pick off, and tidying up behind each other.

In that championship year, Lloyd and Burns experienced a renaissance, Anderson and Woodcock made their debuts as England internationals, and Robertson was without peer as a winger and artistic creator. And Gemmill, in the Argentinean World Cup summer that followed, scored against Holland one of the most sublimely beautiful goals to grace any finals, a goal so memorable that twenty-five years later it was turned into a ballet in recognition of its artistry.

But it was still Shilton who mattered most to Forest. It was his stellar performances, culminating on the April afternoon when a goalless draw at Coventry put them out of reach of Liverpool, that vindicated Clough and Peter Taylor's financial faith in him.

Hard though it is to believe now, Forest's side was assembled on a pittance. A Chelsea player today would earn in a few months what Clough and Taylor spent to capture the League Championship. Frank Clark arrived on a free transfer. Lloyd was bought for £60,000. Of the others, Peter Withe cost £42,000, McGovern £35,000 and Gemmill £20,000. John Middleton (Shilton's predecessor), Woodcock, Robertson, Bowyer, O'Neill and

Jim Wilmer, chairman of Nottingham Forest, welcomes Clough to the club at the beginning of 1975. Wilmer called him 'an energetic young man with an exciting background'.

Clough, with an incredible career scoring record of 250 goals in 296 games, nets yet another for Middlesbrough in the FA Cup against Charlton.

Clough shares a joke with Jimmy Greaves, his rival for the No.9 shirt, at an England team training session in 1959. From left to right: manager Walter Winterbottom, Ron Clayton, trainer Harold Shepherdson, Brian Clough, Tony Allen, Don Howe, Trevor Smith, Maurice Setters, Bobby Charlton, Jimmy Greaves and Edwin Holliday.

Clough and Taylor parade the 1972 League Championship in front of the Derby fans at the Baseball Ground, who had turned up especially to see the trophy.

Clough stands aside the Leeds team – the 'cheats and charlatans' – before the 1974 Charity Shield against Liverpool. From centre to left: Clough, Billy Bremner, David Harvey, Paul Reaney, Johnny Giles, Norman Hunter, Gordon McQueen and Joe Jordan.

John McGovern hoists the 1976 Anglo-Scottish Cup – the one most managers 'didn't want to piss in' – after Forest's aggregate victory over Orient, and starts Forest on the road to success.

Clough and Taylor give instructions from the sidelines at the second leg of the European Cup semi-final against Cologne in 1979.

Trevor Francis celebrates with the European Cup after his lone goal defeated Malmo in the 1979 final.

Clough plays cricket in his underpants at a training session before the 1979 European Cup final.

Peter Shilton signs for Forest at the beginning of their 1977 League Championship season. Shilton, Clough would later say, completely changed the dynamic of the side.

Clough and Taylor, 'the shop window and the goods at the back', playing around at a photo call after winning the 1979 European Cup.

Anderson were already at the club. Before Shilton, only Burns' fee was in six figures – £150,000 from Birmingham City.

The £270,000 invested in Shilton – then a club record – attracted widespread derision. Clough and Taylor were initially castigated for paying an exorbitant sum for a mere goalkeeper. If Shilton was so perfect, said one critic, why had Stoke, who bought him for £325,000 from Leicester, still gone down? Clough and Taylor never doubted the importance of a top-class goalkeeper in terms of both the saves he made and the psychological impact he had on the team. Clough had attempted to sign Shilton at Derby for £175,000. The deal stalled and collapsed. He tried to sign him again at Leeds. The board sacked him before he could push the move through. Shilton wasn't going to escape him a third time.

'We took some stick over Shilton,' Clough told me. We were walking from the training ground back to his office, strolling in the lunchtime sun. His hands were folded behind his back, which made him look like the Duke of Edinburgh inspecting a row of dignitaries.

'We got the lot thrown at us – mostly insults about being irresponsible with our money. I was asked by someone on our board why we should bother to spend so much cash on a guy who might not be in the game for eighty-five minutes.'

Clough had never known such a 'blinkered and barmy' reaction. If necessary, he added, he would have paid twice what he did for Shilton. 'Actually,' he said, qualifying the statement further, 'I'd have paid almost *any* price. If Trevor Francis was worth a million, so was Shilton. It was like buying a painting, like a Constable or a Turner, that you knew in a year or two's time is going to be worth twice what it cost you.'

We had reached the turning into the City Ground when Clough said: 'If you want to know the truth, Shilton won us that bloody title. I didn't tell him of course – one Big Head was enough in our club. We had Robbo, and Woodcock and Burns and Lloyd, and Anderson and the best pros in Frank Clark and Archie Gemmill. Shilton was *still* the deciding factor. He was the difference – honest. He made the fewest mistakes of any-one, including the management.'

Clough was in full flow; I didn't interrupt. 'Just imagine you're a centre forward. You get round Lloyd and Burns, or you beat Anderson . . . and then you have the job of trying to put the ball past Shilton. It's like a bank robber who finds that, once he's inside the bank, there are so many locks and bolts on the vault that he might as well give up and go home. No one who didn't see it would believe how much Shilton did for us. He won matches and he saved them. He was the most significant signing we made that season – by a mile.'

If Shilton hadn't played that game at Mansfield, Clough figured, he wouldn't have joined Forest until much later, prob-ably in the autumn. 'Mansfield? Well, he must have known he'd do better than that. It made our job of signing him far simpler. If we'd had to wait a month or so, goodness knows what might have happened or where we'd have been in the League table.'

Statistics bear out Clough's endorsement of Shilton. Clough and Taylor believed that Forest's crack at a League title had to be based around how few goals they conceded. 'We preached clean sheets morning, noon and night. We preached them until our throats were dry and our lot got sick of us talking about them.'

Forest won four of their opening five matches (losing only at Arsenal) and yet leaked six goals: one at Everton, three at Arsenal and two at Wolves. John Middleton, who played in the opening five games, was a worthy keeper, an England Under-21 international. But he wasn't Peter Shilton. With Shilton in the side, it took Forest fourteen matches to concede another six goals, a run that took them into December. Shilton let in only eighteen goals in thirty-seven League appearances that season (three of them in one match, at Norwich) and kept twenty-three of Clough and Taylor's beloved clean sheets. No team had taken the title with so few goals conceded (24).

Clough was always keen to stress where the impetus to sign Shilton had originated. 'You might think that Peter Taylor was the driving force behind our obsession with Shilton,' he said. To be fair, he added, you'd expect Taylor, as an ex-goalkeeper, to be passionate about buying someone who was in his opinion the finest in the business – or at least potentially the finest when Forest bought him.

'And Taylor was always pressing Shilton's cause,' Clough went on. 'But you have to remember that I was a centre forward – hey, not a bad one either, if you bother to look at the record books. [Clough was always reminding you of his own goalscoring record, such was his pride in it.] A poacher always knows who the best gamekeeper is. Well, the guy with the number nine on his back always knows who the best goalkeeper is – and how valuable he is. I wanted Shilton 'cos I knew, as soon as he was in a decent team, he'd shine in it.'

Clough outlined how he had watched Shilton's career develop. When he was a young lad, 'just a slip of a teenager', he didn't look unsure and nervous like other keepers of the same age. He commanded his box and had a first-rate positional sense. He used to look at him and think, 'How good are you going to be?'

By now we were in Clough's office, and he was pouring a Scotch. 'A team with an OK goalkeeper is always looking over its shoulder,' he said. 'At the back of its mind, it's thinking "It doesn't matter what we do – the fella between the posts might make a mistake." With Shilton in goal, it gave everyone else more confidence. It spread throughout the side. We were full of ourselves. The defenders felt safer, and the forwards thought if we could nick a goal, there was more than an evens chance that the opposition wouldn't score at the other end. That's how you win titles, and that's how we won ours.'

Taylor thought so too: 'We became a different side when Peter Shilton came on board,' he told me on one occasion. 'With him we had a chance. Without him, we didn't.'

On the face of it, Shilton and Clough were the perfect match. The high standards Clough demanded from players, Shilton provided as a basic service. He was the model pro. He was fastidious about what he wore and how he looked. His clothes were always stylish and immaculate (at Leicester he had worn a white goalkeeper's jersey) and he always carried a grooming kit with him. His approach to football was scrupulously well ordered, like a military battle plan. He analysed the game, his own and his rivals', and he trained assiduously, working on his muscular strength as much as essential goalkeeping technique. Just as Clough had done during his own playing days, Shilton chased perfection: every flaw, every blemish was hunted down in an effort to expunge it. Clough said he tried to sign the type of player that he knew Alan Brown would have approved of. 'He'd have liked Shilton. In fact, he'd have stood him in the centre of the dressing room and told everybody to be like him. That's how good he was . . .'

Shilton had left Leicester because he felt the club would never buy the quality players necessary to make them a major force. He left Stoke because he questioned the discipline and commitment of the club and, as Clough had correctly calcu-lated, thought his career would wither in the Second Division.

At Forest, he found at last a management team who bought good players, insisted on discipline and commitment, and shared his lofty ambitions. But even Shilton's consistency didn't stop Forest from being sneeringly dismissed as 'caretaker' leaders of the First Division. The team was treated with the disregard of a pace-setter in a track race. Supposedly, Forest were going to make the First Division competitively interesting by drawing maximum speed out of the chasing group before politely fading from the front.

If you asked me to pick a period when I thought Clough was at his best and his brightest, and at his most confrontational, I'd unhesitatingly choose the Championship season. There was a cocky vitality about him: he was back on top and stuffing his critics, and relishing it. Often, it has to be said, this manifested itself in outlandish and inappropriate rudeness. I would sit for hours in the corridor outside his office waiting for the crumb of a quote. Sometimes he would walk the ten strides from his desk into the main office and ignore me. I knew, or at least I thought I did, that this was a kind of initiation ceremony, a battle of wills, to see how long I was prepared to tough it out. I was determined that nothing would shift me. He would have to tell me to go, and he usually did – with a 'Fuck off'.

In those days Clough played a lot of squash. The courts he used were at Trent Bridge cricket ground. I walked over to watch him one morning. He battered the ball, either taking long, scythe-like sweeps from the back of the court or short-armed jabs from the front. When eventually he saw me peering at him, he yelled at me: 'Bugger off before I wrap the racquet around your head. And I mean it.' His voice echoed around the court, bouncing off the walls, so I heard the message three or four times. Back at the City Ground, another journalist asked him whether he'd had a decent game. 'Yes,' he replied instantly. 'I pretended the ball was your head.'

When he returned well-tanned from a mid-season holiday, I tried to compliment him on looking so healthy. Wrong move. 'I look like this because I haven't had to see you for a week,' he said, disappearing towards the dressing rooms.

At press conferences during the opening half of that season, Clough would jab his finger, like a bayonet, or brandish his squash racket in the direction of anyone who had the temerity to suggest that Forest might not be solid enough to take the title. 'You just fucking wait and see. We're better than you fucking think we are.'

That season, in asking him a question, I referred to Liverpool as the best club in the country. It was like telling Ava Gardner that she wasn't the most beautiful woman in the room. Clough's lip curled. He turned his back on me in disgust and pushed open the door to his office, spitting out his reply: 'Liverpool aren't the best club in the country – 'cos we are.' That quote, which I put out on the wire, went everywhere. He said it again, a few months on, because he knew it was like flicking a lighted match onto dry straw. Of course it rankled Liverpool – a side, like the rest of the First Division, struggling to adjust to Forest's swift ascendancy.

There was no discernible trace of self-doubt in him, just a reluctant acceptance that it would be some time before the rest of us appreciated the seismic movement going on in the First Division. A substantial realignment of power was taking place, and Liverpool, as defending League champions and European Cup holders, were being pushed aside.

The Championship year hardened Clough's antipathy

towards Liverpool. After he left Derby, he was envious of Liverpool's pre-eminence, which followed the end of Bill Shankly's era: Liverpool were winning what Derby would have won if only Clough had still been managing them. When Forest made an impact on the First Division, he felt that Liverpool didn't treat them (or him) with sufficient respect. As he saw it, Liverpool thought 'we were a group of country bumpkins who didn't deserve to be on the same pitch as them. That lot had enjoyed everything their own way for so long, they couldn't handle someone else pushing them out of the way to collect a trophy or two. They hated us for it.'

After nineteen matches, nearly halfway through the season, Forest were a point ahead of Everton and six above Liverpool. The twentieth game was against Manchester United. At Old Trafford, a week before Christmas, the realisation that Forest meant business –indeed, *were* the business – dawned on Liverpool and everyone else. Whipping United 4–0 was a declaration of intent so exquisite, so emblematic of the side's graceful and imaginative form, that those who still harboured doubts about Forest had to put them aside. At last, Clough and Taylor's Forest deserved serious attention. 'We showed all the clever clogs in the media that we were good enough to win the title,' Clough crowed. 'I enjoyed that.'

Clough and Taylor enjoyed something else too. Their last match in charge of Derby had been at Old Trafford. There was a beautiful symmetry in Forest's crushing of United. Years later, reminiscing during a pre-season tour, Clough told me: 'Less than five years before, I'd sat at Old Trafford not wanting to look at, or talk to, Sam Longston. And Sam Longston didn't want to look at, or talk to, me. We couldn't bring ourselves to say a civil word to one another, and both Taylor and I knew it was the end for us. It was a terrible afternoon. So on the way out of Manchester, after we'd stuffed United good and proper, I sat in silence on the coach for a while. I turned to Taylor and he turned to me, and we both knew what the other was thinking. We were just remembering together . . .'

The third of Forest's four goals that afternoon encapsulated the flair and spirit carrying them to the title. Forest counter-attacked lethally. A defensive header from the edge of their own box was picked up by Gemmill, who broke so rapidly that United were woefully overstretched. Their midfield players realised the danger too late. He rode one tackle, carried the ball into the opposition half along the right and flicked an audacious, weighted cross-field ball to Robertson. In space, Robertson took the ball casually round the goalkeeper, just as he might have done in a Monday morning five-a-side practice, and tapped it into the open net. As a contest, the match was over.

Liverpool came to the City Ground on Boxing Day and drew 1–1. Everton were beaten there 1–0 five days later. Here was solid proof that Forest were going to be hard to catch. Neither during the Liverpool game, which Forest threatened to domi-nate, nor after it, did the League champions ever look capable of bettering them. There was a swagger in Forest's step which stemmed directly from the arrogance of the manager. 'I don't think', said Clough, 'that Liverpool could ever quite believe it. I watched them wait all the time for us to trip up and hand them the title back, as if we'd nicked the trophy from the cabinet for an afternoon.'

After Christmas, there was no stopping Forest. Arsenal were beaten 2–0, Chelsea swept aside 3–1, and West Ham and

Newcastle disposed of 2–0 apiece. Fittingly enough, the final game of the season was played at Anfield, a fortnight after Forest had already won the title with four matches to spare. Liverpool, still dazed by it all, applauded them onto the field. 'I enjoyed that,' said Clough, with a hint of mischief. Forest had won the Championship by seven points in an era when there were only two points for a win.

On the April afternoon that Forest were presented with the League trophy, before a goalless draw against Birmingham, Clough and Taylor came onto the City Ground pitch, dressed immaculately in club blazers and ties, to receive medals and the crowd's recognition. Clough's stride was brisk. After acknowledging the crowd, he barely glanced around him until he got his hands on the handsome trophy, which he cradled like a baby in his arms. Taylor, half a pace behind him, took his medal and, ever so briefly, held it half-aloft, as if the act embarrassed him. As the team waited in a straight line across the centre of the pitch, like troops before inspection, Taylor stood beside and slightly in front of Shilton. He half-turned and extended his hand towards him, as if indicating that the crowd should show their appreciation for what the goalkeeper had achieved over the previous eight months.

The Football Writers' Association voted Kenny Burns their Player of the Year. Burns, it needs to be stressed again, had a remarkable Championship season, his first as a central defender. The previous season he'd scored nineteen League goals for Birmingham. The transformation in him, both person-ally and professionally, became an irresistible human interest story, which summed up the scale of what Forest had achieved. It was like a moral fable: a football sinner had repented. Before Forest signed him, disciplinary problems dogged Burns' early career and detracted from his skills. He was perceived as sullen and petulant, someone whose competitive spirit could boil over into combative spite.

The question was whether anyone could manage him firmly enough – whether, indeed, Burns, at twenty-four, wanted to be managed – so that his natural aggression enhanced rather than obstructed his game. The decision by Clough and Taylor to convert Burns permanently from a striker to a central defender said everything about their judgement and their faith in him. The way in which Burns responded to it, taking control of his temper and channelling it positively into his game, said everything about his application and his ability to change. He revealed, too, how astutely he could read the game. It was a season of redemption for him. He was booked only once.

Fellow professionals, however, picked Shilton as PFA Player of the Year, an award then in its infancy, and overshadowed by the long tradition of the Football Writers' accolade – Stanley Matthews was its first winner in 1948 – which is why the vote for Burns generated considerably more publicity. If nothing else, Shilton deserved it for the save that sealed the Championship at Coventry: an acrobatic leap and a clawing hand to deflect a header from Mick Ferguson that was arrowing into the top corner. Ferguson shook his head, unable to believe the miracle he had just witnessed. That one moment defined Shilton at Forest, even more than his impeccable performance two years later in the European Cup final against Hamburg.

From November 1977 to December 1978, Forest went forty-two matches unbeaten, an acomplishment that Clough thought was akin to winning another League title. He was intensely proud of the achievement, and prouder still of a silver salver commemorating the feat. Each result was engraved on it. He held the plate in his hands and gazed into it, examining his own reflection and letting the light catch the names of the teams that were unable to defeat Forest. 'Just beautiful,' he kept repeating, as if unable to believe the record Forest had established.

'I'll tell you how we did it,' he said. 'If we ever got too high and mighty, I just had to call a team meeting and go around the room. I could point to Robbo and say, "You were a tramp when I came here, now you're the best winger in the game." I could tell Burnsy and Lloydy that they'd both have been on the scrap heap without me. I could pick out Frank Clark and say that I'd just given him the best years of his career after Newcastle tossed him aside.

'And if I ever wanted to bring Shilton down a peg or two, I could turn to him in the dressing room and say, "Don't forget, clever clogs, you were playing at Mansfield before I signed you. Fucking Mansfield!" And then I'd ask him, "Would you like to go back there?"'

CHAPTER FIVE

Don't mention the war

When I was a boy, the first game that really gripped me with its drama and sense of grand occasion was Manchester United's European Cup win over Eusebio's Benfica in 1968. I watched it on our sixteen-inch black and white TV, the picture so smoky that the dark figures, sweeping across a grey pitch, seemed to come from another world. One thing I remember is the impudence of George Best's goal in extra time. The goalkeeper was drawn to the ball, like a bull enticed towards a matador's cape, and Best stepped around him and slid it in to an empty net. Another, which stays with me most of all, is Bobby Charlton.

'Watch him,' my father told me. 'He's a Geordie, like you, born a strong corner kick from where you were born.' I remember Charlton's skidding header that gave United the lead, and his second goal, United's last, which killed off the Portuguese side. Most of all I remember how, as captain, Charlton struggled to hold the bulbous trophy as he descended the Wembley steps.

His face was drawn and sweaty, seeming to show more pain than pleasure. He appeared physically and emotionally drained, and the huge cup seemed to overwhelm him. He propped it on to his left shoulder, as if he were carrying a bag of coal. I thought he might drop with exhaustion. I knew nothing about an air crash in Munich, and nothing about what winning the final meant to Charlton in particular; I was just worried that the trophy was too big for my new hero.

Just a dozen years later, I was carrying that same trophy myself. The cup that had passed through the hands of football's masters, such as Puskas and Di Stefano, Cryuff and Beckenbauer, was jammed between my knees on an uncomfortable car ride home from London. I thought about Bobby Charlton, and appreciated for the first time why he had found the cup so awkward in his hands.

The European Cup had been taken to London in December 1980 for a press conference to announce that the World Club Championship would be played the following February in Tokyo. Nottingham Forest, the European Cup holders, had agreed to play the South American champions, Nacional of Uruguay.

Peter Taylor didn't want to carry the cup home. 'You can have a lift back to Nottingham,' he said, after discovering that I had travelled down by train, 'but only if you're responsible for the cup.' I sat in the front passenger seat for the two-hour journey, worried that I might dent the silver trophy if I let go. 'I'll be inspecting every inch of the cup afterwards, and sending you a bill for any repairs,' joked Taylor.

After a while, my hands began to ache and I had to keep shifting position. At one point I wound down the window and heaved the trophy onto my lap so that it lay across me. One of the looping handles poked out of the window, so I had to work it back into the car.

'Think yourself lucky,' said Taylor. 'Every player in Europe wants that cup, and you've got it all to yourself.' He was right, and letting go of it three months earlier – an unexpected defeat to CSKA Sofia in the opening round of the competition in

October 1980 – would prove the beginning of the end for the side that Brian Clough and Taylor had fashioned at Forest.

Clough wasn't with Taylor and me that afternoon; he'd gone on to another appointment. If he had been in the car, I know I'd have heard much earlier his own theory of how, and why, Forest managed to become the only club to have won two European Cups but just one domestic League title.

As the Forest team and staff gathered at the airport to fly home from Munich after winning the European Cup for the first time in May 1979, Clough glanced around the departure lounge. A few hours earlier, Trevor Francis's goal in the Olympic Stadium had enabled Forest to eke out a 1–0 win over the dreary, defence-minded Swedish side Malmö in a final that was, to the neutral eye, more about hard graft than footballing artistry. But the dispiriting quality of the match did not detract from Forest's achievement in winning it. They became the eleventh club to have their name engraved on the trophy, and none of the previous ten winners – who included Real Madrid, Celtic and Ajax – had risen from such a lowly provincial background to become European Champions.

A subdued Clough, complaining of tiredness, glanced from the European Cup, its silver surface marked by many fingerprints, to his players and back again. He told me later that his thoughts were drifting between what had happened the previous evening in Munich, and what had happened on a bitter December night at the City Ground less than two and a half years earlier, in a now-forgotten competition that saw Forest begin their climb from obscurity to the pinnacle of Europe.

The Anglo-Scottish Cup was a trophy, Clough said, that most

managers 'didn't want to piss in'. It was launched by the Football League and the Scottish League to replace the more significant Texaco Cup, which lost its sponsorship. The Texaco tournament was designed as compensation for leading clubs in England and Scotland that had failed to qualify for Europe. The Anglo Scottish Cup was not as ambitious in scope. It became a hands-across-the-border, revenue-generating competition for modest teams with modest ambitions, the type of sides who expected little from a football season other than survival, and perhaps a half-decent cup run and an outside chance of promotion.

The 1976 final was hidden away in the fixture list, as if it were a burden, to be played shortly before Christmas when late-night shopping and office parties were occupying most people's thoughts. After three qualifying group games, and two-legged quarter- and semi-finals, Forest played Orient for a rather plain piece of silverware. There was meagre publicity for the final. The back-page headlines in the 48 hours between the first and second legs focused on Liverpool losing 5–1 at Aston Villa (the club's heaviest League defeat since 1963), Alan Hudson's £200,000 transfer from Stoke to Arsenal, and Trevor Francis, then at Birmingham City, suffering from flu, which ruled him out of the England squad.

A crowd of just over 5,000 watched the first leg at Orient. It finished 1–1. Almost 13,000 saw the return at the City Ground, where Forest won 4–0.

On the plane home from Munich, Clough reflected on something that no one else had properly considered: the importance of the Anglo-Scottish result, and its positive effect on Forest later on. He tried to recall how many of the European Cup final team had also won the Anglo-Scottish Cup for him. 'I remember looking around at the faces – all with smiles as wide as the kids' on Christmas day, and trying to picture the same smiles I'd seen inside our dressing room after we won the Anglo-Scottish Cup.'

When he got back, he checked the two teams. Seven of the side in Munich – Viv Anderson, Frank Clark, John McGovern, Larry Lloyd, Ian Bowyer, John Robertson and Tony Woodcock – had played in one or both legs of the Anglo-Scottish Cup final. Had Martin O'Neill been fit in Munich – or at least if Clough had considered him fit – the number would have been eight. In his analysis of how Forest managed to claw themselves from mid-table in the Second Division to become European Champions, Clough was always grateful to the influence of the Anglo-Scottish Cup, the first trophy the club had won since the FA Cup in 1959.

'Those who said it was a nothing trophy were absolutely crackers,' said Clough with warm nostalgia, like an old soldier reminiscing about a minor battle long ago. I was interviewing him in February 1981, just before Forest flew to Tokyo for that World Club Championship final. I wanted to cover the club's rise over the previous six years. We talked about his arrival, and Taylor's, at Forest, promotion to the First Division, winning the League title and then the first and second European Cups. The Anglo-Scottish Cup seemed to touch him the most. I could scarcely believe it. I had sat in the press box watching Forest collect that cup, wanting to be almost anywhere else. When I rang the score through to the Press Association, the copy-taker at the other end of the phone asked: 'Sorry, what cup final is it?'

I must have betrayed the same thoughts again during the interview – or maybe Clough felt that I wasn't paying sufficient attention. 'Take down every word of what I'm saying,' he insisted, glancing over my shoulder at the blank page of my notebook. 'You look as if you don't believe what I'm saying, as

if I'm only doing it to give you an intro. Don't be daft. I mean it
– I want to see your pen move.'

He carried on speaking. 'The Anglo-Scottish Cup was something to us, to the club and the players. It provided us with a
cup, and players who hadn't won anything with a medal –
players like Woodcock, Withe and half a dozen others who had
got nothing out of their careers until we got our hands on that
trophy. Success of any description was something this club
hadn't known for nearly twenty years. Our lot tasted champagne [for the first time] and found they liked it.' That was the
pay off line Clough gave me.

But whenever he was asked how Forest had been transformed so suddenly, I heard him cite the Anglo-Scottish Cup.
By the late 1980s, when the competition had long since vanished
from the calendar, interviewers with only a vague recollection
that it had ever existed used to give Clough a puzzled glance
when he mentioned it, as if what he had said was a leg-pull.

'Look,' he would say, shaking his head or wagging an index
finger, 'I'm bloody serious. Look in the record books. Talk to
the players.' The demand usually elicited a nervous laugh and
a question to me later on. 'He isn't serious, is he?'

Clough recalled going into the dressing room after beating
Orient, looking at the trophy sitting incongruously on the floor,
wreathed in swirling wisps of steam from the showers, and
seeing the reaction of the players. 'You'd think we'd won the
European Cup *that* night,' he said. 'We were drunk on success
– which, bearing in mind it was the Anglo-Scottish Cup, was a
bit like being drunk on half a pint of shandy. You got the sense,
though, that it was also like we'd been given a shot of something
positive that only a trophy, whatever it is, can bring.'

That competition, Clough said, had the effect of twenty
motivational team talks. 'You could see the lot of 'em, chests

out, backs straight that night. We'd won something, and it made all the difference.'

In the next 16 months, Forest were promoted from the Second Division, won the League Championship and the League Cup. Clough knew that Forest were equipped for the European Cup, but kept relatively quiet about it. The team was solid with international and World Cup experience, and John McGovern and Archie Gemmill had played in the competition before, with Derby. Clough knew too, but again didn't proclaim it, that both he and Taylor were capable of winning a European trophy. But he also knew that very few others, in the media or in management, would share his opinion. 'No one gave us a prayer in Europe. Not one,' he told me.

Winning the trophy in Munich and retaining it twelve months later in Madrid settled three quite separate scores for Clough. The first was with Leeds. As well as a welcome escape from Brighton and the bleakness of the Third Division, part of the glittering allure of Leeds was the free ticket it offered Clough into the European Cup. He wanted to have 'another crack at it', as he explained to Don Revie in a joint interview on television after his sacking in September 1974. By winning the European Cup – the only trophy to elude Revie at Leeds – Clough figured he could cut the umbilical cord that tied the new England manager to his former club. The side would become Clough's Leeds rather than Revie's. Indeed, Clough forced a confession of sorts out of Revie when he got him to concede that the prospect of competing again in the competition (Leeds had been beaten in the semi-finals by Celtic in 1970) had almost persuaded him to turn England down. Eight months later, when

Leeds lost depressingly in a bad-tempered 1975 final to Bayern Munich, Clough was still contemplating how difficult it was going to be for him to revive Forest. A month earlier, Derby, under Dave Mackay, had won the League Championship. It was as though, Clough claimed, a pair of narrow blades had been slipped simultaneously into his heart. Two of his former clubs were prospering while he was on the ropes.

By the time Forest won the European Cup, however, Leeds, were three places and ten points behind them in the First Division, and two other managers had come and gone from Elland Road. Derby finished fourth from bottom of the table. For Clough, there was certainly truth in the old adage that revenge is at its best when it's 'ladled' out cold, as he misquoted it.

Secondly, victory in Munich settled a score not with but on behalf of Derby, and the club's defeat in the 1973 European Cup semi-finals by Juventus – a tie that stuck like a fish-bone in Clough's throat for the rest of his career. A UEFA investigation exonerated Juventus of having had any part in an attempt to bribe the referee in the second leg at the Baseball Ground, where Derby were held to a goalless draw and went out 3–1 on aggregate. The referee told UEFA that he had been offered almost £3,000, plus a car, if the Italians won the match. Juventus, UEFA decided, had nothing to do with the incident: it was the independent work of a Hungarian refugee, Dezso Solti, who had a track record of bribery in Italian football.

Clough was still sceptical, especially since the first leg in Turin had descended into farcical unpleasantness. At half-time Taylor was pushed against a wall by what he assumed were security staff and pinned there until the match resumed. Taylor saw Juventus' Helmut Haller, who had scored for West Germany in the 1966 World Cup final, walking off with the referee, also a German. Taylor tried to follow them so that he could listen to the conversation. He said that Haller elbowed him in the ribs for his trouble. Derby's suspicions had been raised by a message from John Charles. Venerated in Turin, where he played for six seasons, Charles was hired by Clough and Taylor to act as Derby's ambassador and advisor for the tie. When Charles saw Haller enter the referee's room twice before the kick-off, he hurried to tell Taylor.

No evidence exists of any impropriety by, or between, Haller and the referee. Clough still wound himself into incandescent fury over refereeing decisions in Turin which caused both Roy McFarland and Archie Gemmill to be suspended for the second leg after collecting innocuous bookings. For years afterwards, Clough continued to protest about the defeat.

In 1978/79, when Forest won the first of their European Cups, the Italian champions in the competition were Juventus. 'I'd love to go over there and stuff them out of sight,' Clough said, as if the words had been festering inside him for six years. 'And then we could bring them back here and stuff them out of sight again. I want to beat the bastards.' The draw instead paired Forest with Liverpool; Juventus were drawn against Glasgow Rangers, who beat them and denied Clough the closure he sought. It was not just that he neither forgave nor forgot anything easily – particularly a notable defeat that he regarded as a moral wrong committed against him. On top of that was his contempt for what he viewed as UEFA's pusillanimous response to it, which merely confirmed – yet again – his distrust of, and dislike for, authority. Clough decided that UEFA had seriously failed both him and the game. Not even Ajax's defeat of Juventus in the 1973 final appeased him.

Clough regarded Derby's championship side as superior and generally more accomplished on the ball than Forest's. And he often said that the emotion and sense of achievement he experienced after Derby's title win was stronger than the relief and exhaustion that ran through him after Forest's win. He had a far closer emotional attachment to the players at Derby, whom he had nurtured and 'grown up' alongside in his six years at the club. It follows that a lot of the stinging hurt from the result in Turin came from what he felt for those players. The European Cup offered a chance which, for Derby under Clough, would never come again. His resignation a few months later brought a long, mournful reflection on his years there, and on unfulfilled ambitions. The European Cup headed the list. 'We could have won [it] that last year at Derby if it hadn't been for the shenanigans at Juventus. And we would have done,' he said. 'We were good enough . . . and we had the players . . . we had self-belief . . . we'd have been worthy champions.' He said those words to me in 1990, the regret still clearly evident in his voice.

Thirdly, the win in Munich settled a score with the Football Association. The European Cup enabled Clough to demonstrate that he was, despite the FA's misgivings, capable of achieving international success. His managerial abilities extended beyond the domestic game. He explained it like this: 'If you're a club manager – and only a club manager – the way you can partly play at being an international one is to win the European Cup. All hopes had gone for me and the England job by then. If I wasn't getting it in '77, I was never getting it. All I had left was the European Cup. Winning it was my equivalent of the World Cup. Not many managers do *that* twice.'

Some of the things he said in Europe nevertheless confirmed that Clough was unsuited to the diplomatic niceties of the England job. The FA's decision to go for polite, inoffensive Ron Greenwood instead of Clough was vindicated by the looseness of the loser's tongue. Still seething after Derby were beaten by Juventus in Turin, he refused to talk to Italian journalists, announcing that 'I don't speak to cheating bastards.'

After Forest had beaten FC Vorwärts of East Germany in the 1983/84 UEFA Cup, Clough appeared at a press conference. I was standing to one side of the podium, close to the exit. I thought I might catch him when he came past me on his way out. I soon saw that I'd be wasting my time. He was confrontational and ill at ease. Clough gave token answers to the first two or three routine questions before declaring: 'My directors have been swanning around your beautiful city for three days and now they are out celebrating, doing this . . .' (he took an imaginary drink). 'They are the ones who should be here. I've finished my day's work and I want you to know where the directors are. UEFA are wrong to insist that I have to come here.' The German reporters didn't know what to make of it. One of them, who spoke only broken English, asked me afterwards whether Clough was 'mad'. 'No,' I told him 'that's very normal behaviour where I come from.'

In East Berlin, well before the wall came down, Clough talked about trying to walk through Checkpoint Charlie into the West without his passport 'just to see what would happen'. He once referred to FIFA representatives of African countries as 'spear-throwers'. He didn't at first appreciate the gross insensitivity of the comment or how it might be interpreted. 'But I'm not a racist,' he protested.

On trips to Holland (a country he liked enormously), the Second World War was at the centre of Clough's banter. Like Basil Fawlty, he mentioned it constantly. He would regularly use the same line: 'Hey, Hitler only took half an hour to get through this place – and he stopped for twenty minutes to make a cup of tea and to get a bite to eat on the way. The Dutch were waving him through.' Clough would then stand like a policeman at a crossing, waving his arms to direct imaginary traffic. 'Hey, tanks, this way,' he would shout. 'Jeeps down that road.'

Clough suggested that Peter Shilton should 'punch' Diego Maradona as retribution for the 'Hand of God' goal in the 1986 World Cup. It is one thing to think or say such a thing privately; quite another to do so out loud and to see those words reported in print.

As a club manager, a distasteful reference to 'spear-throwers' or a crass comment about punching Maradona – which was actually meant to be good-natured – might make a paragraph or two in the following day's newspapers or an item in a week-end diary. Exactly the same remark from the lips of an England manager, either before or after an international, would have produced a clutch of headlines and a firestorm of protest, fol-lowed by explanations, recriminations and forced apologies. Clough never minded the fact he lived in a glass house. He relished lifting the odd pane to hurl a stone at passing targets. But as England manager, one can only guess at the amount of shattered glass that the FA would have been sweeping up on his behalf if he had accused its international committee of 'swanning around' or going out drinking while he faced the press. Forest's board merely bowed its head in embarrassment and shrugged off Cough's indiscretions with the tame defence of 'Well, it's only Brian. You know what he's like.'

'What Brian was like' would have sent the FA into paroxysms of despair. But if the England job had suddenly fallen vacant in the winter of 1979, rather than two years earlier, the FA would have found it impossible to deny him the post. How those FA councillors must have prayed and given thanks each morning for Greenwood's continuing good health and the reasonable results that brought England unspectacular qualification for the 1982 World Cup in Spain. This was while Clough was calling

Sweden and the Swedes 'boring', saying he hated the French and disliked the Germans and, during the World Club Championship final, disparaging the Japanese. Tokyo's Olympic Stadium was bereft of grass for Forest's 1–0 defeat by Nacional. A fine grit, like harsh sand, kicked up dust clouds. 'Why,' he demanded to know, 'are the Japanese technologically advanced enough to stick a TV in your wristwatch but can't grow grass on a field? It puzzles me. Can someone explain?' Forest's success in Europe suggests what he might have achieved for England – if, of course, his tongue had not got him the sack.

The European Cup was markedly different from the Champions League and before the introduction of a group stage before the knockout rounds. A team played nine matches to win it. There was an added edge to the cup from the first round because the margin for error was minimal: one goalkeeping mistake, one sloppy pass, one open goal missed, and a side could vanish from the competition.

It really was Britain versus Europe. Very few overseas players were bought by British clubs. Journeying into Eastern Europe, especially outside a capital city, made you realise how fortunate you were to live in democratic society. I saw bread queues and food shortages in Romania, where Forest played Arge Piteti. We were fed green chips and horsemeat in the hotel, which had one telephone line. In East Berlin I was followed by the secret police, who looked as though they'd been recruited from Hollywood's central casting – long, black overcoats and wire-rimmed spectacles. In Bulgaria, I spent an hour arguing with customs officers who wrongly believed I'd been laundering money. I was threatened with detention as the rest of the team flew home from an end of season friendly. Ron Fenton came to my rescue.

Before some bright chap invented the Internet, and you could find anything and everything with Google, getting information on European opposition for the newspaper was a laborious task. I would get hold of an international telephone directory and ring a newspaper near the club. If I could get past the operator, making her understand that I wanted to speak to the football correspondent, I hoped someone, somewhere on the editorial floor might speak English so that I could trade team news and results. The popularity of the English game meant that newspapers elsewhere always knew something about Forest and Clough, and were eager to learn more. 'Clough – he's the crazy one, isn't he?' asked one journalist. 'Well he is, but he isn't,' I replied, which confused him.

With their European Cup campaigns, Forest took the view that each tie was a mini-holiday from domestic chores. Clough and Taylor had pioneered the mid-season get-away, for themselves and their players. A quick break overseas with the odd beer, a swim and a soak in the sun defied traditional management philosophy. Most managers thought training in the cold, wind and rain remained the only way to maintain strength and form in midwinter.

'Bollocks.' was Clough's opinion of that. Or, to put it more constructively, he thought it as outdated as the notion that players were hungrier for the ball on a Saturday if it had been denied to them during the week. 'More bollocks. Can you imagine any other profession where not doing something makes you better at it? A pianist learns to play the piano by spending hours at the keyboard. A painter learns how to paint by standing at an easel. And a footballer learns how to become more skilful at his job by practising it.'

His theory behind the mid-season 'holiday' followed the same line of reasoning, which he labelled 'pure common sense'. As the game became more intense and physically demanding, he worried that players would suffer burn-out. 'Do you want frozen mud on your boots, or sun on your back? Which is likely to be more beneficial?' was Clough's then novel way of thinking. It broke the drudgery of routine, which was vital for someone like Clough, who had such a low boredom threshold. 'Didn't someone once say that variety is the spice of life?' he asked. 'He was right.'

Forest, like Derby, were persuaded to consider European ties as get-aways. 'I'm not saying we thought of games in Europe entirely as a holiday,' said Clough, 'but we definitely went out to enjoy them – the trip as well as the match itself. We approached each one as something different from the normal slog and grind of Monday to Friday preparation. We got to see some different scenery.' Not to begin with, however. For Forest in 1978, the first round of the European Cup was a busman's holiday. The win over Liverpool – 2–0 at the City Ground in the first leg, and a typically Shilton-inspired 0–0 at Anfield – underlined Clough's supremacy over Bob Paisley in the late 1970s.

Liverpool had won the European Cup in each of the previous two seasons. Paisley's side went into the opening leg against Forest leading the First Division on the back of five straight wins. When Liverpool arrived in Nottingham on that mid-September night, the air was warm, yet it also contained what seemed to me to be invisible sparks – a rubbing together of tension and a sense of anticipation that I had never felt before. When the match was over and I had finished my report, I watched the Liverpool players file raggedly out of the dressing room towards the team bus. There was no smile, for once, on

Emlyn Hughes' face. Kenny Dalglish looked even grimmer than usual. Graeme Souness stepped out sharply, as if he couldn't wait to get home.

Forest had prised Liverpool's fingers off the European Cup. What the performance did not necessarily do was convince the rest of Europe of Forest's capacity to go on and win the trophy itself. Forest were still a small-town club who had unaccountably managed to slay a giant, probably with a lucky punch. It took the crushing of AEK Athens in the next round (7–2 on aggregate) and a coasting, almost carefree win over Grasshoppers of Zurich (5–2) in the quarter-finals to establish their credentials. Forest's classic style was demonstrated in the semifinal against FC Cologne, in two matches which epitomised the contrasting strengths of Clough and Taylor's team, and of Clough and Taylor themselves.

Forced through their own shortcomings into a first-leg 3–3 draw at the City Ground, Forest seemed to have little hope in the return tie. So certain were Cologne of victory that they reserved hotel rooms in Munich for the final. Looking back on it now, the outcome appears to me as predestined, as if the labour of reaching the final just had to be greater than the effort required to beat Malmö more than a month later.

The first leg at Forest, on an unsightly pitch of thick mud, had swung first Cologne's way (an improbable 2–0 lead) and then Forest's (tenaciously 3–2 up) before a late equaliser from the Germans' Japanese substitute, Yashukiko Okudera. JAP SUB SINKS FOREST, ran a headline the next day, accurately reflecting the bleak prospects for Forest. In the dressing room after the game, the players hadn't even pulled off their boots before Taylor began to spread optimism, reassuring each of them in confidently unequivocal terms what the outcome would be in Cologne, and the straightforward mathematics necessary to achieve it. 'All we need is a goal and a clean sheet to win,' he kept repeating. 'We're going to get both of them.'

Taylor liked horse racing, and he often talked like a compulsive punter who fervently believed that the next horse, the next race, the next meeting, would turn him into a millionaire. With him there was always some blue sky to be found somewhere, even when the heavens were the colour of a bruise. So bullish was he in the aftermath of the draw against Cologne that Clough, worried he was overestimating the odds in Forest's favour, yanked him aside. 'I told him to quieten things down a bit,' Clough told me. 'I didn't want him shouting about it so loudly.' Taylor wouldn't be dissuaded. He wanted Forest's chances in Cologne talking up. And that's what he did, not merely in the dressing room but also to the media. He wanted to sow whatever small doubts he could in the minds of the Germans. 'He was right and I was wrong,' accepted Clough, reflecting on Taylor's tactics a few years after his partner's death. 'We had to make them think we were good enough to win there. Mind you, I think Pete believed it as well. My thought was that we'd scored three goals at home – and still not won it. I was a bit down when I walked back along the tunnel.'

'A goal and a clean sheet' was just what Forest achieved in Cologne. The lone goal was a stooping header from Bowyer, the ball lifted in from the fringe of the six-yard box. At the end of the match, with his prediction fulfilled, Taylor rose regally from the bench and walked calmly back to the dressing room.

When Forest lifted the European Cup it highlighted Clough and Taylor's ability to put together a side from disparate sources.

A victorious team, containing Burns and Lloyd, Woodcock and Robertson, Clark and Anderson, was ample evidence that a fat cheque book was not essential to win in Europe. Granted, the £1 million signing of Francis, in February 1979, was a transfer from the shelves of football's Harrods. But the £2,000 it took to bring Garry Birtles from Midland League side Long Eaton United two years earlier was like a bargain from the bric-a-brac stall at the local market.

Francis was a fixture in the Football League from the moment he made his debut at the age of sixteen. He moved effortlessly past defenders, as if he were gliding. Half-close your eyes and you might think that his studs never touched the turf. If Clough could walk on water, Francis could run on air, with a hint of a vapour trail from his boots.

His signing is still vivid in my mind. A million-pound transfer was football's equivalent of breaking the sound barrier: no British club had ever paid more than £500,000. I'd never seen so many journalists – TV, radio and print – thronging in the City Ground's car park to cover a sports news story. I camped out at the ground for three days, banished from the corridor because Clough got fed up with seeing me there. I still have the Forest programme, published after Francis had arrived, which explains how an 'unobtrusive local journalist' called Duncan Hamilton virtually 'camped' in the main entrance foyer until the manager told him to pack up and 'go sleep elsewhere'. What Clough actually said was, 'If you don't fuck off, I'll kick you out myself.'

The Francis story generated more publicity about a single player than any other story had done for years. I took calls from newspapers around the world. There was a glamour about Francis too. I remember his Jaguar sweeping into the car park, the beige suit he wore on a grey winter's morning and his wife,

Helen, looking like a catwalk model from Paris, swathed in a massive fur coat.

The arrival of Birtles was an altogether lower-key affair. His transfer to Forest just made the back page of the *Nottingham Evening Post*. He had spent his late teens tacking down carpets in homes and offices, and played part-time for two teams in Long Eaton before Forest, recognising him as a late developer, moved in. Clough was asked his view of Birtles after he'd gone to watch him. 'The half-time Oxo was better,' he said, 'but I signed him anyway.'

Birtles soon got himself noticed because he ran at defences, unpicking them with ease. His legs seemed to get longer with each stride.

Birtles was twenty when he first appeared on Forest's team sheet, in an unglamorous Second Division game against Hull in March 1977. He was played out of position, in midfield. I remember that game particularly well because we were both making our debut: I wrote my first real match report that afternoon, and phoned it through to the *Sunday Mercury*. I was working for Matthew Engel, now the editor of *Wisden*, and he lent me his Olivetti typewriter. He pulled my report out of the typewriter as soon as I'd finished, and read it. 'Not bad,' he said, being wildly over-generous.

No one would have believed at the start of the season – with Francis playing for Birmingham City, and Birtles in the reserves at Forest – that the two of them would become integral to the most unlikely European Cup win since the competition began. Birtles scored the first goal of Forest's European Cup run, against Liverpool, and Francis claimed the last and most crucial in the Olympic Stadium. A year later in the final against Hamburg, with Francis injured, Birtles chased the length and breadth of Real Madrid's Bernabeu Stadium to the point of utter exhaustion. By the end of the final his socks were round his ankles, his head drooped like a cut flower, and wide, dark patches of sweat stained his red shirt.

Clough believed that it was always harder to maintain success than to achieve it, and he didn't say that merely as a lame excuse for why, after 1980, Forest deteriorated to such an extent that it took them almost a decade to win another trophy.

In retrospect, just looking through the results round by round in cold type, retaining the European Cup appears far less difficult for Forest than claiming it for the first time had been. Perhaps it was because Forest's and Clough's enhanced reputations gave them a goal start. Perhaps it was because Forest acted like champions, surer of themselves in Europe and more accustomed to it. Perhaps it was because the competition itself, as well as the opposition, seemed a lot less daunting to them.

Easing past the Swedes Östers IF Växjö and Arge Piteti of Romania, Forest tripped briefly against Dynamo Berlin at the City Ground, losing 1–0. In the return leg, Francis's opening goal – a deft, ballet-like turn and a low finish a foot inside the far post – restored equality and launched his side's comeback to a 3–1 win on the night. Ajax were fairly straightforwardly picked off in the semi-final.

The final itself was billed as Clough versus Kevin Keegan, who had signed for Hamburg after Liverpool won the European Cup in 1977. My flight to Madrid arrived at the same time as the Hamburg team's. I interviewed Keegan as he waited for his bags. He was pleasant and polite, and gave me enough copy in twenty minutes for three back page stories. However, I got the feeling that he wasn't terribly confident about the outcome.

As things turned out, I'll always believe the final was shaped not only by Robertson's right-footed goal, which came after Forest had withstood sustained pressure during the opening twenty minutes, or by one pearl of a save after another from Shilton. Crucial to the outcome was the tackling of Burns. Just after Forest scored, Hamburg were impatient and anxious, not quite able to believe that their opponents had caught them on the break. Midway inside the Forest half, Burns went into Keegan with a ferocity that, even watching from a distance, made me wince. Keegan heaved himself off the turf, and seemed to mentally check whether all his limbs were still attached to his body.

Burns had already flattened Hamburg's centre forward. Keegan was the first to remonstrate with the referee, who didn't bother to reach for his book for what today would probably be an automatic sending-off. The two tackles, a clear statement of intent, intimidated Hamburg. As the match wore on, Keegan began to fade. He looked agitated, dropping farther back into Hamburg's half. As the underdogs, Forest were attritional and compact. Shilton, Burns and Lloyd were immovable objects. At the end, Hamburg received their medals as Forest gathered beside them for their team photograph, the European Cup held aloft. As soon as he took his medal, Keegan, gazing at the floor, went silently to the sanctuary of the dressing room.

'You win something once and people can say it's all down to luck,' said Clough, echoing the line he had used when Forest won him his second League Championship. 'You win it twice and it shuts them up.' He would never reach another European final.

Four years later, in the second leg of their UEFA Cup semi-final against Anderlecht, Forest were defending a 2–0 lead from the first leg. They lost 3–0. One of the goals was an absurd penalty

– a theatrical dive, a tackling leg barely in the same postcode as the attacker – but that decision was overshadowed by a greater nonsense. In the last minute Paul Hart buried a strong, perfectly legitimate header in the back of the net. Forest were through on the away goals rule – or so everyone thought. A second later, the Spanish referee Guruceta Muro penalised Hart for pushing or climbing (I was never sure which). In the early hours of the following morning I sat at my desk in the office and studied the evidence: a series of photographs of Hart as he went for the ball and dispatched it beyond the goalkeeper, and then a videotape of the match. Clough had been cheated.

The UEFA Cup was supposed to be Clough's two-fingered reply to critics who claimed that he could not survive without Taylor. He was going to win the thing and use it to beat anyone who had doubted him. On the way back from Belgium, he sat hunched and morose at the front of the plane, refusing to speak. I went forward to try to talk to him. He turned his head and saw me. 'Not tonight, pal,' he said. It was the saddest I had ever seen him. He looked inconsolable, as if there'd been a death in the family.

The truth emerged in 1997: Muro had been bribed. Anderlecht's former president, Constant Vanden Stock, had given the referee £18,000. When the news broke in a Belgian newspaper, Muro was already dead. He'd been killed in a car crash in 1987. The newspaper also reported that money had been paid to individuals who threatened to expose Anderlect. The club claimed that the cash had been handed over as 'loans'.

I have a photograph of Clough's press conference taken the day before the tie. The journalists are sitting on the hotel patio. I am squinting into the lens. Clough, shirt open, willingly poses with us, smiling in the blazing sun, because he wants a souvenir. We'd just listened to Clough voice his concern about the referee who would be in charge the following night. Not because he thought Muro had been, or would be, bribed, but because he knew from experience that referees, especially in Europe, could be swayed by the suffocating influence of a home crowd or by an antipathy towards another country.

'Blow me,' he said, without knowing what was to come. 'You never got that in the Anglo-Scottish Cup.'

CHAPTER SIX

The average FA Councillor's knowledge of football

Long into his retirement, Tommy Lawton, one of the few footballers worthy of being described as a legend, wrote a twice-
weekly column for the *Nottingham Evening Post* which I
occasionally ghosted for him. I got to know Tommy well and
we had long conversations about every aspect of his career.
Tommy was honest enough to say that, during his own playing
days, he was more arrogant than Brian Clough. 'I had a head
bigger than Birkenhead,' he would say 'much bigger than
Cloughie's.'

Like Clough, Tommy was never much impressed with
England managers. Most of his scorn was heaped on Walter
Winterbottom, who was England manager at the end of Lawton's international career. 'The bloke liked the smell of chalk,
loved classrooms and knew nothing about football. Written
down, his knowledge wouldn't have filled the back of a Wood-
bines packet,' was just a sliver of Tommy's condemnation.

On the blackboard, said Tommy, Winterbottom drew 'so
many lines and squiggles you couldn't see the pitch. I got a
migraine looking at the diagrams. Finally, me and Stan
[Matthews] had enough of it. I shouted from the back of the

room, "Look, Walter, let's stop all this guff. It's simple – get the ball out on the wing to Stan, get him to cross it and I'll head it into the net and then we can go home." Stan and me got up and walked out of the team meeting.'

Tommy nevertheless thought he understood why Winterbottom survived for so long, and it turned him bilious. 'Winterbottom wore shiny shoes, pressed flannels, tied a perfect knot in his tie, brushed his blazer and brown-nosed his way through the Football Association. He knew how to doff his cap, bow and scrape. "Yes Mr this, yes Mr that" – and three bags bloody full, too.' And then Tommy would always add: 'Billy Wright used to carry his bag for him – that's how he won over a hundred caps. The pair of them turned my stomach.' Winterbottom, according to Tommy, knew how to 'lick arse' so well that he would have got 'an Olympic medal in it'.

Clough didn't know, and would never consider learning, how to do that. Not only did acerbic bluntness make his appointment as England manager impossible, it very probably cost him a place in the 1958 World Cup squad. Like Tommy Lawton, he didn't much care for either Winterbottom or Wright.

Despite scoring forty-two goals for Middlesbrough during the 1957/58 season, Clough received only tepid support from an influential insider at the club. Harold Shepherdson, the trainer, was Winterbottom's right-hand man. With Shepherdson championing him, Clough's prodigious goalscoring, albeit in the Second Division, ought to have earned him an automatic World Cup place. The problem was that Shepherdson respected but didn't like him. 'I shouted my mouth off too much for him,' Clough told me.

Clough also disagreed publicly with Winterbottom over selection midway through an England Under-23 tour, held a year before the finals in Sweden. Clough scored in the first game, which England lost narrowly to Bulgaria. He was left out of the second match because Winterbottom wanted to give another centre forward, Derek Kevan, his chance. 'I couldn't believe it, and said so in no uncertain terms,' said Clough. We can only speculate about 'no uncertain terms' and what it actually meant.

A month before the World Cup began, Clough travelled with the team to Russia and Yugoslavia for England's final preparations. Winterbottom didn't have a first-choice centre forward, as Tommy Taylor had died in the Munich air crash three months earlier. Clough, fully expecting to go to Sweden, never got his boots dirty. He watched England lose 5–0 to Yugoslavia and draw 1–1 with Russia; Kevan played in both matches.

After Steve Hodge was chosen for England's 1986 World Cup squad in Mexico, where he exchanged shirts with Maradona following the 'Hand of God' quarter-final, Clough talked to me about what had happened to him almost thirty years earlier. He envied Hodge, he said. He would have given 'anything' to play in the World Cup finals.

Clough believed that a conversation in the dressing room had probably cost him his ticket to Sweden. 'Billy Wright was going on about how good the Russian centre forward had been,' said Clough. Wright 'went on and on about it, trying to justify how poor he'd been'. Clough interrupted him and said that he didn't think the centre forward was actually much of a player. 'In fact,' he added, 'I thought he gave up after an hour or so.'

At that point Wright turned away from Clough and carried on his conversation. Clough thought Winterbottom overheard his remarks – a player, without a senior appearance for England, criticising the captain, who had ninety-one caps. If the manager hadn't been eavesdropping, Clough said, Wright would have reported the exchange to him anyway. It was an early sign that free speech was more important to Clough than polite appeasement. 'I just couldn't contain myself,' he admitted, 'it wasn't my nature.'

Clough did go on to represent his country in full internationals, only twice, in 1959. His outspokenness most likely stopped him from being selected again for the national side, just as, eighteen years later, it was certainly what stopped him from being selected to manage it. No doubt, on the pitch, England under Clough would have prospered: disciplined and tight, fluent and stylish. Off it, his lack of tact would have guaranteed heart attacks for those he described as the Football Association's 'blazer-wearing bastards'.

Although he was a fundamentally authoritarian figure himself, Clough mistrusted authority. That was evident not just throughout his managerial career but also before it began. He was seldom comfortable with directors or administrators because he generally held them in as much esteem as a dog does its fleas. While there were individuals he liked and respected, he held the view that directors as a breed were parasitical freeloaders with an appalling ignorance of, and scant appreciation for, both his worth and the game itself. Most, he said to me, fell into one of three categories: duplicitous, devious back-stabbers ('they'd have given Julius Caesar a good going-over'), feckless sycophants ('who hide in dark corners when the flak flies') or egotists ('running a football club gets their photograph on the back page of newspapers – nowt else ever would').

Clough subscribed to the Len Shackleton view. The ninth

chapter of Shackleton's autobiography *Crown Prince of Soccer* was called 'The average director's knowledge of football'. Beneath that title, the page was left blank. 'Most directors are shithouses,' Clough would frequently say in conversation. 'They only know where to find the free drink and the free food. If we win, it's "Oh Brian, lovely to see you!" If we lose, it's "What a bastard the manager is," and lots of muttering behind closed doors.'

The irrational mistrust of directors essentially began for Clough at Hartlepool, a club owned by Ernest Ord, a man so physically diminutive that he could barely see over the steering wheel of his Rolls-Royce. Ord, according to Clough, threatened to sack him 'forty-three times a week' and was bitterly mean-spirited. He would phone Clough's office at five minutes to three to make sure the manager had not 'scarpered home' prematurely. The two of them were perpetually at each other's throats. They disagreed over everything from the performance of the team to the colour of the walls in the manager's office. Ord thought that Clough didn't give him enough respect; Clough thought that Ord was an imbecile determined to dominate everything, including him.

Ord was hostile to the media image Clough cultivated for himself. Searching, as ever, for publicity, Clough took his squad to train on Seaton Carew beach – 'the coldest place on earth,' he called it – and invited a photographer to take pictures of the players running through a typically robust north-easterly wind for the following day's local paper. When the photograph appeared, Ord 'went daft' because 'no one' – by which he meant Clough – had sought his permission. 'He told me he'd be hand-ling all the publicity from then on. He thought he was handling Hollywood, not Hartlepool,' said Clough.

Clough refused to accept that, so Ord sacked both him and

Peter Taylor. With typical bravado, Clough mobilised the board's support against Ord, who eventually had no option but to resign himself. Clough's relationship with Ord, or rather the lack of one, set a pattern for what followed in his dealings with other directors.

Waiting for Clough at Derby was another version of Ord: Sam Longston. Just as Ord had done, Longston became exasperated by the high profile Clough maintained by his non-stop 'publicity', a euphemism for attracting controversy. Longston revelled in the success Clough brought to Derby, and began to treat him like a son. What he didn't revel in, because it embarrassed him, were the attacks Clough made on other managers and chairmen, or specifically on the conduct of the Football Association and the Football League in particular.

Worn down by Clough, and by constantly having to apologise in other clubs' boardrooms on his manager's behalf, Longston became pernickety and dictatorial. His aim, Clough felt, was now to lever him and Taylor out of Derby. Longston had fed ravenously off Clough's connections both inside and outside the game. He constantly asked to be introduced to footballers and managers he didn't know, like Bobby Moore, and showbusiness figures, such as Eric Morecombe, who were linked to the game or who Clough had got to know through charitable work with the Lords Taverners. He accompanied his manager to celebrity functions that would otherwise have been closed off to him. Clough went along with Longston's starry-eyed swooning because it oiled their working relationship. He was slow to cotton on to Longson's burgeoning confidence as a chairman in his own right.

Longston, like Ord, demanded that Clough limit his work for newspapers and TV, and clear anything with him before publication or broadcast. He expressed concern about the amount of alcohol Clough and Taylor were consuming, and ordered that the manager's drinks cabinet should be locked. Clough was drinking heavily. 'We (he meant Taylor too) used it to switch off. We also dispensed the booze to anyone who was passing through – journalists, friends, other managers. We were generous like that. Longston didn't like the size of the bill.'

It was October 1973. Derby were third in the table, and Clough was regularly on TV. With a contract to appear on London Weekend Television's *On the Ball*, he travelled to the studios each week to record his segment of the programme. Whatever issues arose – about either football or politics – Clough would have his say, and no one, especially Longston, was going to silence or control him.

For Clough, hubris took over. He and Taylor quit in a tantrum, a decision he later maintained, very forcefully to me, was the worst of his life. 'Never, never, never quit,' I heard him say, his face pained as he remembered the end at Derby. 'If you're thinking of resigning, go home and weigh things up overnight. If you wake up the following morning still wanting to quit, sleep on it again until the day dawns when you open the curtains and change your mind.'

Clough calculated that Longston would fold as easily as Ord: another terrible misjudgement. The Derby board – despite a players' protest, despite a supporters' protest and despite Clough's protest in the media – had a stiffer spine than Ord at Hartlepool. Longston stayed, Clough and Taylor went, and a lesson was learnt. When the Leeds board abjectly capitulated and pushed Clough out, there was at least the mattress stuffed with money to cushion the fall. But it confirmed to him in spectacular fashion what he had preached all along: 'Directors are shithouses.' The Football Association's hierarchy, stuffily formal, were, he decided, the worst of the worst. 'A bunch of fucking amateurs who couldn't tell Geoff Hurst from their own fat arses,' was how he inelegantly put it to me.

As fortune's wheel turned, Clough found himself at the one club in ninety-two that was unable to prevent a dictatorship. When Clough arrived, Nottingham Forest was constitutionally run like a local cricket team. The club was not a limited company. Instead of directors and shareholders, Forest had members, just over two hundred of them, who paid a nominal sum every year and elected a committee to manage the club's business affairs. In Clough's era the committee consisted chiefly of local businessmen or professionals. The figure of substance was Brian Appleby, a QC, and Clough sensibly opted not to take on his depth and intellect. Appleby's 'Chairman's Report' at the end of Forest's golden season of 1977/78 was as memorable as Shackleton's blank page. Rather than words, he placed two photographs alongside one another: the League Championship trophy and the League Cup.

Clough was de facto head of Forest, and he both relished the position and despised the system. Apart from a membership fee of a couple of hundred pounds, none of Forest's committee were obliged to put a substantial sum of money into the club. The club's financial well-being depended almost entirely on the performance of the team. Clough complained: why should committee members make no significant contribution – by which he meant a six-figure sum – but enjoy the comforts and privileges their status afforded them? At the same time, Forest's anachronistic constitution in comparison to the rest of the clubs in the Football League allowed him the independence he craved. Here, there would never be an Ord or a Longston to lord it over him. Even when the constitution changed, after Forest's two European Cup wins made it necessary, directors and shareholders (209 in total) still owned only one share each.

When Clough first arrived at the City Ground, he asked why there was an empty row of seats at the back of the committee box. 'I found out it was because the supporters spat at the committee. That's the bad shape we were in. I was expected to bail them out.' He called in the debt many times over. He used the story to remind Forest what life had been like before he saved them. 'Hey, don't forget: if it hadn't been for me, you'd still be wiping the spit off your faces,' he would say; usually out of the committee's earshot, of course.

The committee and its meetings were treated with barely concealed contempt because he found the whole thing laborious. If he didn't excuse himself from them altogether, he arrived late or left early. Sometimes I was in his office on the day of a meeting. He would put off his entrance for as long as possible. 'I suppose I'll have to show me face,' he'd say to me, 'but I hate all that hot air. And it's so boring.'

Very few directors went into his office without permission. When one of them did, walking through the door without the courtesy of knocking, Clough greeted him with a 'flame thrower' – a fiery string of invective hot enough to strip the paint from the walls. 'This is my fucking office and I am working. You fucking knock if you want to come in and I'll decide whether to open the door or slam it in your face. Now fucking get out!'

The shocked director took two paces back, half bowing, and closed the door behind him, mumbling an incoherent apology. Clough waited until he heard his footsteps retreating along the corridor. 'Without me this club would be nowt. None of 'em would be able to walk around in a club blazer and tie giving it the "big I am" with a gin and tonic in one hand and a plate full of sandwiches in the other. You'd think the club belonged to them.' It took him a good five minutes to calm down. (The director in question, Maurice Roworth, later became the club's chairman.)

Clough privately vilified directors as 'fucking nonentities', which was enormously unfair. All of them had created success-ful businesses, often from scratch, and were lifelong devotees of the club that now clearly 'belonged' to its manager. I once asked Clough just why he was so intolerant of directors.

'Imagine,' he replied, 'if I walked into *their* premises first thing on Monday morning and strolled around telling them what was wrong with the factory, or the shop floor, or whatever the director runs when he's not here bothering me. The bloke would have every right to turn around and say, "Sorry, Brian, you know nowt about my business. You're a football man." And he'd be right. Now I can say with justification to a director, "You know nowt about *my* business either, 'cos you've never been a footballer or a football manager." It just doesn't stop them poking their nose in, does it? The ideal director raises money, manages it and passes it on to me to spend as I see fit. If they don't like what I do with it, they can sack me and get someone else.'

A few directors did find favour. Stuart Dryden, chairman when Forest beat Malmö to win the European Cup in 1979, ran a village post office until an audit revealed that he had been fraudulently cashing pension books. Dryden had been influen-tial in Clough's move to Forest and subsequently in persuading his more reluctant colleagues on the board that Clough rep-resented an unmissable, once-in-a-lifetime chance for the club. Clough stayed admirably loyal to his friend during the court case and after it, which bizarrely meant that the disgraced Dryden could stroll in to the manager's office and see him whenever he pleased – and he often did – while the directors responsible for running the club were frequently shut out or made unwelcome. What is more, the directors had no option but to put up with it and smile politely at Dryden, who had brought shame on the club, because of his relationship with Clough. 'I don't care what that lot think of Stuart. He's my mate and he's coming in,' Clough said to me.

There was frequently an air of edgy confrontation between manager and board because Clough wanted no opposition. But he found it sometimes in Derek Pavis. He had a gruff manner and gravel-voice, and was the epitome of the successful, self-made businessman. Clough constantly complained to me about him, and all because Pavis was prepared to challenge Clough's dismissive manner with the board, question his record in the transfer market, and, just as Longston and Ord had done, object to his outspokenness when he felt it had been too rabid. Clough hated any interference, as if having the temerity to grill him about the decisions he'd made was an act of insolence. He also hated the fact that Pavis didn't kowtow to him.

In fact, at the time, he just hated him.

Under the company's rules, directors had to periodically submit themselves for re-election to the board. Pavis's seniority also meant he would eventually become chairman, something Clough was determined would never be allowed to happen. 'Working with him would be worse than I could ever imagine,' he told me. 'He's my sworn enemy. If he ever walks in as chairman, I walk out.' When the time came for Pavis' re-election, Clough campaigned vehemently for another candidate, a car dealer called John Smith, to take his place on the board. 'I've got a photograph I want your paper to publish – or you won't get another word out of me this or any other season,' he said to me in a terse phone call. 'John Smith's company is giving the club a sponsored car. I want him photographed with it on your back page. I want people to see I support him.' Clough also lobbied shareholders vigorously on Smith's behalf. He guessed correctly that another candidate, Irving Korn, would comfortably win the ballot. In a three-cornered fight for two vacancies, Smith, a gentle, softly spoken man, represented Clough's only chance of ridding himself of Pavis. Smith's scheme to promote the club was to put Clough in a Robin Hood costume. Smith thought an image of him wearing Lincoln Green, and pointing out of a Lord Kitchener-like recruiting poster, would drum up support. Clough recoiled at the idea of wearing tights. 'I'll get him on the board – but I'm not dressing up,' he balked.

In the election, Clough narrowly got his way: Smith beat Pavis by five votes. 'The air is cleaner now' was all Clough would say about it afterwards. (When Clough retired, though, it was Pavis who took the trouble to write a generous letter, which thanked him for his eighteen years at the City Ground, and what he achieved during it for the city of Nottingham).

Clough was never slow to seize the moment. When a director, a fidgety man named Frank Allcock, whom he disliked, crassly placed a 7:1 bet against Forest – backing Manchester United to beat them in a League match at Old Trafford – Clough used his manager's notes in the following Saturday's matchday programme (an injury-depleted Forest had beaten United 3–2) to begin the process of forcing him to resign. He asked me to dig out a Biblical quote to end his column. It was Matthew, chapter 14, verse 31: 'O thou of little faith.'

Even the one-time chairman, Geoffrey Macpherson, was undermined. Clough referred to him as Dame Margaret Rutherford, the jowly actress who played Miss Marple. 'Well,' he said in mitigation, 'he does look like her and he does sound like her.'

I was sitting next to Clough, gathering quotes for a story, when the coach carrying the directors passed the team bus on the way back from a match. Clough made a theatrical show of waving and blowing kisses from his seat. He smiled broadly, pressing his face close to the window. At the same time I heard him say: 'You shithouses. You think I'm smiling at you. I'm actually telling you to fuck off. I hope you choke on the smoked salmon.'

Similarly withering treatment would have been meted out to the Football Association. Clough was openly hostile towards, for example, Sir Harold Thompson, the FA chairman. With Clough in charge of the England team, the fusty corridors of Lancaster Gate would have been shaken on an hourly basis.

By the time Clough was interviewed for the England job, in December 1977, he ought to have been the automatic selection. Among the serious candidates – Clough, Ron Greenwood, Lawrie McMenemy, Jack Charlton and Dave Sexton – only he had won the League title. He had helpfully been the most remorseless critic of Don Revie, who had resigned suddenly that summer after England had gone five matches without a win. Revie went to the United Arab Emirates to rake in 'fool's gold', according to Clough, who reckoned he was 'obsessed' with money because Leeds scandalously underpaid him. Most importantly of all, Forest under Clough and Peter Taylor were leading the First Division, and on the way to the League championship.

Clough always maintained that he left his interview thinking,

'The job's mine. I didn't so much walk out of the room as float. I was absolutely brilliant. I told them what I'd do and how I'd do it. I was so passionate about the job, I'm sure three lions appeared on my chest as I was chuntering on. I was utterly charming, too. I walked in, introduced myself to them individually and I saw Thompson look so startled I thought his glasses were going to slide of his nose. At the end, I thanked them all very much and said, "Hey, you're not a bad bunch." I went out of the room, back straight, head up, knowing I'd done all I could. Oh, I was full of myself afterwards.'

Clough deceived himself – as he acknowledged to me fifteen years later, in his final season. Anyone on record as saying, as Clough did, that 'an ICI foreman was almost certainly once on the shop floor, a bus inspector once drove a bus. But how many FA officials have ever been footballers?' was never seriously going to be considered for the England post. He was too dangerous for the FA. The FA council was protective of its privileges and perks and of the coldly aloof but clubbably refined atmosphere of Lancaster Gate. The committee held itself in fatuously high regard, as if it were the owner of a grand stately pile, and the manager of the national side merely a hired help, like a handyman or gardener. Clough regarded its attitude towards Sir Alf Ramsey as ungrateful and his sacking as fundamentally cruel. The FA didn't expect its paid employee to be more important or powerful than the organisation itself, which Clough would have been. He was deadly serious when he filled in a profile of himself, and under 'Sports' wrote 'tennis, squash, cricket and baiting directors' and under 'Likes and dislikes', listed firstly 'two man board of directors' and then 'nine man board of directors'.

'I was never going to get that job,' Clough admitted. 'But when the FA saw me, and I wasn't the awful, snarling, spitting,

bombastic bloke they'd imagined, I took them by utter surprise.'
As he reflected on it, Clough imagined the interview panel going
home, flicking through all the old cuttings about him, making a
note of every occasion on which he had criticised someone,
and finally thinking, 'No, he's far too risky, you never know
what he might do next.'

He thought about them ringing friends in football who would
give a sharp intake of breath at the very mention of his name.
'Blimey, the FA would worry that I might want to get rid of
them for a start. And, of course, they were dead right. I'd have
torn the place down brick by brick and rebuilt it the way I
wanted it. After Revie, I was just too risky. The FA wanted Ron
Greenwood – good guy, safe but boring. They wanted the whole
thing kept cosy. They wanted to take their wives on overseas
trips, travelling first class and staying in nice hotels where
cocktails were served on the veranda. They wanted to wear the
England badge on their blazer. Bugger the World Cup. That job
wasn't given on the strength of an interview, it was handed out
to someone who would cause the FA no fuss whatsoever. It
was a carve-up and I should have known it.'

The FA went for the establishment figure of Greenwood, who
had been caretaker manager after Revie's abrupt departure. He
sealed his appointment almost a month before the interviews
took place when England, with three uncapped players – Peter
Barnes, Bob Latchford and Steve Coppell – beat Italy 2–0 at
Wembley.

Well after the interviews had taken place, Peter Swales, the
Manchester City chairman and a member of the selection committee, confirmed that Clough never stood a chance. 'Sir Harold
Thompson didn't want to grant him an interview in the first
place, and promised to sort him out once he got into the interview room. We were 90 per cent against him,' he said, but 'he

gave the best interview of all the candidates – confident, full of common sense and . . . patriotic.'

Clough took Greenwood's appointment as an insult. Greenwood, he reminded everyone, hadn't been a club manager for four years. 'He was a general manager at West Ham, and nowt to do with the team.'

Worse, the FA patronised him. Clough, with Taylor, was made joint manager of the England youth team, which already had a part-time manager, Ken Burton. Clough's job was a token, like a pat on the head to placate a recalcitrant child. He had no choice but to smile and accept it, knowing the doomed nature of the post. If he and Taylor were to make any progress with England, there was bound to be confrontation and aggravation for them along the way; and yet he didn't believe the role, and the extra work it entailed, was necessarily worth it. This job, Clough knew, was a crude sop, which was never going to lead to the one he really wanted. The FA preferred him inside its tent, pissing out, rather than outside it, pissing in. He and Taylor lasted twelve months, a period which covered Burton's resignation, a row with the elderly FA councillors, who took exception to having to wait for Clough and Taylor to finish a team talk in the lobby of a Las Palmas hotel, and another spat with the tracksuited FA representative who always sliced the oranges at half-time. Clough didn't like what he described as the 'hangers on' inside the dressing room, and threw him out of it.

Clough never forgave the FA for its treatment of him, and the average man on the terrace never forgave the FA for failing to give him the job of managing the senior national side, either then or when Bobby Robson replaced Greenwood or, much later, when Graham Taylor was chosen to follow Robson. In fact Robson became so agitated by the public clamour for

Clough to become England manager that he offered to resign in 1983 so the FA could appoint Clough. The FA, very sensibly, rejected the idea.

For Clough, being ignored by the FA was a wound that never healed. He was particularly scathing of Greenwood, who failed abjectly in the 1982 World Cup in Spain. 'If Taylor and I had got that job, we'd have won the bloody thing,' he said. Clough greeted Bobby Robson's succession with deliberate understatement: 'I'm not enchanted.' But his words soon became sharper, and driven in like masonry nails. Robson should never have become England manager ... he was out of his depth ... he had aged horribly since leaving Ipswich ... he had never won the League Championship. Often the denunciation amounted to just rhetoric, rather than a forensic examination. Where England was concerned, he seldom hesitated to say what was on his mind. Rarely did he care whether he offended anybody.

In the run-up to the Mexico World Cup, Clough chastised Robson for arranging for England to play a friendly in Egypt, asking whether the FA wanted to see the pyramids or fancied a camel ride and a rummage in the Cairo bazaar. Perhaps, he added, Robson had developed an interest in archaeology. He advised him to move the FA headquarters to South Yorkshire – 'Barnsley, if possible.' He tried to talk the England manager into taking him to the World Cup in Italy in 1990. He was incandescent that West Ham's John Lyall had been asked to assess England's opponents in the build-up to it. Clough had won two European Cups. If Robson thought Lyall was better, Clough said, then maybe the two of them could put their medals on a table and compare the value of them. Clough offered to pay his own hotel and travel expenses to Italy. Robson was politely deaf to the appeal.

Without escaping Clough's vitriol entirely, Graham Taylor

was more fortunate. Clough was purposefully guarded in his complaints about Taylor because the England manager was, after all, selecting Nottingham Forest's No. 9, a certain Nigel Clough. The father advanced the cause of the son in a peculiar way: he accused the FA, and by implication Taylor, of being influenced in the selection process by what Clough had said about them in the past. 'I genuinely believe that my feelings about the FA have stopped a little bit of progress of my son,' he said in a TV interview. Taylor gave a dignified response.

Although England didn't want him, other countries actively tried to recruit Clough. In 1974 Iran asked him to manage their national side, offering him a two-year contract worth £40,000 tax free with the option of staying on for the 1978 World Cup. Clough flew to Iran – never intending to take the job – and ate caviar from the Caspian Sea and toured the Shah's stables. He did it because, by then, though he was in the Third Division with Brighton, Sir Alf Ramsey's departure as England manager was imminent. Clough deliberately suggested that he was tempted by Iran as a way of reminding the FA of his credentials. It was a transparent and maladroit effort.

Later on, the Republic of Ireland (before appointing Jack Charlton) and Wales made moves for him too. He accepted neither invitation, ostensibly because he was securely tied to a Forest contract on each occasion. In reality, both offers were treated exactly like Iran's – as convenient leverage and for the crafty, subtle manipulation of the situation to suit a wider, personal agenda.

The Welsh were prepared to let him work part-time as a replacement for Mike England in 1988, and Clough, then fifty-two, made a tiresome theatrical show of insisting he would resign from Forest if he was not allowed to combine the two jobs. He called the directors 'a shower' for blocking it, said managing Wales wouldn't affect what he did at Forest 'one bit' and claimed he would be fulfilling his 'life's ambition'. At the time he talked to me about the 'beautiful prospect' of being treated as an international manager across Europe, of how travelling regularly to watch Germany and Italy could impact favourably on Forest's fortunes. He wanted, he added, to have the pleasure of running into Franz Beckenbauer. He dismissed the financial rewards, claiming he had so much money that he could buy the Welsh FA if he wished. What he could not buy, he added, was the kudos. 'From now on I'm taking my summer holidays in Porthcawl and I promise to buy a complete set of Harry Secombe records.'

The humour, which was typical Clough, masked the tactical game he was playing with Forest's directors, indulging his penchant for subterfuge and intrigue. He could be exploitative and unscrupulous in pursuit of the best deal, and almost Machiavellian in its execution. When the Forest board predictably rejected the idea of sharing him with the Welsh, Clough was apologetic about his own climbdown. 'Resigning is for prime ministers and people caught with their pants down,' he said at last, in a U-turn of burning rubber and billowing smoke. He posed for a photograph in his office; a glum looking Clough is captured throwing his passport into the waste-paper basket.

But he got what he wanted. Clough had just four months of his existing Forest contract to run when Wales approached him; he was soon signing a lucrative new one. Clough used the Welsh approach as an effective bargaining chip. The Forest board were hopelessly outmanoeuvred, novices who stood no chance against a grandmaster. In his own autobiography, Clough re-iterated how dearly he wanted to manage Wales. It wasn't, however, what he told me after his retirement. 'Ok,' he said 'maybe Wales did suit a purpose or two for me at the time.'

Ridiculous at it now sounds, two years before Wales' offer, Clough had put himself forward to manage Scotland in preparation for the Mexico World Cup, following the sudden death of Jock Stein. It was the usual stuff. He was serious, and would definitely take the job. I could only shake my head in admiration at his exploitation of the main chance. It was yet another episode of negotiation by megaphone with Forest, another shove in the back for Clough's own directors. As chance would have it, he was about to renegotiate his contract with the club. Scotland's vacancy helped him to do it to his advantage.

'I only ever wanted to be manager of England,' he admitted eventually. 'I'd have made a difference as well, you know. I'd have won the World Cup. Mind you, I'd probably have started a world war in the process . . .' Whenever I thought about the possibility of Clough as England manager, I only had to conjure the picture of a typical post-international press conference in my mind – a green-sweatshirted figure sitting on a podium in front of a roomful of journalists and camera crews – to appreciate how strained it would have been. Like prime ministers, England managers tend not to make headlines with deliberately antagonistic statements. Words that even imply criticism, however mild, are usually carefully picked to soften it at the edges and cause minimum fuss or offence.

With Clough there would have been no diplomatic niceties. Had England been 'crap' (one of his favourite words) he would have said so. Very little would have been held back, either about his own players or about the opposition. And there would have been no banal hobnobbing with the FA councillors for the sake of it afterwards. 'I'd have tried', he said, 'not to give them the time of day.'

CHAPTER SEVEN

Wrestling Sigmund Freud

I travelled with Nottingham Forest on the team coach – a great privilege. Most other provincial reporters I knew who covered a team in the First Division had to make their own way to matches. Managers were generally reluctant to let a journalist onto the coach, thinking there was too much of a risk of them hearing what they shouldn't.

Clough took pity on me. I'd never passed a driving test; in fact, I'd only ever taken a handful of lessons, and so relied almost exclusively for a while on public transport or the benevolence of others. I asked him whether I could cadge a ride one August Bank Holiday when there was a reduced train service. He thought about it for a moment, and then agreed, but with a proviso: 'You have to be on this coach for every match. You miss a game, I kick you off – that's only fair.'

Clough sat in a single seat right behind the driver. The seat reminded me of a throne. I was usually in the window seat just behind him and to his left. He was nearly always the last to board the coach – and woe betide anyone who was later than him. If you were unfortunate to find him already in his seat, the engine of the coach running, you'd get a burst of 'You're keeping me waiting . . .'

Albert, the coach driver and kit man, had the patience of a

saint. Clough would regularly provide a running commentary about his driving. He was always going either too fast or too slow. Sometimes, according to Clough, he was in the wrong lane or hadn't gone through a light on amber when he ought to have done. Clough complained if Albert overestimated the journey time and began to cut his speed. 'You're slow-timing it, Albert,' he'd yell. 'I told you it wouldn't take this long to get here.'

I used to have a bet with myself on the exact minute of the outward and homeward journeys when Clough would tell Albert, 'Hey, get a fag on. I like to smoke by proxy.' Half an hour seemed about the norm. Clough had given up smoking long before I got to know him. He used to smoke Romeo Y Julieta cigars. Albert would light up, and the smoke from his cigarette wafted towards Clough, who threw his head back and sniffed the air. On these trips Albert smoked like a laboratory beagle.

Albert and I used to play pool together. He was full of juicy gossip. He told me why it was that Forest often went to Scarborough to train on the beach or walk along the front. I naively believed that it was for the benefit of the sea air. 'No,' said Albert. 'Peter Taylor's got a flat there. He won't hire a furniture van, so we take his stuff up in the team coach. Last week it was a wardrobe. The time before, it was a couple of chairs and a table.'

Riding with the team meant you kept the team's hours. For a mid-week match, you had to leave early in the morning and sit around the lounge of a hotel in the afternoon and early evening. So much of professional football, I discovered, was about being on the road. I spent hours on the coach, and there were more hours tediously whittled away in hotels or spent in the press room reading and re-reading the programme notes in the matchday programme.

That's why I always brought a book with me. Whatever I brought, though, Clough always borrowed it. I never asked how much of any title he actually read or what happened to the books afterwards – no book was ever returned to me. No doubt my paperback copies of, among others, Anthony Burgess's *Earthly Powers*, A. S. Byatt's *Possession*, Hemingway's *A Moveable Feast* and Tressell's *The Ragged Trousered Philanthropists* are gathering dust in some charity shop or second-hand bookstore. I learnt to buy two copies of any book I planned to take with me because I knew one of them would be going out on permanent loan.

There was, however, one book that Clough made it clear he didn't think much of. We were on a pre-season tour of Holland (Forest, it seemed, always chose Holland for a pre-season tour because Clough liked the country and nearly everyone there spoke English) and Clough, as usual, wanted to look at the book I was reading. He picked it up and for a minute or two stood beside me, glancing through the introduction and the first chapter, then fanning the pages as if something might be concealed between them other than my bookmark. Still standing up, he picked out paragraphs at random and occasionally read out a line or two in a stiff, awkward way. He clearly didn't like it. The book was Freud's *The Psychopathology of Everyday Life*.

'So, you're telling me,' he began, 'that Freud is so good that he can work out what you're really thinking, and all that type of thing, from the way you lose your key?' I nodded silently in response. He sat down next to me and pointed across the room to a group of Forest players who were gathered around a low, glass-topped table, playing cards.

'I don't need a boring book by Freud to show me how to do all that. I've been doing it from day one in management.

How do you think I won two League Championships and two European Cups? I can tell, from the moment I see someone in the dressing room, whether he's off colour, had a row with his missus, kicked the cat or just doesn't fancy it that particular day. I know who needs lifting. I know who needs to have his arse kicked. I know who needs leaving alone to get on with it.

'It only takes a minute to score a goal, and it takes less than a minute to change someone's outlook with a word or two. That's just another form of coaching that you won't find in the manuals, which is why I've never read them. It's a special kind of coaching done only by very, very good managers – like me.

'You have to know what the people you work with are thinking, and you have to sense their mood. You have to read minds, and second-guess them. You have to see right into a player. And then the trick – if it is a trick – is to say the right thing at exactly the right time. Or you just shut up and sit in silence.

'Eric Morecambe used to say to me that the art of all comedy is timing. The art of management is knowing your own players, and I'm not talking about whether someone has a better right foot than his left or can't head the ball for toffee. I'm talking about *really* knowing them, knowing what sort of person you've got on your hands.' For emphasis he deliberately raised his voice when he said the word 'really', and the players looked up sharply from their card game, as if a car had backfired and startled them. Clough paid them no attention.

He handed the book back to me and got up to leave. The assessment he'd provided of himself reminded me of what he'd said about Peter Taylor's ability to 'read minds'. As he was walking away, and without turning, I heard him mutter grumpily under his breath: 'I don't remember Freud winning a European Cup final. Next time, let's see if you can bring something that's worth reading.' I watched him through the window as he went outside and sat in the sun, tilting his face towards it.

Those casual asides prompted by my book on Freud constituted the most eloquent and succinct analysis I ever heard from Clough on his motivational strengths. He was unusually shy about discussing them, or imprecise when he could be persuaded to do so. Ask him to articulate the ability he had to walk into a room and take charge of it merely by being there, as if the sheer force of his personality had actually altered the air itself, and he would struggle for the right words.

I remember him quoting Eric Morecambe another time. We were watching a video of the *Morecambe and Wise Show* at his home. Among his favourite sketches was Eric's dreadful playing of Grieg's *Piano Concerto in A Minor*. André Previn was conducting, or at least trying to. He walks over to Eric and says, 'You're playing all the wrong notes.' Eric says to Previn, 'I'm playing all the right notes but not necessarily in the right order.' Clough thought that footballers could be similarly 'out of tune', as he put it, like a bad pub pianist. 'They have all the right notes – but don't play them in the right order. The difference between a good manager and a bad one is that the good one (a) can recognise they can play and (b) knows how to teach them to put everything in the right order.'

'How do you think we transformed Robbo from a disgrace to become one of the best players in Europe?' Clough paused before continuing. 'I was the best thing to happen to John Robertson's career. This was a guy whose warm-up used to consist of standing on the same spot and shuffling around a bit. He used to shove his hands down the front of his shorts to keep them warm.' I remembered Taylor claiming that *he* was the best thing to have happened to Robertson; the two of them seemed to fight over him like children squabbling over a toy.

Plenty of attempts have been made to work out exactly what it was that made Clough so successful as a manager and motivator, especially as traditional 'tracksuit coaching' – a team gathered around its manager for a lecture – was an anathema to him. Often he didn't take training himself, leaving that job mostly to his coaches. In fact, he was seldom punctual for the beginning of training sessions. He preferred to walk or drive to the training ground, depending on the weather, in his own good time. If I was with him in the morning, he'd often say that if I wanted to continue the conversation I'd have to follow him there. By the time we reached Forest's unglamorous training pitches beside the Trent, the session would already be well under way. Clough would stand on the touchline in his long fleeced coat and flat cap, holding his walking stick. His coaching consisted of bellowed instructions. He might tell someone, 'You're tackling off the wrong leg – and you'll end up on your arse!' Or, 'Take him to the corner flag!' Or, 'You're a crap shot because you're not keeping your head still. Everything in sport comes from keeping your head still.'

As for motivation, it is a gross oversimplification to say, as many did and continue to, that Clough ruled by fear. Fear, or at least an apprehension of him, was part of it, but it was not the full essence of his style. I have seen international players, alerted by the sound of his voice in the distance, dive through the nearest door or shrink into a corner to escape him. Some would ask me, 'What's he like today?' and sweat over the answer. You didn't want to meet Clough when he was in a bad mood, certainly not in the confined space of a corridor.

As I sat in the corridor waiting for Clough, as I often had to, I watched young apprentices who had been given his shoes to shine leave them nervously outside his office door, like the night porter in a hotel, rather than knock on it and go in. I watched directors go warily past his door in case he appeared unexpectedly and caught them off guard. At training, players who were taking it easy would suddenly run like hell, as if a rocket had been tied to their backs, as soon as he came into view.

But instilling fear only produces unwilling, cowering re-cruits, and Clough was aware that that alone would guarantee him neither loyalty nor consistent performances. Respect was essential. So was awe. I saw those around him hanging on his every sentence. 'Some call it psychology. I call it intuition,' said Clough. 'I'm on the same wavelength as players.' In the 1970s and 80s, that intuition set Clough apart from other managers. While he didn't concern himself too much with tactics or train-ing techniques, he did think at length about how an individual player's mind worked, his likes and dislikes, and how he lived his life. Having bought a player, Clough wanted more to under-stand the attitude of his new arrival, and what made him respond positively, than to fill his head with arid tactical theories.

The first thing Clough always did was to ask his new player to list his number one vice. 'I'd want them to tell me, is it the birds, is it the booze or is it the betting. 'Cos most of us are susceptible to one of those things, and I'd find out about it sooner or later . . . If I find out that someone likes a bet, I can watch the size of his wallet. If I find out someone likes to chase women, I can see whether his fly is undone. If someone likes a beer, I'll get close enough to smell his breath in the morning. Now that's management . . .'

Clough also always strived to invent fresh ways to generate a reaction from his players. Not all of it was off the cuff. What appeared to be spontaneous, such as a put-down or a devastating quote that created a headline, had often been worked out and rehearsed beforehand. Clough was like an actor, polishing and repolishing his lines.

Although he didn't play the sport himself, Clough likened his philosophy at Forest to a golfer's swing. The more complicated the swing, he argued, the more chances of it going wrong. A manager's first job in Clough's book was to prepare his players properly, which in his case meant relaxing them, whether with bottles of beer, a glass of champagne or a long walk before a match.

Before one game against Liverpool at Anfield, Clough took the team to a pub for a drink – 'two half pints each' – and a round of dominoes. Before the European Cup semi-final in Amsterdam, he walked them around the red-light district. At the entrance to a sex club, Taylor made a fuss of trying to get a group discount to watch a show, bartering with the doorman, who became increasingly wide-eyed at what Taylor was proposing. Taylor had no intention of taking the players inside: it was just a comedy routine, and a bonding exercise. Their attitude was 'if one of us does something, everyone has to follow'. As ever, the plan was to take the players' minds off the match itself, and afterwards in the hotel to get them talking about something other than football.

On a pre-season tour of Holland, Clough actually led his players into a sex club. The club was as dark as a mine, with a stage at the front and a small bar at the back. Downstairs, there was a plunge bath. The girls walked around in short, white costumes like mini-togas. Clough sat himself on a sofa, which was pushed against the left-hand wall, buttressed on either side by two 'minders' who made sure he wouldn't be caught, as the *News of the World* might say, 'in a compromising position'. I hid as much as possible at the bar. The players watched a couple of shows and then went back to the hotel. Clough believed any shared experience – providing it was a positive or pleasant one – fostered a team spirit.

Clough never forgot what happened to him in the dressing room before his League debut for Middlesbrough. The manager, Bob Dennison, told Clough that now he had finally been chosen for the side, the rest was 'up to him', as if Dennison himself was offering no support and making little effort to put the debutant at ease. The burden, Clough felt, ought to have been taken off him, or at least eased. All Dennison needed to say was that he believed in him, or to tell him not to worry about playing in his first game. But the phrase he used had a discomforting and flattening effect on Clough, making him worried. His core dictum as a manager – 'make sure you've got players who are relaxed' – sprang out of that moment of thoughtlessness from Dennison. Clough wanted to reassure players: 'You're in the team 'cos you're good enough, son.'

Another strategy, typified by the haggling at the door of the sex club, was always to do the unexpected. 'I didn't want anything to be predictable' was Clough's line. Some of his management was not so much unorthodox as downright eccentric. Punching players in the stomach, usually at half-time, to signal his displeasure: Stuart Pearce, Neil Webb, Roy Keane and Nigel Jemson all experienced it. 'As I recall,' said Clough, 'all of 'em deserved it. They were lucky I didn't hit them harder.' I have no idea how that peculiarity squared with his idea of relaxing players. Grabbing someone by the balls: virtually everyone experienced that, including visiting managers and coaches. Beating his hand on the desk in his office, or staring someone out – a game to see who would blink first – as a form of intimidation. Telling established internationals, such as Peter Shilton or Trevor Francis, to brew tea or collect shirts in the dressing room. Banning Francis from attending the second European Cup final because he was on crutches. 'I didn't want our lot, preparing for a major final, watching someone on a pair of those,' he explained to me. Francis watched the match on holiday in the South of France. Ordering the squad to run through stinging nettles and cowpats close to the training ground. Asking Lee Chapman, nearly thirty years old, whether he had washed his hands after he had seen him coming out of the toilet. 'Well,' explained Clough, 'that's what my mam used to ask me.' Enquiring how much a shirt, or a pair of shoes, or a suit cost a player, and then replying: 'I come from Middlesbrough. You'd have fed a family of eight for a month or more on what you've just spent. Just remember how lucky you are, young man.' Asking whether you wanted a whisky but then pouring it anyway, whatever your answer. 'It'll keep out the cold,' he'd say. 'But Brian,' you would protest meekly, 'it's April and I'm wearing a short-sleeved shirt.' 'Well,' he'd reply, 'think of it as fuel for November. The forecast says it's going to be a freezing winter.' And, of course, kissing nearly everyone, male or female, young or old, ugly or beautiful. I saw him grab countless people by the wrist and pull them towards him before planting a kiss on their cheek. They'd try to escape at first, like a boxer leaning away from a punch, before succumbing to the inevitable. 'A kiss is just a kiss,' he'd say, as if he were singing 'As Time Goes By'.

Some of his antics were crude displays of authority – just a way of emphasising who was boss. But it underlines that with

Clough almost every waking minute was a performance, almost every action was performed for an audience. 'Some people say I do odd things,' he told me. 'Well, I never do *anything* without a purpose behind it. I plan a lot more than I ever let on. Sometimes I just pretend to be angry so the word will go round that Big Head's in a bad mood, and you'd better stay well clear. No one ever really gets the hang of me. I don't want them to. I want them guessing instead.'

When it came to individual team members, Clough's deliberate 'keep 'em guessing' technique was tailored to the personality of the player. Take Martin O'Neill, for example. Clough was wary of his intelligence. O'Neill had studied law at Queen's University in Belfast and was an eloquent speaker. In the early 1970s, the sports editor of the *Nottingham Evening Post* wrote a column critical of O'Neill, the implication being that he was another thick-headed footballer who ought to be grateful for the living the game had given him. The reply O'Neill wrote for publication, pointing out his law studies, was a cogent put-down.

Sitting in his office one day, Clough was reading a story about O'Neill in a newspaper. By this time O'Neill was in management, at Wycombe Wanderers. Clough used to insist that he never paid any attention to anything that appeared in print, and was never much concerned by what newspapers wrote about him. The fact he owned a newsagent's a mile from the City Ground, and was often seen selling papers there on a Sunday morning during the summer months, made the claim ridiculous. I knew the opposite applied. One of the things that gave Clough an edge was that he seemed to have read *every-*

thing anyone wrote about him. He regularly threw it back at you.

'Who's the Irish writer no one can understand?' Clough asked me. 'The guy who wrote that very long book . . .'

'James Joyce,' I said, guessing that the book might be *Ulysses*.

'Aye, that's him. Martin O'Neill was like James Joyce. He used words I'd never heard of.' He tried to remember two of them. After several stabs, we decided between us that the words in question might have been 'pedantry' and 'obfuscation'.

'I don't know what either of them really mean. Especially the second one,' laughed Clough. 'He was a smart-arse, that Martin. So I decided to handle him by pretending he was thick. I thought that way I might just shut him up. Of course, it didn't always work, 'cos here was a bloke capable of talking for Ireland. One day he'll be manager of this club [Clough was by then in his final season], and I'm going to buy the biggest dictionary I can find, pick out a few words he doesn't know, and when he invites me over for a beer I'm going drop them into the conversation. I want to see his eyes roll,' he said, laughing again. Clough respected O'Neill. In him he had found someone who challenged his watertight opinion of himself.

Clough had difficulty dealing with any player who did not match the stereotypical profile of a footballer. That was certainly the case with Justin Fashanu, the first openly gay player in Britain and whose facade of self-belief disguised a confused, vulnerable character in need of support rather than criticism. Off the pitch, Fashanu dressed in what Clough thought were outrageously flamboyant clothes and extravagant jewellery. 'If he wants to show off,' said Clough, 'why doesn't he just do it on the pitch?' Fashanu was charming, well-mannered, lucid without being academically bright, and took part in fashion shoots and cut a record. He employed his own masseur.

'He's got a fucking screw loose. He's barmy and he tells lies,' was Clough's verdict, bitter that Taylor had not done his homework sufficiently before buying the player. Clough was adamant: 'Whenever anyone mentions Justin Fashanu to me, I say one thing. I didn't buy him. It had nowt to do with me. The person who did buy him didn't do his job properly. We signed an idiot.'

Fashanu became so terrified of Clough that he broke into a panting sweat just talking about him. 'It's the way he looks at me,' Fashanu would tell me. 'You just know you're about to get a right bollocking. He doesn't like me. Never will.' He began going out in Nottingham until the early hours. Once he rang me at 2.30a.m. 'Couldn't your paper get me a move to Notts County?' he pleaded. 'I like Nottingham but I don't want to stay at Forest. Not with him.' (Clough).

Clough had handled footballers who fell into marriage or relationship problems through infidelity. He had sobered up a lot of grown men. He had successfully rescued others from gambling debts; Colin Todd thanked him in print for it. But he wasn't used to players who went to what he described as 'puffs' clubs'. That Fashanu was gay, and later became a born-again Chrisitan, made his situation at Forest untenable as far as Clough was concerned. He had no practical solution to the issues raised by Fashanu's religion and sexuality: he didn't know how to handle either of them.

In later years, Clough would think back to the May night when he won the European Cup for the second time and try to work out why and when the club subsequently began to unravel. After his retirement, he concluded, at least to me, that it was in the summer and autumn of 1980, and the publication of

Taylor's book about him. From that moment on, he said, the trust between them was shattered. But the signing of Fashanu twelve months later, he added, also had a profound effect. It finished the partnership off. Clough was embarrassed by the transfer, most of all by his obligation to defend it. Finally, he didn't bother.

When Forest, to Clough's utter relief, finally managed to offload Fashanu to Notts County for £100,000, a member of the board asked the chastened manager if he knew how much the deal had cost the club. 'I hung my head in shame,' he said. Clough was used to 'man to man, cards on the bloody table plain dealing' about everything. He had done as much, he added, with Burns and Lloyd and Gemmill, each of whom 'would scrap like a dog to win an argument'. 'But,' he said, 'I couldn't do any of that with Fashanu. Especially when he used to burst into tears if I said hello to him. Here was a slip of lad, twenty-one or so, who had so many personal problems that a platoon of agony aunts couldn't have sorted him out. Hey, I'm a football manager, not a shrink. I couldn't talk to him 'cos I didn't know what I could say that would make a difference. He *looked* like a million quid – but he sure wasn't *worth* a million quid.'

With Fashanu scared of Clough, and Clough unimpressed with and apprehensive about Fashanu, the two of them could never communicate. The relationship between player and manager descended into simmering conflict. Fashanu's emotional turmoil steadily worsened. When he pulled out of a game three-quarters of an hour before kick-off, claiming he wasn't fit enough to play, Clough 'whacked' him on the side of the head with a flailing arm. Who knows what might have happened if Fashanu had struck back? When he turned up for training after Clough had explicitly told him to stay away, the police were called. Fashanu was escorted out of the City Ground. 'He was weeping buckets,' said Clough. 'I can't imagine how he'd have coped in Middlesbrough in the 1950s.'

The awful sadness is that, ultimately, Fashanu didn't cope. He hanged himself in a lock-up garage in Shoreditch in May 1998. His suicide note read: 'I hope the Jesus I love welcomes me, I will at last find peace.' A seventeen-year-old in Maryland had accused Fashanu of sexual assault. Fashanu believed that police in America had a warrant for his arrest. At his inquest, four months later, it was made clear that no such warrant existed. I remember hearing the news of his suicide on the radio. I'd last seen him at Brighton when, after a match, he'd come to the press box, snappily dressed as ever and smiling. We chatted for a quarter of an hour. There was an exuberance about him that night; he seemed genuinely content. That's the image of him that stays in my mind.

When his son Nigel emerged as a First Division player, Clough revealed another uncertainty that surprised me. For months, he would not refer to him by name in interviews. Nigel was 'our number nine' or 'the centre forward', nothing more. He wouldn't let him speak to the press. Nigel was signed as an amateur – the only one in the First Division – so as to break him gently into the professional game. And Clough made sure that he continued, as an amateur, to play for his brother Simon's Sunday league side, AC Hunters, where the family gathered on the touchline of a park pitch on Sunday mornings to watch matches, and Clough was heard to yell 'Run, you bloody clown!'

The overprotectiveness increased, rather than lessened, the clamour for interviews generated more interest in how the father–son relationship worked. In private, usually in his office, it was different. Clough spoke about Nigel constantly – so much in fact that I longed for him to stop. 'His name's Clough and that's why he'll get attention. I'm just trying to take a bit of the heat off him,' he would say. 'The sins of the father shouldn't be heaped on the shoulders of the son – but he'll get a fair amount of that in any case, no matter what I say. But it'll be slightly easier for him if I say nowt for the time being.'

Clough was understandably concerned that Nigel's selection would be viewed as nepotism, which is odd when you think how well he played: he finished top scorer in six out of seven seasons between 1985 and 1991, and again in 1993 when Forest were relegated. His first touch and distribution were exceptional. What he lacked in pace he made up for with the speed of his football brain. He may have been one step behind defenders in pursuit of the ball, but he was two thoughts in front of them. He had the vision to see how the game was unfolding ahead of him and could exploit it with a beautifully weighted pass or a slanted run.

'He can play,' Clough said regularly. 'Wait till he gets a dozen or so games under his belt, and sticks in the odd goal or two. Everyone will soon find out what I'm talking about. Judge him then, not now. It takes time for somebody to adjust to the First Division. After his debut, I asked him what the most difficult thing was about it. You know what he said? It wasn't the tackling or the pace of the match. He said it was the noise – the constant din of the crowd. You tend to forget things like that because you're caught up in it every week. Anyway, he'll be stronger, physically and mentally, to play ninety minutes, when he gets some regular training in.' And then he would say, 'Just don't publish a word of what I've said or I'll punch you . . .'

When the *Nottingham Evening Post* carried a photograph of Nigel planting a diving header into the net, Clough asked for several copies for friends. 'What's so special about this picture?' he asked. There were a handful of people in his office. Around the room the question was met with baffled head-shakes. 'Look at it closely,' he told us. 'Pick out one thing.' Various possible reasons were suggested. No one gave the right answer. 'You're all thick,' said Clough. 'It's his eyes –they're wide open. You'd be amazed how many players head the ball with their eyes closed, 'cos they're scared of it. Our Nige isn't scared. He's brave.' In that moment, he was just a typically proud father.

Clough was prouder still when the team accepted Nigel as one of their own. When the players got to know him, there was no suggestion that he might 'snitch and run home to dad' or pass on dressing-room gossip or complaints. He was polite, well educated and modest – the polar opposite of his father. His father was right, too: he was brave, a fact he proved by playing in the centre of defence during his father's final season as manager. 'He can play anywhere,' said Clough.

A football team is always a work in progress, and two points stand out about the sides Clough created. The first is how he managed to make the ordinary extraordinary. Players who were regarded elsewhere as no more than solid journeymen, lacking enough potential to attract First Division interest, blossomed under Clough's tutelage. Until he took over at Forest, no one was much interested in Viv Anderson, Tony Woodcock, Martin O'Neill or John Robertson; though Don Revie, believing Roberstson was English, did list him in one of his England get-togethers. No one else came in for Larry Lloyd, Peter Withe or Kenny Burns, and each of them would go on to win League championship medals. And no one was pounding on the door to sign John McGovern, John O'Hare or Frank Clark, who Newcastle allowed to leave on a free transfer, thinking his career was nearing its end. When Clough rang to sign him for Forest, Clark was talking over a possible move to Doncaster Rovers. Among the side of the mid-eighties, Clough identified Peter Davenport, Stuart Pearce and Des Walker as potential internationals long before word about them had spread. Walker, as fast as an Olympic sprinter, had been released by Tottenham.

The second point is that no other club successfully brought back so many of the players it had sold. Garry Birtles, Steve Hodge, Neil Webb, Ian Bowyer and John Robertson all returned fairly rapidly to Forest after leaving, and always for a fee lower than the one Clough received for them. Also, John McGovern, John O'Hare, Colin Todd and Archie Gemmill had previously played for Clough when he bought them for Forest. If Clough was so abusive and tyrannical, if the City Ground was like a chaotic mental institution and its manager resembled one of the inmates, why would any of those players so willingly sign for him again? After all, Clough's methods were hardly classified information to them. He didn't like the jelly-boned; the more disinterested he seemed about something, the more interested he actually turned out to be; he was good at feigning indifference; his temper could be apocalyptic; he was stubborn over minor issues; if someone called him 'Mr Clough', he would tell them to call him 'Brian' and if someone called him 'Brian', he would tell them: 'It's Mr Clough to you.'

He always set out to claim the psychological high-ground. Rough treatment was meted out in newspapers to players who displeased him. He enjoyed communicating through the megaphone of print journalism. He didn't care if it embarrassed anyone.

Withe's request for the ball after scoring all four goals against

Ipswich in the League championship season was met with these brusque words: 'You'll get it when you learn how to play with it.' Withe did eventually get the ball as a souvenir.

Davenport exasperated him by often wanting to return to his parents' home in Birkenhead rather than stay in Nottingham. He was told to 'meet and marry a Nottingham girl and settle down with her – here.'

When Clough wanted to puncture Nigel Jemson's ego, he said: 'He's the only one with a head bigger than mine,' and added, after Jemson had scored two goals, 'He's gone to the crowd both times to celebrate. If he wants to race anywhere after he's scored, let him use his surplus energy in coming to me. I pick the side.'

Gary Megson was more caustically dealt with. 'When he learns how to trap and kick a ball, I'll play him,' Clough said, insisting later that it was a 'joke'. Some joke.

At least his put-down of Brian Rice was relatively mild: 'I'm not saying he's thin and pale, but the maid in our hotel remade his bed without realising he was still in it.'

In the dressing room, Clough always had to have the final word. Shortly after Pearce's arrival, as he recounts in his autobiography, *Psycho*, Clough accused him of 'being a lying bastard . . . a drunk and . . . homosexual'. On the day Pearce was chosen for the England squad for the first time, Clough called him into his office. 'I said to him that I didn't think he was good enough for international football. I was just trying to make sure we didn't have a cocky bastard on our hands for the next month.'

After Roy Keane had unexpectedly played his first League match at Liverpool, Clough made a point of making him polish the manager's boots, 'just to let him know who's boss'. Keane had only previously appeared in an under-21 tournament, briefly in two pre-season friendlies for the reserves and then for ten minutes (again for the reserves) just 48 hours before his League debut. I hadn't seen the match at Liverpool. When I went to interview Keane two days later, I had to ask Ron Fenton to identify him for me. Clough picked Keane for Anfield on the evidence of twenty minutes that he'd watched him play at non-League Sutton-in-Ashfield a week or so earlier. 'I can spot 'em that quickly – usually in a minute,' he said.

Clough was in the habit of making players who were either off-form or out of favour sit next to him on the bench: 'The best coaching lesson of them all,' he called it. 'They learn very quickly how the game ought to be played. After 90 minutes of listening to me yell at everyone, whoever it is knows me better than he's ever done before.'

For Clough, it was all about discipline. Larry Lloyd's fine for not wearing his blazer after a European Cup tie in Athens – Lloyd said it was at the bottom of his case and too much trouble to take out and put on – typified his zero tolerance of minor infringements. 'If you sort out the small things, the big ones won't bother you,' he said. Forest's players described those fines as The Red Tree – the letter telling them they'd been fined arrived in an envelope marked with the club's badge. Lloyd was nevertheless adamant: 'If the gaffer asked me to take a diving header through a plate-glass window, I would give it a go.'

Some observers thought that such devotion from his players was football's equivalent of Stockholm Syndrome: the player forming a bond with the manager who frequently gave him a verbal lashing. But, it has to be remembered, Clough was also staunchly supportive of his players. In his book *Anatomy of a £1m Player*, Trevor Francis recounts how, during his clandestine and illegal appearance for the Forest youth side following his million-pound signing (he wasn't registered with the Football League), one of his shots widely missed the target. A spectator on the touchline shouted 'Got to do better than that, Francis. Clough, says Francis, ran more than fifty yards to tell the spectator: 'Trevor is his name.'

In fact, Clough had a thing about the use of surnames. When I asked him once about Peter Shilton's future, I knew – at that moment – that I wouldn't be able to say 'Peter': my stammer made it impossible, and the P-sound would just stick on my tongue. So I called him 'Shilton'. Clough looked at me so coldly that I thought a hoar frost might descend over the room. 'He calls you Duncan,' he said tersely, and turned his back on me.

He regularly rebuked fans for criticising players. I remember one supporter we passed in the car park turning to Clough and saying, 'I hope Brian Rice starts to play a bit better this season.' The fan, a stout, podgy figure with a pockmarked face, was wearing a Forest scarf that trailed to his waist. Rows of enamel badges were pinned on both lapels and the tail of the scarf. There were badges from an assortment of countries, which suggested that he was a veteran of the European Cup campaigns. The fan obviously thought he was making a shrewd tactical remark rather than being hostile. Clough felt otherwise, and the fan was given a two-minute lecture: Rice 'is a young man trying his balls off for people like you. He works hard at this trade – harder than you've ever worked at yours, I'd bet.' Clough's final line was: 'Go home and lose some weight. Next time, be more respectful.'

'Respect' was a word Clough used a lot. I covered reserve matches from an executive box which was almost directly in front of the manager's dugout. For one game Clough decided to sit on the bench beside Archie Gemmill, by now the reserve coach. I wasn't paying much attention. I used the first half to catch up on my reading: I began with the *Guardian*, and made notes from the game when necessary. I only had a few paragraphs to file, after all.

The following day, Archie stopped me. 'You were lucky last night,' he said. I told him I didn't know what he meant. Archie explained that Clough had noticed a figure in the executive boxes reading a newspaper and took it as a personal insult. He said something along the lines of 'Look at that bastard – he'll be writing to me to say the team's not good enough, and he hasn't even watched the fucking match. I ought to go round there and wring his neck for such a lack of respect'. Archie saw the blood drain from my face. 'It's OK,' he said, 'he didn't know it was you. But I did – and I didn't let on, so you're in the clear.'

His backing for anyone he considered to be supportive continued long-after the player had left the club. Clough arranged for two ghosted columns to appear under his name about Clark, who had become manager of Orient. The columns eulogised his management style, his professionalism and then, as the dramatic clincher, picked him as his successor at Forest. Clark's Orient, and particularly Clark himself, had experienced a tortuous two and a half months. When the first of those columns appeared (which I wrote for him), Orient had taken only five points from the previous ten matches. Sensing Clark's vulnerability, Clough moved to make sure that Orient's directors couldn't sack him.

On countless occasions Clough used newspaper columns to vigorously promote either former players for management jobs or to push current ones for international recognition. It was the least he could do, he said, and it cost 'nowt' except a 'wee bit of time and trouble'. 'I'm a manager players generally like because I win them things,' said Clough. 'No one wants to go through their career without winning a medal. Anyway, most of 'em who come back probably missed my singing as well . . .'

Clough had charisma, a hypnotic presence which compensated for his disregard for what he called 'fancy' tactics, and the players were desperate to win his approval. 'A word of praise from him in the dressing room was like having a gold coin pressed into your palm,' said one player. 'There was never any bullshit,' said another. And no Freud either.

CHAPTER EIGHT

There may be trouble ahead ...

Brian Clough liked to sing. I would often hear him humming to himself, usually something by Frank Sinatra, before the words broke into the air a few bars later. If it wasn't Sinatra, he might croon a line from Nat King Cole or Tony Bennett – in fact anything from the Great American Songbook. He was particularly fond of the musical *Guys and Dolls*. I think he either wanted to be Nathan Detroit, the character Sinatra played in the film, or he just liked the sound of the name and the pinstriped suit. 'Luck Be a Lady Tonight' was a Clough standard.

Another of his favourites were the Ink Spots. The track of theirs he particularly liked was 'I Don't Want To Set The World On Fire'. 'It's not true,' he said, 'I do.' Sometimes, especially if he was pouring a drink, I would hear Dean Martin's 'Little Ole Wine Drinker Me'. He also sang songs you'd never heard of from acts you never knew existed, such as Nellie Lutcher, and then chide you for your ignorance. 'Hey, she's at the top of my chart,' he would protest.

Clough would sing down the phone at you. It wasn't unusual to answer a call and find him warbling away at the other end in an impersonation of Sinatra. I once picked up the phone and heard the first couple of lines of 'I've Got You Under My Skin'.

When he finished, he said, 'Somebody's putting it around that I'm barmy.' The obvious retort was that it wasn't me, but I decided to say nothing and laugh instead, and that turned out to be the right thing to do. 'I've phoned about half a dozen people – including some of our players – and said the same thing to them. All of them said "It wasn't me." You're the only one who's laughed,' said Clough. 'That's a gold star for you.'

He would sing while writing out his team sheet, breaking off in mid-sentence. He would sing to his dog. 'I really wish,' he lamented with a shake of the head, 'that I could play the piano, so I could sing along to my own playing, like a scene from *Casablanca*.'

I have never come across another manager who would select lyrics – and then sing them repeatedly over a season or two – as background music to reflect the position of the club. But then I always considered the City Ground to be an island separated from the rest of the First Division by the quirks and the imagination of the man in charge.

There was one song frequently on Clough's lips during the early and mid-1980s. 'There may be trouble ahead,' he would sing, whenever bad news surfaced, '. . . but let's face the music and dance.' I half-expected Forest to run out onto the pitch with it blaring from the City Ground's PA – in fact I'm sure that at one point Clough considered the idea himself. There was trouble, and Forest were dancing – in this case to the rather bleak music played by their bank manager.

In the early 1980s, as Forest stumbled out of one era and into another, Clough did something that brought him no medal or trophy, or much in the way of congratulatory headlines. He

The 1978 First Division Champions and League Cup winners line up with their trophies, together with members of the local police constabulary who were placed in charge of the cups by Clough.

The 1980 European Cup winning side pictured immediately after the game. Captain John McGovern has his hands on the trophy.

Clough poses in front of the hoard of Manager of the Month prizes.

The foul-mouthed Clough requests a cleaner City Ground, accompanied by threats of resignation in the media if the fans didn't tone down the language.

The Gentlemen respond.

Ever the master of publicity, Clough poses with his British passport over the bin after the Forest board disallowed him from taking his first international post as part-time manager of Wales. He would, however, sign a lucrative new contract shortly after having yet again threatened resignation.

The infamous entrance to the 1991 FA Cup final between Forest and Spurs, where Terry Venables and Clough walked from the tunnel hand-in-hand.

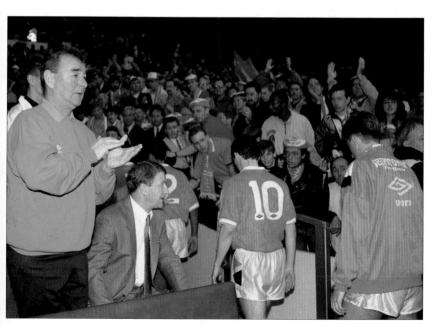

Clough applauds his defeated players from the pitch after losing the 1991 FA Cup final. He had controversially decided to stay in the dug-out at the end of full-time and not speak to his players.

Nigel Clough planting a diving header into the net. It was this picture about which his father took great pride, pointing out his son's wide-open eyes and boasting about his bravery and awareness.

Towards the end of his career, Clough would rarely be seen without his dog at his side.

Clough revels in the adoration of the Forest faithful shortly before his last game in charge in May 1993.

balanced the books. Given the rest of his achievements, it seems prosaic and barely worth recording until you stop to think what would have happened to Forest – and to Clough himself – if it hadn't been done. Until relegation and alcohol abuse brought about his resignation, this was the biggest crisis he faced in his managerial career.

Winning two European Cups made the club complacent. Success had, to all appearances, come so easily. Surely there was no reason why it shouldn't continue, as it had for Liverpool? In fact, Forest were the new Liverpool – even Clough thought so. But the club was in turmoil, and Clough was largely to blame. After years of plenty at Forest came years of famine, a parched period of scrimping and making do – the consequence of dreadful decision-making and monstrous rows.

The club had overstretched itself financially. Repayments on a grand, newly built Executive Stand, which Clough had pushed through on his own insistence ('I wanted to play in a palace,' he said to me), were a monthly drain on a bank balance soon starved of European gate receipts, Wembley ticket sales and trophy-winning bonuses, and the TV money that went with them. In 1982, Forest were around £2m in the red. The club also had to pay off £2.5m it had invested in the Executive Stand. Its skeletal frame dominated the skyline, a constant reminder that Forest had to play well to pay for it before interest charges began to bite. The irony is that the club eventually chose to name the stand in Clough's honour.

More worryingly, the beginning of Forest's financial difficulties coincided with the collapse of Clough and Peter Taylor's working relationship. As it became increasingly impossible for the two of them to agree on anything – apart from their dislike of each other – they made appalling management decisions about which players to sell and buy. It was as though the

European champions had passed into the hands of novice coaches.

The European Cup winning squads were dismantled far too hastily. Kenny Burns, Larry Lloyd, Martin O'Neill, Archie Gemmill, Trevor Francis, Garry Birtles and Ian Bowyer were all sold without being adequately replaced. By 1983, Peter Shilton had also left because the club needed hard cash quickly. What ought to have been a gradual, piecemeal rebuilding programme – so incremental that it was hardly noticeable – turned instead into a wholesale stripping away of almost everything that had made Forest successful.

Clough later conceded that he ought to have copied Liverpool's best practice: replace one or two key players per season, and leave the rest alone. 'We were wrong,' he said to me when we went back over that stage of his career. 'In fact, we were so wrong I can't believe it. We lost our sense of proportion, and paid for it. We were too worried that some players might age too quickly. That was barmy. We'd never worried about age before. We'd only been concerned about talent. And I suppose we got too big-headed. We believed that everything we did was right.' Taking the wood-chopper's axe to the team, rather than the pruning shears, left Forest unbalanced. The side finished below mid-table in 1982, when Taylor left. Forest's final home match that season drew a crowd below 16,000. In Clough's words, a two-year 'nightmare' followed.

With the remnants of that European Cup team – and the re-purchase of Birtles after his goal drought at Manchester United – Clough managed to take Forest to fifth place in 1982/83, and third the following year. But saving money became paramount, which is why the club experienced another three seasons in the nether regions of the First Division between 1985 and 1987. Forest travelled to most away matches on the day of the game rather than stay overnight in a hotel. The team were served soup and sandwiches en route and picked up the occasional bag of chips on the way home. The coach would stop outside a fish and chip shop early on a Saturday evening, the players filing off the bus to collect haddock or cod wrapped in paper. Clough claimed that it made him feel slightly nostalgic, as if he were starting again at Hartlepool or Derby.

On other occasions, particularly after a defeat, Clough's frustrations shot to the surface. I remember him pummelling his fist into the headrest of his seat on the coach. 'If I have any more soup,' he complained, 'I'm going to look like a tin of fucking Heinz. I am a fucking European Cup winning manager – and here I am going to a match in the First Division on soup and sandwiches and a bag of chips on the way home. What the fuck am I doing here?' No one, when he was in such a mood, was capable of calming him down. You had to wait until the fire went out of him. I decided not to go and ask for a quote.

Contemporaries such as Joe Fagan at Liverpool and Howard Kendall at Everton were dining with napkins and silver service. Forest ate off plastic plates and drank from polystyrene cups. But the Scotch still flowed – 'We have to keep our spirits up,' said Clough. The Forest team bus, ageing and slow and smelling of chips, couldn't be replaced. There wasn't enough cash, so it was patched up and kept on the road for a while longer. 'It's so old we could enter it in the London to Brighton rally,' Clough moaned.

Forest had to fill blank mid-weeks of the season with lucrative friendlies abroad to places such as the Middle East. Clough hated the travelling. With home gates now usually below 20,000, and sometimes less than 15,000, Forest constantly fretted over money. There was a sense of panic around the club. Whereas a successful side attracts investment and hangers-on, there is little interest, financial or otherwise, in a team in decline. At the start of the Thatcherite era, when the economy was ailing and recovery seemed a long way off, Forest's overdraft hovered close to £2 million. Speculation that Clough would follow Taylor out of the club began to dominate the sports pages.

Reflecting again on that fraught time, Clough said to me: 'I think the board probably thought about sacking me at least once a week. After all, I'd wasted millions in the transfer market and I was still an awkward bastard. I also earned a lot of money. Sacking me would have saved them a few bob eventually, once my contract was paid off. The truth is, we were so hard up we couldn't afford to buy a box of teabags without going on our knees to the bank first. What saved me was that the club couldn't afford to give me a cheque and tell me to bugger off. I'd have bankrupted them.' As a manager used to buying and selling million-pound players, Clough found himself with a spending limit of £100,000. 'I couldn't buy a midfield player with one leg,' he moaned.

Clough reckoned that, once Forest were solvent again, the creation of a new team – eventually good enough to win two League Cups, reach two FA Cup semi-finals and one final – was equal to his winning two Championships with different clubs. He didn't think that either of the managers he most admired, Bill Shankly or Jock Stein, would have been able to match what he had done in such circumstances. It was one thing, Clough argued, to build a side from nothing when 'you'd come from nothing', quite another to rebuild it when you'd once been 'on top of the heap'. The rhetoric may seem overdramatic. But the prospect of managing single-handedly with a patchwork side, with virtually no financial resources to speak of and in the knowledge that his enemies were circling, was more than daunting for Clough.

I sensed a fear within him. He thought the club might go bankrupt. 'If we had done, it'd have been the Third Division for us – and for me,' he admitted. At one point, he said, he felt as if he had indeed plummeted back through time to his days at Hartlepool: switching off the light in the office when he left at night so the club could cut its electricity bill; sweating over whether there was enough in petty cash to pay the milkman at the end of the week; worrying that the gas man might turn up one morning and disconnect the central heating.

As Forest began to slowly change, so did Clough himself. What emerged were two distinct Cloughs, the contradictions in his character more sharply defined than ever.

The first was the overprotective, suspicious Clough, who went around, like Margaret Thatcher (whom he found politically repugnant), rooting out anyone he thought was 'not one of us'. It created a bunker-like mentality, with Clough fiercely defending those within the circle who were 'on side'. 'When we won the titles, Archie Gemmill used to utter a phrase in our dressing room that was so perfect I pinched it from him. When our backs were against the wall, maybe we'd lost a match or played badly, Archie said it was time to "close ranks". That's what I did for a while after Taylor went,' he explained.

The second was the less aloof, slightly friendlier Clough. The abrasiveness was still in his voice, and the temper still broke loose occasionally. He remained fundamentally an argumentative, unpredictable and exasperating man. I grew to recognise whether he was in a bad mood or uncommunicative before I spoke to him. If he came towards me and didn't want to talk, he would look to his left and give the swing doors in the corridor a heftier push than usual. Then I'd tread carefully, knowing that I had to wait my turn – and that he'd have to speak to me eventually.

But Clough also mellowed noticeably. It was, I think, done reluctantly because he regarded the adjustment in his approach almost as a sign of weakness. He thought it betrayed a lack of confidence, which he fought to disguise with deliberate bluster and self-deprecation, as with his regular rendition of 'There may be trouble ahead . . .' He would say that he stood a chance of winning something 'if there was a bad manager of the month award'. Or that he did not select a team, he 'just hung around to see who turned up for training' because there were not enough players from whom to cherry-pick. Suddenly he was a suffering mortal like the rest of us: nervous and wary, with his position as manager and his authority at Forest called into question for the first time.

'It was daft,' he would say. 'Peter and I had shown over a number of years that two men, not one, were needed to run a successful club. But at that time, when we had nowt in bank and not much on the pitch, I was doing it on my own. I didn't even have Jimmy Gordon [the first-team trainer] beside me. Football managers work every Saturday in front of thousands and thousands of people. But no one who hasn't done it under-stands how lonely the job is. You're totally isolated, and that's the way I felt at first. It was like being back at square one. You tried to laugh, 'cos if you didn't, you'd cry.'

To me, Clough began to go out of his way to be conciliatory and helpful. He would phone me with stories. He appeared, odd though it may sound, to be less intimidating, and less conceited, in the views he expressed. He got involved in fewer public arguments with his directors and with the Football Association.

If he was rude, or kept me waiting, he would make up for it with a lunch that provided half a dozen stories. I began to work on his ghosted columns too. Eventually, his office was always open to me.

'I've been around football long enough to know that the evening newspaper is more important in my current situation than half a dozen nationals,' Clough rang me to say. 'You're a useless bugger, who ought to be covering cricket or writing book reviews rather than covering football. But this is your chance to dip your bread. You'll have so many stories you'll have to ring W. H. Smith to double your notebook order. Ta-ra.' In another call, he said: 'When I say I'm worried, I mean it. This isn't a lot of bollocks to get your sympathy.'

Just as he had done in 1975, albeit in very contrasting circumstances, Clough now had to rebuild his reputation. His stock had now plummeted to a troublesome low. He knew he couldn't go on apologising for the mess he'd created. People had to know how much he wanted to put it right, and how difficult it was going to be.

There were incessant mutterings about whether Clough could cope without Taylor's support. There were whispers that, in any case, his judgement was shot. And some expressed their doubts about whether he had the drive and the will for another effort. He understood that he needed friends, and he would have to recruit them himself. The friends he most wanted were on the terraces. If Forest's crowd began to turn against him, he felt the board would weaken and begin the search to replace him. With typical panache, like a politician trying to smooth-talk voters, he began a charm offensive on the supporters.

The new Clough used his newspaper columns to explain, with wit, the parlous state of Forest, admit his role in it, lightly criticise the board when necessary and, most importantly, advance his own cause. Expectations out there were high, and he was anxious to demonstrate, as softly as possible, that for the time being there was no possibility of fulfilling them. Forest could no longer compete in the transfer market, and the idea of challenging Liverpool or Everton was too preposterous for words, he said.

Clough became an avid but regularly annoyed reader of the letters pages in the *Football Post* (the *Nottingham Evening Post*'s Saturday night sports paper), which he used as a barometer of opinion. It showed how sensitive he had become to criticism – just like Taylor in his final six months at Forest. Previously, criticism and abuse had just bounced off Clough, but not now. 'I'm fed up reading all the bollocks in your paper,' he yelled at me down the phone, quoting at me the headlines on two or three letters. 'I'm tempted to ring this shower [the letter writers] myself and ask them to come and pick the team. Or just to fuck off and let them do the job instead of me. The people of Nottingham got too much, too soon. We spoilt the bastards – and now all I hear is grumbles. They'd have been grumbling a lot more if I'd never come here in the first place.'

The fact Clough stayed at Forest when he was financially secure enough to have walked away says two things: how much he felt personally responsible for the club's predicament and, more pointedly, how much he needed to be involved in football. With his usual flourish, he said that if he quit he would never get a good night's sleep again. He was, I believe, more concerned with how his resignation would be perceived and the quality of whatever job he might get after it. However much he protested to the contrary, posterity was important to him.

Even after a League title and two European Cups, history's

view of Clough would have been markedly different if, like Taylor, he had opted to leave and let Forest fend for themselves under a new manager in 1982–83. There would have been the obvious accusations that he was unable to carry on without Taylor and, by implication, that Taylor's role in the partnership was greater than Clough had ever been willing to publicly concede. The last thing Clough wanted was to swell someone else's ego – and certainly not Taylor's.

He had been annoyed enough by the mere suggestion that Taylor, and not he, had been the determining factor in Forest's climb out of obscurity. It was a tricky point to argue for Clough, for the basic facts suggested that that was indeed the case. Taylor's influence did make the difference. After he arrived, went scouting and took the edge off Clough's extremes, Forest were promoted and won the League title in less than two years. Asking Clough about it was to invite one of those penetrating, disquieting stares. When the heavy silence was broken, he might wag his finger at you and go on at length about the players who were already at the club before Taylor arrived (which was true) and the players he had already targeted to bring to it (which was partly true).

That Clough took the trouble to defend himself so adamantly, as if he were on trial, was indicative of how prickly the question was for him. Taylor was exactly the same. Mention to him that Forest might have climbed out of the Second Division, and up to the summit of the First, whether he had joined Clough or not, and he would push his tongue into his cheek and turn it around like a corkscrew. Then he'd give you a sideways look and talk about Burns' defending or Shilton's goalkeeping, which was his way of saying that neither Shilton nor Burns would have been at Forest without him.

Pride was always going to prevent Clough from leaving

Forest in the immediate aftermath of Taylor's departure. Having mocked Taylor's mental and physical tiredness after his abrupt return to Derby, Clough couldn't reach for the same excuse to quit Forest, and in any case, he would have been too worried about what was said about him as a result. The stain on his CV would have been impossible to shift: walking away from his failures in the transfer market and from the slovenly decisions that allowed a European Cup winning side to slide downhill so rapidly. However much Clough hated to contemplate it, many people would have believed that Forest's success was somehow diminished by the management's inability to sustain it – that the side Clough and Taylor had fashioned was capable of just a brief flash of glory. Clough would have spent the next decade trying to explain why Forest had imploded so spectacularly. That *would* have spoilt a good night's sleep.

After his awful experiences at Derby and Leeds, Clough neither wanted, nor could professionally afford, another period in the wilderness. Forest, after all, had been the only club to court him seriously after he was sacked from Leeds. He didn't speak a foreign language, and would not learn one, so it was imposs- ible for him to manage abroad. Anyway, he had no in-depth knowledge of overseas players or European clubs, just an acquaintance with the teams that Forest had faced in the Euro- pean Cup. He was not going to land a job at a major club, such as Manchester United or Newcastle, because he was too erratic and outspoken. He was still only 47, far too young to retire. He didn't want to move away – or at least very far – from his home in Derby, where his family were settled.

His options boiled down to this: rebuild Forest, resign and

move to another club of a similar size and ambition, or abandon management altogether to accept a role in television punditry, a route he had turned down almost a decade earlier. 'I don't really like doing TV,' he used to say. 'You sit in a chair and get made up, you sit in a studio and get hot. The whole thing bores me. I'm not a TV man. I do TV under sufferance and for a few bob.'

Derby, a club then as impecunious as Forest, and where Taylor was back in charge, handed Clough his only serious invitation. Taylor wanted Clough to rejoin him and re-create the past together. In the week that Taylor signed his contract, the two of them met on the Embankment, a mile and a half from Forest's City Ground, to discuss the possibility of Clough moving back to the Baseball Ground. But there was never any realistic chance of Clough working again with Taylor. It would have ended in another bitter scrap. Derby also had far less going for them than Forest, and for Clough to drop into the Second Division so soon after winning the European Cup would have represented a loss of status too heavy for his dignity to support.

So, for the sake of his sanity and self-preservation, Clough began the painstaking restoration of his team – and of his own image. He went on a mission to build bridges. After matches, win, lose or draw, Clough could still be awkward and tetchy, shutting out the press. Now, though, he was keener to dispense the Scotch to those who a year or two earlier, when public relations was far less of a priority than winning trophies, would have had the door slammed in their faces.

The new Clough was a convivial host rather than a hostile, remote one. A would-be sponsor, despised privately as an 'oaf', had his ego massaged with a tour of the ground. Another was told to sit behind the manager's desk so that he could experience what it felt like to 'be in charge'. Clough was the model salesman – persuasively charming, solicitous and attentive – and the product being sold was himself. He was able to use the two European Cups as security to buy himself some time.

Over the next few years, with his back against the wall, I came to see Clough's greatness as a manager: the way he could take a raw team and mould it, his ability to recognise buried talent, his knack – through vigorous self-promotion – of being able to bend public opinion, and his skill at inspiring, cajoling and terrorising in equal measure.

With his erratic timekeeping, Clough was frequently dismissed as a kind of footballing version of Ronald Reagan, who once said: 'They say hard work never killed anyone, but I say why take the chance?' Clough was known for arriving at the City Ground late in the morning, often after training had begun, or sometimes not arriving at all. He kept distinctly odd hours. He would often turn up just to write out the team sheet, or appear, as if through a secret door, in the dressing room at quarter to three on a Saturday afternoon.

In those post-European Cup winning days, however, he was tireless – but often exhausted. One afternoon I found him sitting in his office, his eyes closed, the lines on his face more pronounced. He had taken off his trainers and socks and rolled up his tracksuit bottoms to the knee. If you had put a knotted handkerchief on his head, and planted him in a striped deckchair, he could have passed for a figure on a Donald McGill seaside postcard. 'I am absolutely knackered,' he sighed. 'I have not an ounce of strength left. You'd have to stick a gallon bottle of Scotch in the dugout as an incentive to get me to sit in it. And even then, it might take a week for me to get there, a week for me to pour the Scotch, and another week for me to lift the glass to my lips. I'm fat and finished, and my legs ache. Fuck me, what am I doing this for?'

With the return of Bowyer, bought back midway through Taylor's final season, Birtles and then eventually Robertson too, Clough managed both to create a youngish side and to forge a link with Forest's recently illustrious past. Colin Todd's signing brought in another player he trusted as well as someone he didn't need to coach. Relative unknowns such as Peter Daven-port, Steve Hodge and Chris Fairclough began to flourish. So did a goalkeeper barely anyone in England had heard of: Hans van Breukelen, who went on to win a European Championship with Holland and a European Cup with PSV Eindhoven. From the raked ashes of Forest's European Cup winning team came what Clough called 'lovely blooms'.

'I did one thing that was important. I didn't sign any shit-houses. We had players who you'd want to take home to meet your mam and dad and who knew how to behave in polite company,' he said to me. He just wasn't prepared to take on any difficult customers, like Larry Lloyd, who he complained used to interrupt his team talks, or Kenny Burns, who required firm management. Increasingly, I sensed that he wanted a quieter, almost docile managerial life. Perhaps it was his age. Whatever the reason, there were seldom instances of ill-discipline at Forest. Few dared step out of line and incur his disapproval.

As a journalist, it was bliss. Every player's telephone number was in my book. If I wanted anything, I simply rang them at home. There were no agents to go through, no hoop-jumping and no reply of 'What's in this for me?' It truly was a different era. Even after the undemonstrative Davenport won an England cap in 1985, playing alongside Gary Lineker, you would occasionally see him coming out of Nottingham's Central Library carrying a pile of books. I once walked with him to the bus stop after a game. He was returning to his digs close to the City Ground. I think of that now as nicely illustrating what top-flight football used to be like. I remember Davenport's proud father, who went to every match and waited afterwards without any fuss for his son to emerge from the players' entrance.

The editor of the *Nottingham Evening Post* asked me to arrange for a Christmas photograph of Stuart Pearce. He wanted Pearce in a Santa outfit alongside his horse. Can you imagine Pearce in a Santa outfit alongside his horse? Well, Pearce willingly agreed and didn't ask for a penny for it. A month or so after Italia '90, when Pearce's was one of the penalty misses that saw England lose the semi-final shoot-out against Germany, I asked him whether he would talk to me about the letters of support he'd received. 'I don't have much time today,' he said, 'but jump in the car – I'm going your way and I'll take you back to the office.'

Pearce *was* Nottingham Forest. He was one of those players with whom the crowd identified. They loved his raw commitment. The desire to win shone in his eyes: playing for Forest was a crusade for him, not merely a job. The devastating free kicks he struck were the garnish on his basic game. Fearful opposition wingers would hang back, or take a step in-field, as Pearce steamrolled towards them. Not since Burns had Forest seen anyone who tackled so hard, and not since Robertson had there been a Forest player able to form such a special relationship with the crowd, as if it kicked each ball with him.

A lot of it came, I think, from Pearce's grounded and unpretentious approach to the game, and the fact that fame didn't discernibly change him. He played his punk music. He was prepared to talk to people. He even, in the mid-eighties, advertised his services in the club programme as a qualified electrician. Working-class fans recognised something of themselves in Pearce, who had known what it was like to get up early and graft for a living before football became his livelihood.

Pearce and Nigel Clough were the heart of the team that won the League Cup (then with its Littlewoods tag) in 1989 and retained it the following year – the first trophies Clough had claimed without Taylor. By then the club was healthily 'loaded' again. 'We've got more dosh than John Paul Getty,' boasted Clough, his tone understandably self-satisfied. What he never looked like regaining, though, was the League title. A substantial gap in spending power had opened up between small provincial clubs such as Forest and those in the big cities of London, Liverpool, Manchester and Newcastle.

Whether or not the League Cup mattered on football's calendar, it was nevertheless particularly good to Clough: four wins in twelve seasons – two with Taylor, two without. This new Forest side were also refreshingly entertaining to watch, playing the quick and simple style that Clough preached so passionately. But the garlanded praise Forest won for their style, along with those League Cups, was still a consolation prize in his eyes. What he'd done in the past was always going to outshine what he was capable of winning in the future. Next to the European Cup, most football trophies look pitifully inconsequential.

Clough was always talking about the League Championship. He spoke of it in a reverential way, as if competing in it was akin to taking the sacrament. He'd go misty-eyed over it. In his eyes, it was the true test of footballing strength and skill, and a team's resolve, which is why so few managers had won it, as he had done, with two different clubs. 'It takes enormous effort to create two different teams in two different places,' he'd say.

I have a clear memory, the season after Forest won the League title, of the trophy sitting majestically on Clough's desk. I passed his open door and gave a double-take, as if I'd seen a mirage. That beautiful piece of silverware, with its ornate, filigree-like decoration, stood where he usually kept a pile of paper. He was sitting in his chair reading a letter. He looked up when he saw me. 'I'm looking after it', he said flatly, 'in case someone tries to whip it from us.'

'You never give up hope,' Clough said to me a month or so before relegation in his last season. 'You think about the Championship, you think about another European Cup. I don't know how many great teams one manager can create in a lifetime. Two? Three at most? The thing is, though, you never stop trying. It's like an actor wanting to win another Oscar, a mountaineer who wants another crack at scaling Everest. I'm like that.'

He broke off and began to sing: 'There may be trouble ahead . . .'

CHAPTER NINE

Walk around and booze

Brian Clough drank to celebrate. He drank to lift himself out of a dark corner. He drank because he was bored. He drank to forget. Finally, he drank because he forgot what he was drinking for. He drank whisky. He drank champagne. Like all alcoholics, he made excuses, and specialised in evasions. He snatched at chances to drink when he thought no one would notice. And, as time went on, he drank surreptitiously because he knew he had to hide his drinking or, at best, disguise how much alcohol he was pouring into his system.

Even when it became sadly obvious – from the red blotchy face, from the ravage marks spreading across his skin and from the trembling right hand, which he would bury deep in his tracksuit pocket – Clough refused to accept that drink had taken him over. He was a casebook addict, one who proved the adage that drink finally takes the man.

It got to the point where the only way to rid himself of a hangover was to start drinking again. That early-morning shot of gin or vodka, or glass of white wine, took the sting out of the headache. Just briefly, it brought focus to blurry eyes and gave the impression to outsiders, as well as to Clough himself, that a period of clear thinking and relative sobriety had begun. All it did was make him worse. The more he drank, the more dependent on drink he became and as he moved from his forties into his fifties, he became less able to deal with the amount he was drinking.

I heard Clough argue in his defence that drink was a lubricant for his mind. Like football's equivalent of Inspector Morse, who used a few pints to solve crimes, alcohol was essential to help him 'to think'. It also enabled him to unwind after what he described as the unbelievable pressures of management, and the expectations he placed on himself.

Clough began an intimate friendship with the bottle early on, and a pattern was set. After the knee injury that prematurely ended his playing career, he embraced drink as an anaesthetic to dull his depression and confusion. It became a constant comforter. 'I went berserk for a time. I drank heavily. I wasn't very manly,' he admitted in the mid-1960s.

At first, Scotch was the drink of every day, poured at a time in the morning when office workers were thinking of a second cup of tea or a first mug of coffee. Scotch kept in the warmth during winter. It took away the autumn chill. It was necessary fuel to lift Clough's tired spirit in the spring, when eight tough months of a season were behind him and another month still to come. In the summer, it was a reward for 'surviving' the long football season.

If I asked him how he was doing, the answer I'd always get was that single word: 'Surviving.' 'You see,' he would say, 'that's what we all do, isn't it? We survive first and try to prosper afterwards. I survive, day to day, month to month, year to year. No one does any more than survive.' Near the end of his managerial career, the word took on a darker meaning. He was *just* surviving. Indeed, survival was everything.

I watched Clough take pleasure in preparing to drink, the ordinary rituals of pouring and tasting: breaking the seal of a new Scotch bottle with the twist of a wrist, the splash of golden liquid filling the bottom of a heavy glass, holding the glass up to the light and watching the sparkle of the glass and its contents.

Clough used to complain whenever Peter Taylor brought his black Labrador, Bess, to the club. The dog would wander along the corridors and often into Clough's office, from where it was promptly sent back to its master. After years of protesting that he would never buy a dog himself – 'dirty, filthy things that crap over your carpet' – he arrived unexpectedly one morning at the City Ground with a Labrador retriever. 'I was forced into it,' he said without much conviction. 'It's my daughter's dog – the family call it Del Boy.'

The dog went everywhere with Clough. He took it with him to training, where it stood with him on the touchline. It lay beside his desk, yawning occasionally when he spoke. It was the most photographed dog in the history of the Football League. At the beginning of one season, it appeared in a team photograph. He doted on it, as if it were a grandchild. He fetched it water, fed it biscuits and chocolate.

On a Friday morning, when he wrote out the team sheet so it could be pinned up near the dressing room, he went through a routine with the dog. 'Now, dog,' he'd say, leaning down towards it. 'Who's our goalkeeper this week – Sutton or Crossley? One bark for Sutton, two for Crossley.' The dog would look up at him with watery black eyes, and bark. 'You are a genius!' Clough would tell it. 'I tell you what, I'll sack the coaching staff and make you my assistant manager. If any of that lot [the players] get out of line, bite 'em on the arse!'

It was all innocent and playful until Clough started to use the dog as a way of pouring himself another drink, as though he needed an excuse to do so. He would finish one glass and then look at the dog, talking to it in the same offhand, jovial manner. 'Don't tell me you want another Scotch. Haven't you had enough? And isn't it a wee bit early in the morning? You know something, if you carry on like this, you're going to have a drink problem. But, OK, just this once.' Clough would trot off down the corridor to the chairman's room where the Scotch was kept and return with his glass charged. He would tell the dog to stay in the office. On other occasions he would deliver a one-liner as he poured the Scotch. 'If there was a European Cup for drinking, we'd still win it.' Of course, by 'we' he meant 'I'.

Drink too often dredged up the dark silt of Clough's personality. His alcohol consumption began to explain everything about his behaviour: the irrational moments, the mood swings and the demonic aggression, both physical and verbal. Most of the bad stuff happened behind closed doors. As his alcoholism worsened, his tantrums increased in their severity: no longer the mild, quick outbursts of his fiery temper, but long storms of rage from which there was no shelter.

At Luton's Kenilworth Road, after Stuart Pearce's debut, Clough boarded the team coach ready for a speedy departure. He never liked hanging around opposition grounds after a match was over. But a car was blocking the Forest coach's exit. Irritable and impatient, he shouted out: 'I'll show the bastard who's done this to us.' The car owner was still inside the ground, and Clough sent someone to get his keys. The driver willingly surrendered them, probably expecting the vehicle to be moved to another vacant space in the car park.

Clough, his temper boiling over, drove the car out of Kenilworth Road himself and left it in a side-street. For the ten minutes or so that it took him to leave the car park, abandon the car and then be driven back in another vehicle, a hush descended inside the Forest coach. There were whispered mutterings about what was going on. 'What's he doing now?' I heard one player ask from the back of the coach. Clough returned and ordered the coach to set off. He still had the car keys in his hand.

The engine of the coach revved up. There had barely been a quarter-turn of the front wheels when Clough turned to Ron Fenton, who was sitting across the aisle from him, and in front of me. 'Ron,' he said with a jerk, as though an exclamation mark was attached to Fenton's Christian name, 'do you know what I've just done?' Wagging his finger, he didn't wait for him answer. 'I have just stolen a car. I am now a felon. A criminal, in fact. And I have a vision of the police knocking on my door tonight and arresting me, and bringing me back here. I think I'd better go and get the car. That's sensible . . .' Clough shouted for the coach to stop, and the whole process was reversed: he was driven to pick up the car and bring it back, and the keys were returned to the driver.

Turning in my seat, I looked back to where the players were sitting, in the rear seats. I caught sight of Pearce, and Ian Butterworth, who had also just made his debut. I saw two pairs of eyes spinning like reels in a fruit machine. I'm sure some of the players could not have looked more stunned if Clough had levitated in front of them. I shrank back into my seat.

In January of the same season, Forest ineptly lost 3–2 in an FA Cup replay at Blackburn Rovers, then in the Second Division. When Clough climbed onto the coach, he looked as if he was about to pick a fight. The eyes were narrowed to blazing slits and the mouth gaped open, flecks of spittle and foam at the corners. The skin was pulled tight across devil-red cheeks. He clenched his fists so tightly that I thought blood would seep from his palms. And then he began to yell, and the sound came from the back of his throat, and it was a roar of bile, the way you might imagine the last trumpet blast of the apocalypse.

'You fucking lot . . . We're going home with the fucking lights off. No fucking lights on this coach – understand. Not one fucking light. You're going to sit in the dark like children, 'cos you played like children. You were fucking pathetic. You were fucking spineless. You made me ashamed. You let down our club. You let me down. You deserve fucking nothing.'

He emphasised each syllable, stretching out the words. As he spoke, he chopped through the air with his right hand as if he was a butcher hacking apart a carcass. Even when he took his seat, it was not the end of the performance. Every few minutes during the next half-hour or so, he would spring up again and launch into an abbreviated version of the same tirade until, finally, the lava flow of abuse abated.

I can't remember being brave enough to go and ask Clough a question. I staggered off the coach in the early hours, as though I'd just been freed from a long jail sentence. For a week or so afterwards, until he quietened down again, I considered whether I ought to give up the job and cover another sport instead. It didn't seem worth the hassle any longer. Clough offered a tame explanation rather than an apology. 'I lost my rag a bit, not at the result, but at the manner of it.' That was no consolation for those of us who had endured that horrific journey.

Another outrageous tantrum came during a pre-season tour of Holland. Forest were staying in Zeist, where the Dutch national squad trained. Clough had given a red and white sports holdall to one of his friends for safe keeping. 'Don't let it out of your sight,' he ordered. The holdall was packed with cash. I knew that because his friend had shown it to me. 'Brian says it's expenses for the trip,' the friend said. I didn't believe him. He unzipped the holdall, revealing crisp £10 and £20 notes tightly packed in clear plastic money bags. By my conservative estimate, there was about £15,000 in there.

As the holdall was lugged from one match to another, some of the players became curious. Word began to spread about what was inside it. Clough, who had been drinking steadily for a few hours before the evening meal, mostly beer and the odd glass of wine, heard that the secret was out, and when the meal began, so did his fury. He banged his fists on the table. 'You all keep your fucking noses out of that bag,' he ranted. 'You keep your fucking hands off it, or I'll chop the fucking fingers off you.'

Just like that drive back from Blackburn, the meal took place in an embarrassed, numbed silence. Clough's anger gripped the dining room like a vice, and the only noise was the scraping of cutlery on plates and a slight shuffling of feet. I don't remember much eye contact. After Clough went off to his room to sleep off the alcohol, it took half an hour or more for the atmosphere to return to normal. At first there was just small talk, with nervous glances in case he re-emerged unexpectedly. It was as if no one wanted to talk about what we had all just witnessed.

Those outbursts were not isolated incidents. I was there when Clough used his walking stick to strike the calves of a fisherman who dared to come too close to him during an early spring stroll along the banks of the Trent. He grabbed Maradona by the testicles before a pre-season friendly in Barcelona. 'It was playfully done,' he argued. He pushed journalists he did not like out of the main doors of the club – sometimes with a boot in their backside.

Clough had a terrible habit of intercepting supporters' enquiries from the phone on his desk that were meant to go through to the ticket office. If he saw the light flicker, and he had nothing better to occupy his time, he would press the button and pick up the phone. 'Nottingham Forest Football Club . . . You want tickets for when? . . . You want to know how much? . . . How do I know? . . . Call back later when there's somebody here to help you.' He would carry on taking calls until he got tired of it. I always wondered how many callers recognised his voice.

Sadder still, and infinitely more worrying than his rudeness or eccentricities, was Clough's physical attack on supporters who ran onto the pitch after Forest had beaten Queen's Park Rangers 5–2 in a League Cup tie. The TV cameras caught Clough landing one blow after another. The assaults were euphem-istically described by his then chairman, Maurice Roworth, as a 'cuffing' or a 'clip on the ear'. The Football Association fined him a paltry £5,000. Clough tried to defend his action, explain-ing his motives, and went through the ridiculous motion of offering his resignation, knowing full well that Roworth would decline it.

I witnessed shouting fits, violent arguments, slamming of doors and throwing of cups and glasses. You never knew what sort of mood you might find him in, or how alcohol might have influenced it.

There is a view that Clough's behaviour got worse, and his drinking far heavier, as a result of Taylor's death. Some of his friends thought that the sudden onset of his alcohol-fuelled tirades and escapades were expressions of Clough's remorse for his failure to repair their friendship and for the acrimony between them. 'He talks about Taylor a lot, you know,' I was told. Taylor's death may have accelerated Clough's drinking, but he was already a hard drinker by the mid-1980s. Before a pre-season tour in 1987, I'd scribbled a note to myself. 'Believe it or not,' I wrote, 'he drank nothing stronger than coffee. The question is: has he kicked the booze?' The liver transplant he eventually had to undergo answered that question for me.

One of the requirements of my job was to sink a largish Scotch with him – usually one or two fingers – often as early as 9.30 a.m. The more you drank, the more copy you got because he stayed with you in the office. I often went back to my desk in a worse state than he went to training. I smelt like a distillery, and had to sober myself up with many cups of foul-tasting coffee from a machine. At the end of the day, Clough got someone to drive him home. I took a corporation bus that seemed to sway over a rubbery Trent Bridge.

One morning I was not feeling well, and tried to refuse the drink he was offering. He ignored my protests at first, talking to me as he poured it. I took small sips from the goblet, hoping he hadn't noticed that I didn't want a large Scotch on an upset stomach. 'It's medicinal,' he said. 'Get it down you in one. You'll feel a lot better.' At that moment, he was mercifully called away to speak to someone else, and I tipped the contents of my glass back into the bottle. Clough came back into the room, saw that my glass was empty and poured the whisky I'd just abandoned back into it. 'I told you you'd feel better after drinking it. But if you have two, you'll feel even better than you do now,' he said.

In his final few seasons, Clough began to drink vodka instead of Scotch. It did not linger on his breath like the Scotch did. He used to pour himself enormous vodkas and pretend he was

PROVIDED YOU DON'T KISS ME

sipping water, or dilute them with a drop of orange juice for appearance's sake.

A few months before his enforced retirement, I found him in his office. He had decided not to go to training, he told me. It was an unseasonably mild day for early spring, yet Clough was sitting in his long fleeced coat, zipped up almost to his chin. He was wearing his flat cap and his spectacles sat on the bridge of his nose. A spirits' tumbler, half-full with what I presumed was vodka, was at his right hand. His head was bowed over a piece of paper and he was scribbling on it, which was unusual for him. I watched him write something down and then cross it out again.

As he wrote, he sang the same verses of 'Fly Me to the Moon', as if the needle had caught on a scratch. 'As I sing, I'm hearing Frank Sinatra in my head,' he explained. I asked Clough what he was writing. Without looking up, he said he was trying to cheer himself up by writing down the best players who'd been at the club since he became manager. He began to sing again: 'Let me play among the stars. Let me see what spring is like on Jupiter and Mars . . .'

Clough stopped singing. 'I'm doing it', he said, 'to remind myself of what life used to be like here, which seems about half a century ago. 'Cos at the moment . . . well, let's just say a lot of people seem to forget what I've done for this club – on and off the field. There's a lot of people who think I'm past it. Some fans believe this club will be better off without me. Most of 'em are ungrateful little shits. You do something on their behalf – something like winning them a championship or European Cup or two – and what happens? On the day itself there's the backslapping and the champagne and the "He's a jolly good fellow" bollocks and the "We'll never forget what you've done 'cos you're a legend here . . ." And then we have a season like

196

this one, and you hear the moaning behind your back, the whispers that "Maybe he's not up to it anymore", or "He's just crap and ought to go now" and "Doesn't the world move on" and "Shouldn't we lock up the drinks cabinet to stop him having a swig". Or, "Maybe, shouldn't we just lock him up instead and throw away the key . . ." I've been hearing that for months – and I'm sick to the stomach of it. I ought to tell this club to fuck off. Just get on a plane to Spain and fuck off. Or stick the Vs up and then walk out.'

He reached for his glass and took a long swallow. 'Hang on a second. I'll be back,' he said. 'Don't go away.' Clough vanished for a minute or two and returned with his glass refilled. 'You can have a coffee if you want one,' he said to me, almost apologetically. He began to sing again – belting out the words to 'Fly Me to the Moon' – and his body moved almost in time to the lyrics. When he reached the line 'Darling, kiss me', his head back rocked back, and he let it hang there, like a decorator examining the ceiling to see if it needed another coat of paint. The glass was still in his hand.

After a pause, he continued. 'Football is a terrible game, you know. It's got a bit of Sky TV money now, and a lot of people are coming to games who wouldn't know Stanley Matthews from Bernard Matthews. The stands are full of people who can't tell you anything about the game unless it happened after 1990. They're either so conceited or so stupid that they believe football was invented just five minutes before they became interested in it. I can see them looking at me and thinking, "Aye, it's not his era any more. He's stuck in the 1970s. Possibly the 1870s. And he likes a drink too much. And he opens his mouth too much. And he isn't part of the great new game we want to create." I look around at football and I don't recognise what it's changing into.'

197

Clough was always fond of two photographs. The first showed Trevor Francis seconds before he connected with John Robertson's far-post cross to head Forest into their European Cup win, over Malmö in Munich. In the second, Robertson is about to score himself a year later and retain the Cup in Madrid. The photographs used to hang in the corridor, where I usually spent hours waiting for Clough to appear.

'You can't argue with those photographs. But in the last few months, I've lost count of the number of times I've had to point out what I've done here, what I've achieved – all this at a club that eighteen years ago couldn't beat Notts County in the end of season friendly. It's as if I have to give people a history lesson. You know, grab them by the lapels and say, "Hey, I'm the bloke who ought to have taken England to a World Cup. I'm the bloke who took *two teams* from nowhere to win the League Championship. I'm the bloke who did in Europe what Shankly and Revie couldn't do once, and what Busby and Stein couldn't achieve twice."' It was odd to hear him sound so sorry for himself.

Football, Clough, went on, was 'so full of sycophants and slime-balls' that nearly every day he wanted to 'throw up when I meet them'. He began talking about directors. 'Do any of 'em in the entire Football League ever consider what it takes to be a manager? Not a bit of it. I can't think of many who would put up with half the amount of stick I've taken – and will continue to take – this season. I can't think of many of them capable of withstanding the pressure, of trying to fulfil expectations. I'd like them to sit in my chair for a day and not feel the overwhelming burden of the job. The walk from the dressing room to the dugout on a Saturday would kill 'em. They'd run and hide themselves in a cupboard out of sheer fear.'

His glass was already half-empty. Clough took off his spectacles and began to massage his temples, as if to revive the thinking part of his brain. He shook his head slowly – more from regret than anger, I imagined. He gave a throaty mock-laugh and slapped the palms of his hands on the desk, and then started to sing and speak at the same time. His index finger tapped the desk with each beat.

'Fly me to the Moon . . . And don't get me started on the players . . . Let me play among the stars . . . I'm telling you, in a few years' time, managers will have no power at all. We'll be redundant . . . Let me know what spring is like on Jupiter and Mars . . . The players will be in charge. They'll have wardrobes the size of houses, houses the size of castles and more cars than Formula One. What's more, they'll have so much money that most of 'em won't know how to spend it. They'll have agents and hair stylists and some lass in a short skirt to do their publicity. I'm glad I won't be around for all that crap – 'cos the manager won't get a look in, and that's not my way . . . In other words . . . darling kiss me . . . Hey, don't laugh – I'm deadly serious.'

As he said that, his voice rose like the Mad Hatter's, and he slid down in his chair, his drink still perfectly weighted in his hand. The words of the song trailed away. 'I'm a tired old git, and there's nowt worse than hearing an ageing football manager talk about the glory, glory days,' Clough said. 'If I'm not careful, you'll think I want to go back to the days of baggy shorts and a lace in the ball. I don't. I just want a bit of respect. When I retire or I'm sacked, I'll have the satisfaction of knowing that, hey, I bought and sold some decent players and won a bit of silverware too.'

Clough stared intently at the list he had written, as if the ink might be about to soak into the paper and disappear. His eyes became glassy, as though a film of water had spread across

199

them. 'Now,' he said, 'what about this lot? We've got Shilton in goal. We've got Anderson and Pearce – when fit. We've got Burns and Walker. We've got Keane, McGovern, Gemmill. We've got the little fat fella Robertson. We've got Francis and Woodcock. There's also the centre forward – if I pick him. If I could only send that bunch out on Saturday . . . oh now, we'd be in business then, wouldn't we?'

Clough sank the dregs from his glass and fetched himself another. 'Don't worry,' he said. 'I'm not upset. I'm angry – that's different.' He looked again at the names he'd written and put down his glass. He stood up, snatched the paper off the table and screwed it into a tight ball. I hoped he wasn't going to throw it at me. Instead, he lobbed it carefully into the far corner of the office. I watched it loop across the room, the ball of paper spinning gently in flight before it dropped out of sight. He sighed, and rested his hands on his hips.

In his first autobiography, Clough was coy about his drinking. While he accepted that he drank too much, he maintained that alcohol had never affected his judgement. In his second autobiography, which began with his liver transplant, he had no option but to confess to using alcohol excessively. But he was still partly in denial: he protested about the terms 'alcoholic' and 'alcoholism', as if trying to distance himself from the dictionary definition of the two words. By this time, he was gaunt and grey and weak.

Towards the end of his career at Forest, there were very few dry spells. In his final season it became glaringly apparent that you were witnessing the sad afterglow of a career, a star flickering out, and there was no possibility of saving it or dragging him back from the brink. There were just too many occasions when he was caught with a glass in his hand.

I heard a middle-aged woman, who knew nothing about football and didn't know Clough, innocently ask him what he did.

'Me?' he replied. 'I just walk around and booze.'

CHAPTER TEN

Even Clark Gable gets
wrinkles

The walls of the office had been stripped bare, the desktop swept clean of photographs and personal mementoes. An untidy heap of cardboard boxes and black bin liners lay in the corner, eighteen years of accumulated memories wrapped and packed up, waiting to be taken home. With all the personality removed from it, the office was austere and unwelcoming, like a room in a budget hotel. I glanced around and couldn't even see the stuffed toy that used to sit in Brian Clough's chair when he was out of the room. It was a chimp in a waistcoat and flat cap, a cigar in the corner of its mouth.

The man himself sat facing me, a fatigued expression across his crestfallen face. His eyelids drooped, and the eyes themselves betrayed the exhaustion of what had happened to him during the previous few weeks. Now, as the small hours approached, here was Clough in his last moments in management, saying his final goodbyes, his regal domination of one club almost over. An hour or so earlier, after an inconsequential reserve match against Stoke City ('What a bloody stupid way to finish,' he groaned), Clough had headed for the sanctuary of his office, which was already being prepared for his successor.

He settled himself into a comfy seat, put Frank Sinatra on the 'gramophone' – 'My Way' at full volume – and began once more to sing and drink. At first he tried to fling his cap onto the coat stand in the corner, and then he picked up a cricket ball and began juggling it in his hands. He clearly wasn't ready to go home. When the song ended, he sat quietly for a while, sipping a small vodka. The silence in the room was broken only by the loud, repetitive ticking of the clock, its hands closing in on midnight.

A small group of journalists and friends were gathered around him in his City Ground office for the last time. It was a sad, achingly lonely scene. I felt privileged to be there to witness the very last minutes of one of the longest managerial careers in modern football. But I also felt the grief and the wrenching loss of the occasion.

Clough's gaze wandered across the office, and then he began to examine his glass in a puzzled way, as though it might refill itself if he looked at it hard enough. None of us could think of anything meaningful to say. 'So this is how it ends,' Clough said distractedly to himself, as if, like the rest of us, he couldn't quite believe the prosaic nature of it.

The end came for Clough on May 12, 1993. He'd gone through the misery of relegation compounded by the ignominy of forced resignation and the indignity of so forcibly having to deny that he had a drink problem. On that poignant, bitter night, as I reflected on the calamitous nine months that led up to it, I knew what had gone wrong for him, and why. His drinking was to blame. The dependence on alcohol, which he had managed to conceal for so long, had begun to manifest itself in his physical condition a year to eighteen months earlier. The face began to look ravaged, the body shaky. In that final, wretched season, it robbed him of his wits.

In that season, Forest won only ten league matches and conceded sixty-two goals. The side had been rooted in the bottom three of the table since the opening Saturday of September. A team supposedly 'too good to go down' clearly wasn't good enough to stay up, and it was Clough's fault. As early as October in that relegation season, Clough flicked a V-sign at his own jeering supporters after a home defeat to Ipswich. By November he was describing the side as 'crap' and himself as 'being in the shit'. By January, he received that kiss of death – a vote of confidence from the board. In March he made another two-fingered gesture at his own fans.

Clough became even more unpredictable than usual, and remote too. He seldom went to the ground, and when he did it was usually a fleeting visit. When I went to see him shortly before Christmas, he kept losing the thread of what he was trying to say to me. He would start a sentence but be unable to finish it. Sometimes he slurred his words. He couldn't remember the name of a player: 'You know, the big, tall lad,' was the best he could do, and I assumed he meant Carl Tiler, the central defender. Halfway through a conversation he got up from his desk and walked out of his office. 'I'm popping out for five minutes,' he said. I let almost an hour pass before I decided that he wasn't coming back.

Clough could no longer perform the basic tasks of management. A manager who had been involved in ten million-pound-plus deals no longer trusted his own judgement. Forest were weak after the sale of Des Walker to Sampdoria the previous summer and Clough's inexplicable decision to let Teddy Sheringham go to Spurs, when the season was still in its infancy, without a replacement lined up. Stuart Pearce, newly appointed as England captain, was missing from January onwards because of injury. Forest had insufficient power up front and a lack of resources in defence. The club was linked with a succession of players who were capable of keeping the team afloat, including Andy Cole, Dean Saunders and Craig Short, as well as the possible return of both Colin Foster and Nigel Jemson. None of those players were bought. For months, in a bout of anxious hand-wringing, Clough deliberated over whether or not to sign Stan Collymore from Southend. 'I can't make my mind up about him,' he admitted to me, defending the decision to do nothing and repeating one of his favourite sayings: 'Sometimes the hardest thing in life is to do nothing.'

Doing nothing when Forest were so dire condemned them to Premiership death. Early in the season, after a lacklustre draw at Manchester City, I suggested in a match report – without using the word 'relegation' – that Forest's path to safety, if negotiated at all, would be slowly achieved. After reading it, he rang me: 'You're a bloody idiot,' he barked. 'There's more chance of Trent Bridge falling down than us going down. You didn't say we'd be relegated – but we all know that you meant it.' He ended the phone call before I had the chance to respond.

Clough didn't like anyone to mention relegation: he thought it was disrespectful to him. At first he treated the evidence of the League table as if it was down to typographical errors or the table had somehow been published upside down. 'We're playing better than our position, and we're playing better pure football than most of the teams at the top,' he said in an effort to convince himself that Forest would, eventually, climb out of trouble.

But results got worse. The season had begun with hefty defeats: 5–3 to Oldham and 4–1 to Blackburn, followed by losses to Arsenal, Ipswich and Everton, all by a solitary goal. It was Clough's worst ever start to a season as a manager. A 4–1 win over Leeds in early December briefly revived Forest. In March, however, first Everton and then Norwich won so convincingly against them, 3–0 apiece, that the stench of relegation clung to the club and its increasingly desperate manager.

The more I watched Forest, the more I became convinced that I was witnessing the disintegration of a man as well as a team. The side could neither score goals nor stop conceding them. And it was evident that Clough was struggling to cope with his drinking: I could see how much of a strain it was for him just to function, so much so that he became but a poor impersonation of his old self. I also began to learn more than I ever wanted to know about how someone with a drink problem manages to get through every day. The result was always going to be carelessness and disorganisation.

Clough, it seemed to me, missed the very obvious danger signs that led to Forest's and his own demise. He lost touch with what was happening in football. Forest became tactically naive and anachronistic. As tactics became more complex and varied, it was no longer sensible, as Clough had done for so long, to ignore the opposition and to regard their formation and strengths as irrelevant. Breaking down his own team into its constituent parts and explaining straightforwardly each player's job left them unprepared against teams run by managers who had studied in minute detail Forest's by then orthodox and predictable approach.

It wasn't enough simply to rely on absorbing pressure and striking back on the break, especially when Forest possessed neither the defenders to withstand a pounding nor the strikers to counter-attack and score. He was reluctant to adapt Forest's formation to take into account the strengths or style of play of other teams. For months he maintained that Forest were good enough not to overly concern themselves with the opposition.

Training was generally less rigorous than at other clubs. I could see that a stiff walk along the banks of the Trent followed by passing practice on the training pitch would never be enough to steel Forest against highly trained and very fit rivals. Even pre-season training seemed to me to be not particularly taxing. Clough didn't see it that way, of course, and was reluctant to change the routines he'd employed since the 1960s. He used to tell me a story about a former First Division manager. Sometime in the late seventies, certainly after Forest had won the Championship, Clough ran into him during a break in Spain. According to Clough, the ex-manager told him that Forest weren't fit enough. 'I could make your players sick in fifteen minutes,' he said. Clough gave him a disdainful look. 'I don't want my players to be sick,' he replied. 'I want them to be relaxed. We're training for a football match, not a world war.'

Clough didn't understand, or chose to ignore, the new realities of a game which by this time was embracing the nascent demands of the Premiership. There was more pressure on players and the financial incentives for clubs were far higher than before. Sky's endless hours of television coverage examined football more intensely than ever before. In contrast, Clough still seemed to be stuck in the early 1980s.

He also had little in common with his younger players, and struggled to relate to their lifestyles. The old tricks, like the bellowing 'motivation', the calculated bullying, the sudden appearance in the dressing room, didn't work any longer. As the season progressed and the situation became worse, it demanded something different – a major signing or two, or a tactical reappraisal. Clough was in no fit state to provide either. The alcohol had too strong a grip on him. Slowly, his authority drained away.

On a calm April night, Forest lost 3–1 to Blackburn. Clough looked burnt-out and disconsolate. At half-time he sat alone in the dugout rather than return to the dressing room with his players. The *Nottingham Evening Post* published a photograph of him smiling broadly, as if he wasn't really part of what was happening around him. A day or so later, when I caught up with him, he couldn't properly explain either the smile or the decision to sit in isolation.

A month and a half before the season ended, Clough received the Freedom of the City of Nottingham. The gesture, though manifestly well meant, was regarded as another sign of his imminent retirement. He was obliged to make a succession of visits to places of his choice during a long, arduous day, which ended with speeches and a presentation in the Council House.

The media gathered like predatory undertakers, and Clough knew that his best behaviour was called for. What under normal circumstances would have been an undemanding exercise in hand-shaking, well synchronised with a smile, threatened to become a trial – even for someone, like Clough, familiar with the art of self-defence. He began the day being doorstepped by a tabloid journalist enquiring whether he might be better off resigning. Had he thought about it? The reply can be guessed at: you could count its syllables on two fingers.

Halfway through the day, Clough suggested that the two of us go back to the City Ground. 'Come for a chat,' he said. 'We'll have a seat in comfort.' We sat alone in his office for more than an hour. He dealt perfunctorily with some paperwork, took a few phone calls, drank a cup of tea. He warmed his hands comfortingly around the cup, and dipped his head over it so the hot steam rose up to his face. He seemed so bone-weary that I thought he might begin to doze off. Looking at him sitting in the chair, it was as if his entire world had shrunk into the room. He showed no signs of wanting to leave it again.

'Let's work,' he said at last, in a tired voice. 'We'll get it out of the way.' I sensed that I wouldn't have to ask any questions, and took out my notebook.

'This is in two parts,' he began. 'There's the part you can write for tomorrow and the part you can save for your book. Which would you like first?'

I stared at him, not grasping what he meant. 'What book?' I asked.

'Look, you're a journalist who reads a lot of books. One day you'll write a book. About this club. Or, more to the point, about me. So you may as well know what I'm thinking right now, and save it up for later when it won't do any harm to anyone.' Clough had always been harsh on anyone who wanted to write a book about him. I'd always thought that if I'd said I was writing one, he'd oppose it. Now here he was giving it his seal of approval.

The first part of my interview, for public consumption, was a defiant 'I'm not resigning.' He'd put too much into the club to give it all up . . . he wouldn't walk away . . . whatever happens, he would be at the City Ground next season. He ended with a reference to the singer Paul Robeson. 'He did "Ole Man River",' said Clough. 'Well, that's me, I just keep rolling along.'

The second part was an honest appraisal of his own situation. He'd thought about resigning 'a million times in forty years,' he said. 'But the temptation is always to hang on. To think you'll have one more year and see how it goes. To think you'll be better if you can just get over the next hurdle. You saw the same thing happen with nearly all the great managers. The hardest thing in life is to decide when to resign. Even when Bill Shankly resigned, so suddenly it was stunning, he found he didn't have enough to do. He missed the game, he missed the people. There was a hole in his life. You see, people like Bill and me are football men. We really know nowt about anything else. And you can't turn someone into something they're not. So when we quit as football managers, it means years of sitting in front of the TV, pruning the roses or taking the dog for a walk.'

He rang for another cup of tea. 'I've always thought I'd go at the time of my choosing. But now I've got supporters belly-aching, some of the same supporters who were bellyaching nearly twenty years ago when I got here. You see, nowt changes. Whoever said history repeats itself was a genius. I've got direc-tors giving me sideways glances – and saying nowt to my face. And now I've got you lot [the media] saying I've shot it. Hey, maybe I have.' He moved forward, to the edge of his chair. 'Do you think I'll be here next season?'

I shook my head. 'Not if you're sensible,' I said instinctively, and then wondered if I'd been too candid.

There was a long silence, as if he was turning over in his mind all the things he had just said. 'It's an honest opinion,' he replied finally, not looking at me. He finished his tea in two huge gulps and then asked me to pour him a glass of water. I found a bottle and brought it back to him.

'I didn't sign a striker,' he said. 'That's where I went wrong. Selling Sheringham at the start of the season wasn't the prob-lem. I had my doubts about him as a player,' (a dreadful miscalculation, I thought). 'But not replacing him properly was stupid. I could pick up that phone now and buy that bloke Stan Collymore before the transfer deadline. We've got the money. I just don't have the inclination. I don't know if he's right for us, I'm not sure he can play. And yet the thing is I used to know. I used to know who was perfect and who could play. I'm just knackered – mentally, physically. But the only option when you're in the boat we're in is to keep rowing, to keep telling people you can get to the shore. But you know what I think? You can get relegated in October as easily as you get relegated in April or May. And we didn't play well enough at the start of the season.'

He paused. 'Who was the guy who said we'd all get fifteen minutes of fame? Andy Warhol, wasn't it? Aye, well I've had a lot more than fifteen minutes' worth, so I can't complain. But this is almost the worst time – certainly worse than Leeds, worse than Derby. Just not as worse as when I got injured and knew, right at the end, that I wouldn't play again. Now that was like having a crushing weight on top of you. But relegation is like falling off a cliff. You don't know how to stop yourself sailing through the air. You pass everybody on the way – and they smile and wave at you, and you try to wave back.' He gave a weak wave at this point, his face flat and expressionless.

'I'm telling you, we've been absolute, total shit for most of this season. I've never been so depressed, so down. I'm getting older, the players are getting younger, the game is moving on. Even Clark Gable had to accept in the end that he'd got a few wrinkles. I have to accept I'm not as good as I was.'

Clough accepted something else that afternoon: that he ought to have resigned two years earlier. When Forest at last reached Clough's first and only FA Cup final, against Tottenham in 1991, there was a tide of sentimental support for him. The

FA Cup was the only major domestic trophy he had never won. I'm certain that, had Forest beaten Tottenham, Clough would have basked in the success and a week or two later announced his retirement.

'I could have done it,' he said, 'gone and had a life, 'cos I wasn't at my best then health-wise. But it's that thing about hanging on again. It's temptation. You think about what you've done in the past. You think you might – just might – be able to do it again. Or at least you think you've got half a chance.'

The Forest–Tottenham final is remembered for Paul Gascoigne's brutish tackles, first on Garry Parker and then the scything chop on Gary Charles, for Pearce's blazing free kick, which gave Forest the lead, for Mark Crossley saving a Gary Lineker penalty, and for Walker's headed own goal.

I think the turning point – not just for Forest that afternoon but for Clough's management career over the next two years – was his decision to remain on the bench before extra time began. The players wanted, and waited for, the adrenalin kick his words might have given them: an inspirational line to match Alf Ramsey's in the World Cup final of 1966 – 'You've won it once, now go out and win it again!' – or merely an arm placed reassuringly round the shoulders. With Clough, some of the players probably expected an extravagant kiss on the cheek. Instead, someone who had built a reputation and won trophies on his motivational powers sat motionless and mute on the sidelines, a good thirty yards from his team, arms folded and staring straight ahead. When he did get up it was to walk down the tunnel to chat to a bemused policeman.

That was one of the crassest decisions he ever made. It was not, he admitted, even an attempt at reverse psychology: 'Just a mistake,' he said lamely. In his first autobiography, Clough argued that the players didn't want him alongside them on the pitch. He said that he felt the cameras would be too intrusive for them.

That afternoon he told me a different story. He said that when he returned to the bench after half-time and sat down, the strangest sensation swept over him: 'I thought we weren't going to win, and that somehow whatever we did that day wasn't going to be enough.'

This passive acceptance of what he imagined fate held in store didn't sound like Clough. I believe his concern about the TV cameras was greater than he admitted; that he imagined the cameras focusing on his every twitching move and casual hand gesture, and the commentators trying to lip-read what he was saying. He knew he'd be the centre of attention – odd, since that is usually what he wanted – and it disturbed him enormously. I thought it was an illogical argument. How would it have adversely affected the passage of extra time? Had Forest got through it unscathed and earned themselves a replay, it was Clough's belief that Spurs would have been 'murdered' in it. 'We couldn't play that poorly twice,' he said, which makes you wonder even more why he ducked out of a team talk.

A week before the final, Forest had beaten Leeds 4–3. The Clough I saw after that game was so subdued and unimpressed by what he had seen that you would have thought Forest had been soundly thrashed. He sat hunched in his chair, his face grim. He was worried that the side had peaked too soon – that the football that ought to have been saved for cup final Saturday had been spent lavishly the previous month. As I left him, he

213

said, wagging his finger at me, 'I want to the win the FA Cup very badly – but don't say that unless we do win it.'

Watching Clough as he walked out at Wembley, incongruously holding Terry Venables' hand, I thought back to that line and how nervous he seemed about the final and the thick cloak of history around the competition. He had grown up, as a boy, and as a player and a manager, during a time when the FA Cup final was almost, as Danny Blanchflower once described it, like a religious ceremony, with its own rites and strict order of service: the slow drive down Wembley Way, the twin towers, the spongy lushness of the turf, the red carpet, the royal guest, the week-long round of interviews and hype. Clough had won two European Cups and two League Championships, but in almost forty years as a manager he was experiencing the FA Cup final for the first time. He was a Wembley 'virgin', and he wanted to win the FA Cup so badly that he felt nervous about admitting it publicly.

After the final I stood near the door of the dressing room waiting for him to emerge. He barged past everyone, eyes lowered, and silently boarded the team coach for the journey back to Nottingham.

Forest returned to Wembley the following year – in the League Cup – and lost again, Manchester United beating them 1–0. Yet another chance to retire, reputation burnished, was passed up. So when I left him on the afternoon of his receiving the Freedom of the City, I was not convinced that he would resign. I had heard that speech, or a version of it, so often before. He was always threatening to resign – I had a file full of stories that said so. I thought that if Forest went down, Clough would feel obliged to spend at least one season trying to push them back up again. And if Forest survived, the pull for 'another go' in the Premiership would have been irresistible.

It's my feeling that whenever Clough considered quitting, one of the factors that dissuaded him was Peter Taylor's experience. Taylor was so bored in retirement, and so consumed by football, that he could not compensate for its loss without returning to Derby. Surely Clough would go through an identical, frustratingly empty phase? The prospect certainly ran through his mind. 'Lots of times I told Taylor that when he quit, he'd be sitting at home pining to put his coat on and go to work,' he said. I knew there was no possibility of Clough moving from the East Midlands. He was too old, too set in his ways; far better, he decided, just to stick it out. And stick it out he did – for two seasons too long.

The further I step back from the Clough years, the crisper the picture I get. I know now that I didn't fully appreciate at the time his brittle nature. That he drank far more than was humanly good for him was obvious enough, but no one reported it explicitly until his final months at Forest. Had they done so, medical help would have arrived much earlier than it did. Forest were too fearful to do anything about it, to the extent that when he ought to have been sidelined, in the November of the relegation season, Clough was given a one-year extension to his contract.

Having asked for trouble so blatantly throughout his career meant that the last act for Clough was to become a grotesque cause célèbre, full of embarrassment and recriminations. That the catalyst for it was a Shredded Wheat commercial turned it into black comedy. Indeed, the last act was so preposterously chaotic that I've always imagined it being accompanied by circus music.

What has stayed with me about the twenty-four hours during which his fate was resolved – beginning on April 25 – is not the *Sunday People* headline AMAZING PLOT TO KICK OUT BRIAN CLOUGH. (The 'amazing plot', insisted the newspaper, was a boardroom coup to unseat him at the end of the season). Nor was it reading, with no surprise, the very specific and very damaging allegations about his drinking made by a director called Chris Wootton, including the claim that Clough had nearly died twice because of his alcoholism. It wasn't the audiotape that Wootton possessed on which Clough, evidently drunk, horribly slurs his words as he tries to record his lines for the Shredded Wheat TV commercial. And it wasn't even Clough appearing in *The Sun*, his grinning face peering from the front page, his skin red and welted, beside the headline I DON'T HAVE A DRINK PROBLEM (he ludicrously claimed to have a drop of sherry and the odd glass of white wine). What has stayed with me is the response of a city to one man's dreadful misfortune.

When Clough formally agreed to retire, the morning after the *Sunday People* story, he told me that he had done so in the belief that the announcement of his decision would not be made until the season was over. The chairman, Fred Reacher, emphatically told me otherwise. Within hours, Reacher had called a press conference and made Clough's retirement public. That the press release appeared so soon after the stories about his drinking made it very hard to claim that the two were not linked. More to the point, it gave the impression that Forest were eager to push a drink-soaked Clough out of the door before he changed his mind. The timing of Forest's announcement could hardly have been worse for him or his family.

I'd written Clough's football obituary two weeks earlier. The editor asked me to do it as a precaution. All I had to do was read it through one last time and send it to the subeditors. The *Nottingham Evening Post* was soon printing a commemorative edition. An hour later, I walked out of the office and into the city centre for some fresh air.

On street corners, in bars and cafes, I saw people engrossed in the newspaper. I watched as others heard the almost indecipherable cries of the inky-fingered vendors, or saw the headline on the news-stand, and reached for their loose change. The news dominated conversations everywhere: 'Brian's going', 'Cloughie's quit'. I listened as people talked about him like a personal friend fallen on hard times. 'It's not true, is it?' I heard one man, with a mop of greying curls, anxiously ask a newspaper seller, who replied without needing the question clarified. ''Fraid so,' he said, handing over the paper. The man read the story in a dismayed silence.

In the days that followed, it was reported that Clough had recently been found asleep in a ditch close to his home. A *Spitting Image* sketch mocked him. His rubbery puppet had scarlet cheeks and moved bottles of spirits around a drinks cabinet as if each one was a player on a tactics board.

If nothing becomes a man like his leaving, then Clough restored his dignity the afternoon Forest were relegated. His final League game at the City Ground saw an outpouring of compassion from the crowd, a raw demonstration of the emotional attachment which existed – and probably always will exist – between him and his public. The whole afternoon belonged to him to such an extent that the defeat against Sheffield United was almost irrelevant. That Saturday, the tannoy boomed out songs symbolic of the occasion, like some celebratory *Desert Island*

Discs, including 'My Way' (naturally enough) and 'Please Don't Go'.

During the match, Clough stood straight-backed outside the dugout like a captain determined to be on the bridge when the ship went down. He went through an assortment of gestures to acknowledge the accolades that came from all corners of the City Ground: thumbs up, a modest bow of the head, arms theatrically raised. There were kisses and handshakes from supporters straining to reach him from behind the perimeter wall, and resounding chants of 'Brian Clough's a football genius!'

After the whistle, the crowd spilled on to the pitch. Clough was pressed to come back onto the field by the Trent End, its supporters refusing to go home until he appeared in front of them. In one photograph, Clough, on the verge of tears, appears in the centre of the passionate thousands who were determined not to let him go. Afterwards, he accepted a flower from a young girl, as distraught as a mourner at a funeral. He looked at her, his head on one side, and said tenderly: 'Hey beauty, no tears today, please.'

'Can I have a word from you, Brian,' asked a desperate TV interviewer outside the ground. 'Of course,' said Clough, walking briskly away. 'Goodbye.'

———————

The following afternoon, a clear-skied spring Sunday, I went to Clough's home with my family. He'd called in midweek to invite me. 'Come for lunch. You might get a line out of it,' he said nonchalantly, as if nothing out of the ordinary was happening. 'But bring your bairn – I want to sit her on my knee.'

My daughter Sarah, who had just turned four, did sit on his knee, and he took his flat cap and tried, unsuccessfully, to skim it like a frisbee into the chandelier. His own grandchildren's toys were scattered across the floor, building bricks behind the sofa, a fort in front of it. Later on, he took Sarah outside and watched her chase his dog around a garden that resembled a golfing fairway, the soft folds of the Derbyshire hills visible in the middle distance.

'You know,' Clough said, turning towards me. 'That is bliss. If you want to know what life's really about, it's here right in front of your eyes. A lovely garden. A lovely bairn enjoying herself. Oh, so precious.'

After lunch, which he helped to cook, he told me that one of the saddest phone calls he'd received had been from Alan Brown, his managerial predecessor at Forest. Brown was then seventy-seven. 'We had a weep together,' said Clough.

He decided he wanted to change his clothes for the photograph to accompany the article we wrote together. He disappeared and came back wearing an immaculate suit. 'Appearances matter. We have to look good,' he said, and then settled down in the breakfast room and began to talk.

Clough dismissed the prospect of becoming a director of the club or its life president because he didn't want any more titles. Worried that he might be treading on the toes of his successor, and with a deliberate reference to Don Revie's interference at Leeds, Clough added that he knew what it was like to follow a manager who had been entrenched at one club, 'to walk around the ground he built, to stare at his photograph on all the walls, to hear his name whispered in corridors.' He wouldn't join the board for the same reason. His replacement 'would feel like a husband who'd got his mother-in-law living in the spare bed-room'. We agreed on a final phrase, 'You'll need a telescope to find me next season'.

As soon as it was published, Clough's declaration that he

would cut all ties with Forest was dismissed as arrant nonsense, a piece of showboating for the sake of it. But he kept his word. He said to me that he'd tried, as best he could, to line up Archie Gemmill for the vacancy, and he wanted Ron Fenton as general manager. Viewed in profile, Fenton looked stern and rugged, like one of the stone carvings on Easter Island. He had done much to protect Clough and worked unselfishly hard for him. He was Clough's friend, and I admired him enormously for his loyalty.

'I wanted to be loyal to the people who were loyal to me,' Clough explained. But the board was in no mood to listen to his recommendations. That's why, on the night that Clough left his office for the last time, Frank Clark was ready to take over the following morning. 'Hope he likes the office,' was all Clough said.

After being gently nudged to leave by a friend, Clough got to his feet, placed the glass on the desk that no longer belonged to him, and gathered together a few odds and ends. He hugged everyone in the room. On the way out, he glanced back, as if there might be ghosts lurking in the corners. Another friend of his whispered to me, 'He'd have stayed here all night if we'd let him.'

CHAPTER ELEVEN

Don't forget me

'So,' I asked, 'are you missing football?' Clough looked at me as if he didn't understand the question. I had gone to visit him at his home. He opened the door himself. He was wearing a smart V-necked sweater and an open-necked shirt, and looked thinner and much paler, as though he had just recovered from a heavy cold. The red blotches had vanished from his face, which was drawn, and his slow body movements suggested that his hand and knee joints were stiffening. He insisted on wearing his tweed cap inside the house, which made him look like a gentleman farmer or a retired jockey.

I followed him into the lounge. Sitting on the sofa, surrounded by a heap of newspapers, he started to talk about his garden, his grandchildren, the letters he still received and the games he watched on TV so that he 'could shout at the screen when anyone said anything stupid'. It was odd to see him in casual clothes and outside the cosseted, cloistered environment of a football club. Such cosy surroundings made him look a far less severe character.

The media weren't particularly interested in Clough at this stage in his retirement, and his public voice had fallen silent. Allegations about financial irregularities, which began in summer 1993 immediately following his retirement – when

Tottenham's then chairman Alan Sugar said in the High Court that Clough liked 'a bung' – had all but died away, though the claim grievously wounded his reputation. It was briefly damaged again in September of the same year when the TV programme *World in Action* accused Clough of dealing in black market tickets (although the club's internal investigation cleared him).

Forest, under Frank Clark, had shot back into the Premiership at the first attempt, riding on the back of Stan Collymore's goals. Clark had bought him within weeks of taking over for £2.25m. The Clough era, and stories of his drinking, seemed to belong to another century. I got the feeling that, around the club, Clough was being dismissed as yesterday's man. A lot of people seemed mightily relieved that he was out of the way. He wasn't seen at all or spoken about very much.

We sat for a while drinking coffee, and then Clough took me into the front room so we could look at his mother's washing mangle, beautifully restored, which he later used as the leitmotif in his own autobiography. He seemed to have forgotten that he'd already shown me the mangle, on an earlier visit just a few weeks before. He reminisced briefly about his boyhood and washing day itself, the sharp scent of soap and powder accompanying the furious cranking of the mangle's handle, a woman-powered machine that to him epitomised his proudly humble beginnings and the honest graft of the ordinary working family. I could almost see his mind cutting across time, the vision of his 'mam' in front of his eyes.

Beside the mangle Clough had placed the scroll he had been given by Nottingham City Council which declared him a Freeman of the City. The two objects together represented where he had come from and what he had achieved. In a corner of the room was a cardboard box containing letters from fans.

Some of the envelopes had been neatly computer-printed, others were addressed in scratchy handwriting. One of them read 'Sir Brian Clough', an honour he'd never receive.

'You don't think you've got old until you begin to count the years one at a time,' Clough said. 'That's when you realise how much you've seen. It doesn't seem five minutes since I started in football. Now I'm finished with it.' That was when I asked him if he was missing football. He was caught in transit between his old life and his new one, playing with his grandchildren, sometimes helping out in his son's newsagent's shop. 'I don't miss you lot,' by which he meant the media. He paused, and tugged down the peak of his cap, as if he was hiding his eyes. 'I love retirement. I love living quietly for once.' I wasn't sure whether I believed him.

He loved his garden, the trees in particular. Sometimes Clough would hire a team of apprentices to sweep leaves, weed the flowerbeds, cut the grass and prune the bushes. He would return home and inspect the work as if he were the head of the Royal Horticultural Society. He loved cricket, but didn't seem to watch a lot of it except on TV. When he did go, usually to Trent Bridge when he was manager of Forest, he sat for just an hour or two before heading back to his office. One of his friends also told me that he'd never known anyone who enjoyed holidays as much as Clough. 'You can see it in his face. He's a really different person,' he said, as if he felt obliged to make a case for Clough's benevolent side.

I knew that Clough was committed to his family and had told me that he wanted to spend more time with them, but his reply still didn't convince me. So many people must have put the question to him that I think he developed a reflex response to it. Anyway, my expression must have betrayed my reservations. He fixed his gaze on me. 'You don't believe me, do you?' The cap was pulled down again, so far this time that its peak was almost touching his nose. He tilted his head towards me. 'Aye,' he said phlegmatically. 'Some days you get up and think you should have a team to pick. It soon passes, and you begin to walk in the garden and admire the plants and the trees and the scenery. I've done my bit. I've had enough of football. I'm enjoying life. Honest.'

That brought the conversation temporarily to a dead halt, and Clough turned to walk back into the living room. He paused beneath the lintel of the door. 'And no one will ever do what I did at Nottingham Forest. Now that's something to keep you warm at night.'

I knew what he meant, and of course, he was right.

Clough slid into sad decline in the first season of the Premiership, just when football was on the cusp of its revolution – the time when it finally broke away from the slightly seedy glamour of the seventies and eighties and threw itself into an era of showbiz glitz, carried along in a ticker-tape procession on the juggernaut of television money.

It is inconceivable that another Brian Clough could ever emerge from the swamp of banknotes that is modern football. To achieve now what Clough did between his first League title in 1972 and his second European Cup eight years later – with or without someone as capable as Peter Taylor beside him – would be impossible. No team from a backwater, such as Nottingham Forest or Derby County, is capable of gaining, let alone sustaining, a competitive edge over clubs that are run as vast corporations.

The polarisation of the game almost guarantees that no one

learning the managerial trade in the present League Two would
be able to take over a mid-table Championship side and steer
them to the Premiership title on slender financial means and
crowds that seldom topped 25,000. The feat was astonishing
enough when Clough originally pulled it off, which emphasised
his unique individual skill. A solitary Championship at Derby
could be easily dismissed as an outrageous fluke. But when he
repeated it with a different club and then twice won the European Cup, he set a gold standard against which the rest of his
career was judged.

When I hear anyone talk dismissively about the last, largely
barren years of Clough's career (for two League Cups amounted
to a meagre return on the financial investment he made), I think
about Joseph Heller, the author of *Catch-22*. When Heller was
told – a phrase he heard repeatedly – that 'you've never written
a better novel than *Catch-22*', he would nod his head sagely in
agreement, and then reply with a smile: 'But who has?' No one
in British football has come close to matching the incredible
transformation that Clough wrought on two clubs that had
almost nothing going for them apart from the formidable talents
of their manager.

When Clough is remembered now, it's often for a cutting or
jokey one-liner he once used, for the mimicked catchphrase
'young man', for the green sweatshirt, which became a trade-
mark, for 'bungs' in brown envelopes, or for the haggard, crim-
son, alcoholic face. Sadly, Clough the vaudevillian obscures
Clough the master manager, and the taint on his character
obscures the debt so many owe him and the legacy he left.

So much of sport is ephemeral. As the years click by, the
faded photographs and footage of cup finals and individual
performances begin to look dated and irrelevant in the eyes of
a new generation which bows to its own heroes. To them,

a sepia-tinted past has no significant bearing on the brightly coloured present. I'm not so sure.

Clough was prickly and introspective, and a strange mix of talent, ambition and bombast. But you could forgive him his bad points because he had a burning sense of purpose that was not wholly fuelled by the prospect of personal financial gain. Far more than most, he cared about the spirit of football and the need to play the game stylishly and without cynicism. He saw nobility in the figures he most admired: Raich Carter, Len Shackleton – Sunderland's Championship and FA Cup winning goal-scorer of the 1930s, Jackie Milburn, Alan Brown and Clough's hero, Middlesbrough inside forward Wilf Mannion. He set out to copy them. Furthermore, he was conscious of football's history, what the game meant to the ordinary man, and the pivotal role it played in so many people's daily lives. He was also realistic enough to know that once his part in it was over, the historical current would flow on and wash away all but his most notable contributions.

'After I've been gone for a while,' he often said, 'it'll be as if I never existed in football. You start off in the game thinking you're indispensable. It never occurred to me that I wasn't indispensable at Derby, for example. I even told them so. I soon found out I was talking crap. There's always someone who can sit in your chair. I don't know anything about art. But I do know that one artist influences another artist, persuades him to paint in the same style or use the same colours. I reckon if I can influence just one manager to look at what I did, and then try to do exactly the same thing himself, then I'll take it as a compliment. I'll know that I was half-decent at my job.'

In a piece published in the late 1950s in the *Empire News*, Clough was quoted as saying: 'Publicity is not my strong point. Some footballers constantly like to see their names in the headlines. I don't.' It's the most preposterous statement he ever made. Clough adored publicity, and loved his name in lights. He became his own Dictionary of Quotations:

'I wouldn't say I was the best manager in the business. But I was in the top one.'

'If God had wanted us to play football in the clouds, he'd have put grass up there.'

'There are never any disagreements with players. We talk about it for twenty minutes and then we'd decide I was right.'

So often football indulges in inappropriately emotive language to describe what happens within and around it. The words 'tragedy' and 'tragic' are attached too frequently to events – such as the loss of a cup final, relegation or even an open goal carelessly missed – that don't remotely deserve them. That Clough managed only the smaller fish in the pond has been described as tragic. In public, Clough vociferously agreed. All his football life, he acted as though he wanted to be somewhere else. He always gave the impression that the view would be infinitely better, the grass of the pitch greener, if he was sitting in the dugout of another club. In private, he conceded that he was infinitely more suited to the hand fate had dealt him.

No season, apart from his last, went by without Clough being linked, tenuously or otherwise, with a move to another club. 'Clough ready to quit' or 'Clough for (insert the name of almost any club here)' stories consumed acres of newsprint, gallons of ink. At Derby, he was supposedly on the brink of going to Coventry weeks before the League title was secured. After winning it, with Derby progressing through the early rounds of the European Cup, he complained about Sunderland's decision not to approach him following Alan Brown's departure for the second time from Roker Park. 'I'd have gone there,' he said. 'I've always had a passion for Sunderland.'

At Forest, there were constant threats to resign, either as a consequence of boardroom disagreements over something Clough had said or done, or because there was a vacancy to be filled somewhere: Manchester United, Manchester City, Sheffield Wednesday, Derby, Barcelona, Valencia, Gijon, the Greek national side, clubs in America's nascent North American Soccer League . . . the list went on and on. As only he could, Clough made capital out of all of them, manipulating each opportunity to suit a purpose. He exploited them to strengthen his domination over his board of directors, to add leverage to his contractual demands or just to make mischief.

With Sunderland, for example, he knew that one of the men he most despised, Bob Stokoe, was next in line to become manager. Stokoe was on the pitch, playing for Bury, on the afternoon that Clough's playing career ended. Clough was in agony, clutching his knee and screaming in pain. Thinking he was faking the injury, Stokoe yelled at him to get up and carry on. Clough never forgave him.

Putting himself in contention for the vacancy at Sunderland was done solely to get back at Stokoe. Sunderland, after all, were near the bottom of the Second Division, and there was no way that Clough was going to abandon a League Championship winning side for them. He hadn't climbed the ladder, rung by desperate rung, only to voluntarily descend it again. He couldn't believe that, just six months later, Stokoe had won the FA Cup. 'But he's crap,' he said.

With Derby, both in 1977 and then when Peter Taylor returned there in 1982, Clough's practised eyelash-fluttering at the board gave them the impression that he just might go back if the offer was good enough. He deliberately created a false sense of expectation. 'Derby deserved it,' he told me, 'for letting me leave in the first place.'

The same flirting technique was used to handle approaches from television and the handful of constituencies that sounded him out to become a prospective parliamentary candidate. But Clough as MP was about as likely as Clough as archbishop. He wouldn't have survived long in the rarefied atmosphere of Westminster, and he knew it. His combustible nature was never suited to the protocols of its gothic corridors and the arcane procedures of the House of Commons; acute boredom and a sense of detached helplessness would have dogged him. What is more, Clough – though intelligent in many ways – didn't possess the scalpel-sharp intellect required to understand complicated bills, the patience to tackle basic constituency work, and I couldn't imagine him spending long nights studiously sifting through the red boxes of cabinet responsibility.

He talked about politics with me a lot because he knew I was passionately interested in it. He was a socialist, albeit a champagne one. In the 1970s especially, he was often asked to give his opinion on current affairs, from Edward Heath's Tory government to Harold Wilson's resignation, and from the royal family to social deprivation. His knowledge and political philosophy, however, wouldn't have withstood in-depth scrutiny.

Even in the unlikely event that he had become a parliamentarian, Clough could never have travelled far from the back benches. For someone used to being locked in at the centre of things, it would have been a restricting and suffocating experience. He nonetheless milked the publicity accompanying each round of speculation about his future as a possible MP. He did it to comfort himself.

As Taylor stressed in his own book, Clough wanted to be

wanted. He craved the affection of others and needed to be told how good he was, how brilliantly he had spoken. However spurious an offer of alternative employment, he saw it as another way of gaining the upper hand on someone who had rejected him in the past: Sunderland, for sacking him as youth coach; Leeds, for dismissing him before he'd unpacked his case; Forest, for approaching him only after his forty-four days at Elland Road; the perpetual rejection by England; the refusal of any major English club – Manchester United, Liverpool, Arsenal – to consider him as manager. To the big clubs, Clough was radioactive, not to be touched at any cost. But the courtship of other clubs was his reassurance, an endorsement of his value and self-worth. He never saw how brightly it illuminated his vulnerability and the insecurity that Taylor so presciently identified.

So much mythology has built up around Clough that it is difficult to get close to the man himself. Put aside the crude stereotype of someone slightly unhinged who turns into a cor-rupt, alcohol-dependent mess, and think instead of a troubled visionary, private pain never far from the surface. He did dwell on the unfulfilled promise of his playing career. He did hold grudges, whether real or imaginary. A small part of him did believe that he hadn't been properly appreciated and was often under-paid by many of those who had employed him.

Aside from what Derby and Forest did so gloriously in his name, the thing to remember is that Clough was essentially an attention-seeker, and someone who wanted constant reassur-ance. He craved recognition and hated being ignored. Whenever I walked into a store or a bar with him, I would see people glance up, blink in disbelief and then nudge one another. Once one person had the courage to come up and speak to him, others followed, slapping his back and asking for his autograph.

Clough revelled in it, and reacted to such occasions as if he were giving a one-man stage performance. He was usually charming and talkative, the relaxed manner and hand-shaking a prelude to some well-rehearsed lines that usually made the recipient feel much better about having met him. 'Hello beauty,' he would say to women, irrespective of their looks.

If for some reason he wasn't being noticed, he had a tendency to talk very loudly or start singing, or even move furniture around a room – anything, in fact, to get people to look at him. It never failed. Once, in a hotel on Brighton sea-front, he astonished the dozen or so guests in a hotel bar by picking out stories to read aloud from the *Guardian* and then trying to engage the barman in conversation about them. The bar was twenty-five yards from our table, and his voice filled the room. He cleared it very quickly.

The question of whether Clough would have been as successful in today's football is easily answered – he would not. Clough was always at his best when he was in total charge. Nowadays he would be unable to exert total domination over a club, as he did at Nottingham Forest, so that it snapped to attention as soon as he arrived through its doors in the morning.

He would be answerable to a board of directors – many of them vastly wealthy businessmen and investors, far more powerful and articulate and well connected than those he was used to. His decision-making, especially in the transfer market, would be under much stiffer scrutiny. His insouciance about what he said and when he said it would be viewed with acute suspicion, especially if the repercussions of one of his verbal attacks made the share price shudder or upset sponsors or advertisers. His drinking would be curbed, or at least more carefully monitored, and his self-indulgent whims would not be pandered to so readily. He would be obliged to blunt the maverick, volatile streak that ran through him, for today's football's governing bodies would not be as lenient with him over his destructive tirades against authority.

Clough would find it nauseating to have to deal with the demands of players' agents, and to do so in the knowledge that the balance of power had swung from the manager's office to the dressing room. Inside the dressing room and on the training pitch, he would need to be less abrasively dismissive of players, who – as the board and shareholders would be quick to remind him – were the club's chief financial assets. He would not be able to treat them so roughly or bypass any contractual negotiation through intimidation or humiliation. Financial independence and the Bosman ruling have made players completely aware of their worth and marketability, a state of affairs Clough would struggle to accept.

Odd though it may sound, for someone who was so publicity-savvy in his era, the voracious demands of the modern media would be a burden for Clough. With the clamour from rolling news and radio, the thicker sports supplements, and with the Internet churning out both sophisticated analysis and the raw views of supporters, Clough would find it impossible to trumpet unopposed his own opinions or version of events. On a practical level, the mere act of dealing with the 24/7 demand for quotes would place a considerable strain on him.

Clough's preferred method of communication was to talk to a small number of journalists, mostly ignoring the rest, and to put his name to ghosted columns for a lot of money. David Lacey of the *Guardian* once wrote that no one since Ibsen had made more use of ghosts. Clough used the space newspapers made available to him like a soapbox at Speaker's Corner, for blatant propaganda or settling scores.

I began to write a column for Clough that appeared under his name in the *Nottingham Evening Post*. He would ring or buttonhole me, make two or three points about what he wanted to say and then tell me, 'Make up the rest – and make sure you put a few jokes in there. I like to laugh when I read it.' The success of the column was judged by how many national newspapers picked it up the following morning.

After a month or two, Clough called me into his office. 'I'm embarrassed that I'm getting so much money, and so much capital, out of a column that I'm not actually writing,' he said. 'I've written to your editor to ask him to pay you part of my fee. So why don't we start writing more of them . . . and then you can start paying off your mortgage.' I received £125 for every first-person piece I wrote with him. At least twenty-five appeared each year, which made me an extra £3,000 – then a quarter of my basic salary. Halfway through a speech at a testimonial dinner, he broke off to publicly ask my editor to pay me more money.

Clough would take journalists out to lunch, pay for the meal and then give them the receipt. 'Put it on your expenses,' he'd say. 'Buy your bairn something with it.' That was typical of his generosity, which he spread far and wide, and often to people he barely knew. I saw him pay for strangers' groceries when he was queuing in a shop. I saw him buy meals and bottles of wine and beer for people in pubs that he'd never met before. He wanted to 'spread a bit of happiness'.

On the whole Clough liked to help journalists, despite making painstaking efforts to avoid them, and took a good deal of pleasure in coming up with an intro or a final paragraph. He enjoyed reading newspaper columns by writers he believed wrote with style and authority. He liked to read aloud from their columns, savouring the roll of their words on his own tongue. Phrase-making fascinated Clough: the way a piece of writing took shape in the mind before it assumed permanent form on paper. As well as words on the page, he was drawn to oratory – Labour politicians such as Bevan, Foot and Benn – and he usually worked out what he wanted to say long before the sentence, finely chiselled, left his lips.

But an insatiable, clamouring press, far greater in number and descending on him in a twice-daily swarm, would have been Clough's idea of hell. In his later years he had to take a drink – often a hefty one – before embarking on a set-piece TV interview. He did it because of the pressure. 'I'm the barking seal,' he quipped, 'and I have to perform.' He knew what was expected of him: a shining, memorable line or a machine-gun burst of bile.

'When I sit down in front of a TV camera for half an hour,' said Clough, 'it's as if I'm the prime minister. I have to say something significant. I can't be boring. Eric Morecambe once told me about the sheer bloody pressure he was under. Wherever he turned up, people expected him to be funny. If he wasn't, they went away disappointed. Imagine that! Every time you leave your own home and walk into the street, or into a room, you have to become what other people assume you to be . . . now that's wearing.' With modern football's rigidly organised press conferences and the constant presence of the TV cameras, I doubt he would have had the patience to endure what is required of a contemporary manager.

So picture a subdued Brian Clough, often subservient to his board of directors, regularly glad-handing sponsors and advertisers, tempering his criticism, going through the polite motions of answering one tedious question after another (and with no industrial language) during a press conference televised live on Sky. That would be Clough with his soul scooped out. It just wouldn't have happened.

Clough left football management at fifty-eight, an age when contemporaries such as Alex Ferguson and Bobby Robson were still lithe and fit and working. He died of stomach cancer at sixty-nine, and contributed only fitfully to the major debates about the game in the dozen years of his retirement. That was only partly because of ill-health. Worried by the shadow he cast at Forest, Clough deliberately avoided the City Ground until, rather too belatedly, as if it was an afterthought, the club renamed its Executive Stand in his honour. Crossing Trent Bridge from the city end, with his name spelt out in bright red letters, the Brian Clough Stand dominates the low horizon. There is – disgracefully – nothing comparable to mark Peter Taylor's contribution to the club's successes.

Clough explained to me his decision to cut himself off. 'When I was at Leeds, it seemed as if Don Revie was still living over the shop and nipping down every morning for a coffee. When I left Derby, Dave Mackay must have thought I was on his shoulder, 'cos I still lived in Derby and his team were friends of mine. Looking back on it, I didn't do Dave as many favours as I should have done, mostly 'cos I was jealous of the fact he'd inherited a team so good that I used to wake up in a cold sweat thinking about the chance I'd missed by resigning. It's unfair to hang around and lurk in the background. I had to make a clean break from Forest, in fairness to the club, the players and the blokes who had to try to follow me.' Of course, no one could follow him – or ignore him.

On that wintry morning at his home, our conversation ranged from football memories to politics and the definition of 'working class' (he still regarded himself as such). After it was over, I remember him standing on the doorstep waving his sombre goodbye to me as I climbed into my taxi. Outlined in the door frame, his figure looked tragically small.

'When you come back, we'll sing a Sinatra song,' he called out, and then chimed up with 'You make me feel so young . . .' He clicked his fingers in time to the music playing in his head. Finally he took off his cap and began to wave it. He yelled out: 'Hey, don't forget me!'

And I thought, how could anyone ever do that?

The greatest manager of all time ... even if I do say so myself

Monday, 20 September 2004

I am sitting at my desk at the *Yorkshire Post*, glancing through a copy of the Press Association's afternoon news schedule. I am deputy editor of the newspaper, which is considered to be one of the most prestigious outside of London. The paper has recently marked its 250th anniversary. It has also (to use football parlance) just parted company with its editor – a fact that almost no one else on the editorial floor is yet aware of. After less than a year in Leeds, where the *Yorkshire Post* is based, I suddenly find myself in charge of the paper until a formal announcement is made of the editor's departure and a new editor (which I know will not be me) is appointed. I don't have much time to think about anything else.

A decade earlier I'd decided to give up writing about football. I was sick of it. I couldn't bring myself to sit through another match, either live or on television. I cancelled all my football magazines. I parcelled up the football books I intended to keep – about 500 of them – and stored them in my loft. The rest – another 500 – went to local charity shops or were sold at the village fete. I couldn't wait to get rid of them. I began to read newspapers from the front page rather than the back.

An American journalist once said that reporting on sport is journalism's equivalent of working in the 'toy shop'. He wasn't belittling the job – it was his way of expressing the inherent pleasures to be found in covering sport: you can take something relatively unimportant, such as a contest between sweaty athletes, and imbue it with a meaning far beyond its real significance; you get paid for watching an event from the best seat in the house; and most of all, for a lot of the time it is pure fun – if you don't get too carried away, and understand that sport doesn't matter very much in the vast scheme of things. It's just there to be enjoyed. Well, I had stopped enjoying it.

Whatever the cause of my acute disillusionment – arrogant players, rude, dismissive managers, clubs who welcomed reporters as they would an outbreak of anthrax – I decided that I never wanted to sit in another press box or attend another pointless post-match press conference. I couldn't listen to another manager or player complain about a referee or offer one of those stale, formulaic descriptions of what I'd just watched on the pitch – about 'the lads' and 'giving it 110%' and all sort of other crap from the Football Book of Clichés. I didn't want to ask another player how he was feeling, whether he intended to support his manager during a bad run of results (obviously he was going to say yes). I didn't want to hear anyone tell me that team spirit was good 'in the camp' or 'honestly – we're just taking one game at a time right now'. I certainly didn't want to write any of it down.

The style of football reporting had begun to seem frivolous, and football itself pointlessly trivial. To my horribly jaundiced eyes, everyone in the game was cynical, manipulative and grotesquely grasping. The game's charm had gone. Everything about it was focused on money. I could not get enthused about the new season. Who cared which team won the Premiership or the FA Cup? Not me, not anymore. The winners barely had time to lift a champagne flute to their lips before another League season began, another cup competition was already drawn and under way. Football was too profitable a treadmill ever to slow down. The summer seemed to consist of a single Saturday in early June. You were either winding down at the end of one season or winding up in anxious preparation for another.

The daily mechanics of football reporting had changed too. You couldn't just phone a player at his home: you had to go through an agent, who wanted to know what angle you were pursuing and why, and what might be 'in' your story for the benefit of his client – usually either money or favourable publicity. Cooperation from the agent and player was dependent on one or the other. And unless you asked the most anodyne questions, the equivalent of underarm bowling with a tennis ball, you began to be viewed as a snoop or a troublemaker. A spoilt and sneering arrogance descended on football, as if it was the only sport that mattered.

I had always been interested in politics and the arts, especially literature. I'd collected books for many years, and now my house was stuffed with them, from floor to ceiling. You get typecast as a sports reporter. Leaving sport to write about anything 'serious', such as politics or literature, would be like an actor in a soap taking up Shakespeare: everyone would remember you in your previous role. But if I was going to change the direction of my career, I had to cut every tie I had with sports reporting. I wouldn't write about it, I wouldn't talk about it. I wouldn't – if at all possible – even read about the damned thing.

That's why I stopped thinking about Brian Clough. The mention of his name – even the suggestion that I might have to relive any of the previous sixteen years by writing about it or him – was enough to induce a tightness in my stomach. Clough belonged to a past that I no longer wanted to be a part of.

I knew he'd resented a decision – for which I suppose he blamed me – not to let him write a one-off column for the *Nottingham Evening Post* after his retirement. Clough wanted to have his say on the future of the club. He phoned me about it: 'Get yourself over here, I've got plenty to say.' The *Evening Post* had recently been bought by another newspaper group. The paper wasn't keen to pay the money Clough had previously received for his columns, which was quite understandable: the fee for one of his columns – around £500 – would have paid for five or more of anyone else's. When he rang back, I had to tell him about their refusal. He didn't say anything in reply; all I heard was the gentle click of the handset being replaced. Slights remained with Clough like visible scars. Grievances were filed away and remembered. If you crossed him – or if he thought he'd been crossed – he cut you dead. He never spoke to me again.

I caught occasional TV appearances, which merely confirmed Clough's slow, sad decay. By the time he reached his mid-sixties he looked a decade older. His hair was so thin and brittle that it looked as though it would all fall out if you combed it. His eyes were sunken. He seemed to need new suits and shirts to fit his diminishing frame. There was an unsteady roll to his gait, as though he were walking across a ship's deck during a minor storm.

But if you heard Clough on the radio, the voice was still hard and punchy. You could be easily fooled into thinking that he was a healthy and vigorous man who was talking from the chair in his office with a glass of Scotch at his right hand and his dog at his feet. He hadn't lost his comic timing, and certainly not his argumentative streak. He was still capable of mounting a head-on assault against anyone or anything that displeased him.

It had never occurred to me that he might die. If he did, I figured, he'd be at least ninety and would have turned by then into a cantankerous old cove wrapped in a tartan blanket. I pictured him yelling across the lounge of an old folk's home at a nurse: 'Hey, shithouse! Where are my pills?'

And then, of course, it happened. The *Yorkshire Post*'s news editor walked into my office. 'Have you heard?' she asked, very softly. I thought for a moment that she was about to tell me the identity of the new editor.

I shook my head. 'Heard what?'

'I thought I'd better tell you. Sky News is saying that Brian Clough has died. You knew him quite well, didn't you? I just felt you needed to know before you came out and saw it on the TV. I thought you might be upset.' There was a pause. 'Are you all right?' she asked.

In that instant I could see him walking towards me, pushing aside the double swing doors in the corridor at Nottingham Forest with one hand, sweeping back his hair with the other. His dog followed. His face was flushed. He wore his green sweatshirt and tracksuit. I saw him standing in front of me and heard him say, 'Are you here again? Don't I get any fucking peace from you? Go on then, you'd better come in. I bet you'll want a drink.'

The image dissolved, and I became aware that the news editor was asking me another question. 'Is there anything you want me to do? About the story, I mean?'

I shook my head, and said I'd think about it and come over to see her shortly. I got up from my desk and stared out of my office towards the TV that sat on top of the metal filing cabinets beside the newsdesk. Clough's face filled the screen. He was laughing. The picture suddenly changed to a black and white shot of a much younger Clough, in his early thirties I guessed, being interviewed in a dressing room.

Time froze. I could hear the beating of my own heart, my blood pounding in my ears. For a while I sat alone in my office and rearranged the papers and books in front of me. Then I rearranged them again. I went through the Press Association copy on Clough. I logged on to the Internet and scanned the early reports on the BBC website.

When I walked into the newsroom, a debate was in progress about how much space we should give the story in the following day's paper. 'I'm not sure I'm the best judge of that,' I said. 'I'm too close to it.' The chief subeditor and the copy-taster persuaded me to put his death on the front page. We agreed to run a page-length obituary inside, an appreciation on the sports page and a brief editorial. 'Are you sure that's not excessive?' I asked, unsure of whether anyone apart from me cared about Clough.

I went into the vacant editor's office, turned on the TV and began to channel-hop through the satellite news stations. There were already cameras at the City Ground, where supporters – a few in tears – were arriving with flowers and cards or to tie scarves and messages to the front gates. The flowers were laid reverently, as if at the tomb of a martyr. Blank-faced fans were milling around, not quite sure what they should be doing apart from sharing their sadness with one another.

A few ex-players were being interviewed. I recognised John McGovern, still trim and neat, and Kenny Burns, his face and neck fatter with age. Later on I caught sight of Peter Shilton, who hardly seemed to have changed at all. Other ex-players were being interviewed by phone, each of them shocked and fumbling for words that might convey something profound about their former manager.

Most expressed the same thoughts. He was a genius . . . he was a legend . . . he was a one-off . . . you'll never see his like again . . . he had a 'gift' no one can explain. A lot of the same stories were told and retold: that he didn't mind players drinking before a big match . . . that sometimes he scared them half to death. . . that you were never properly relaxed in his presence.

Highlights of Clough's career were being played on an endless loop, as if his life were being relived. There was monochrome footage of him as a thin, athletic player, banging the ball into an empty net during a training session and leaping upwards, like a diver at the edge of a springboard, after scoring a goal for Sunderland. The terraces behind him were packed, all the men wearing caps and hats, the youngsters at the front swinging wooden rattles.

There were other shots. Clough barking 'You're a bloody disgrace!' and 'That's crap!' from the touchline at Derby. Clough rising from the bench in Munich after winning the European Cup, turning and shaking Peter Taylor casually by the hand. And a much older Clough, in early retirement, with his arms aloft acknowledging the applause of a crowd, many too young to have been alive when he won either of his League championships.

It was peculiar to watch, with such a sense of dislocation, a drama being played out in a place I knew so well but was now so detached from. It was like looking at a familiar scene from behind a thick pane of glass. Landmarks came and went: the brown waters of the Trent, Forest's floodlight pylons, the pediment of Notts County's Meadow Lane ground in the middle distance, the dove-grey dome of the Council House, the bleak slabs of the Market Square beneath it, and the blue and red tiled roofs of Nottingham city centre.

I could picture the frantic goings-on at my old newspaper in Nottingham: a re-plate for the front page, delivery vans dashing back from the press in Derby to catch commuters on the way home, a meeting around the conference table to decide what to do with the following day's tribute edition. I thought of the scene time and again as I watched the same moving images on TV for more than half an hour, and read and re-read the breaking-news banner along the bottom of the screen: BRIAN CLOUGH HAS DIED. HE WAS 69.

The combination of words and pictures ought to have confirmed to me that he was dead. And yet it didn't feel real. Any moment, I thought, the presenter would suddenly announce that Brian Clough was on the line, ringing in to say that reports of his death were, like Twain's, exaggerated. I expected to hear that voice again. When, an hour or two later, the news had finally penetrated my brain and I'd begun to accept it, I wondered what he'd think of the things now being said about him.

A fan had been urging the club to build a memorial for him at the ground. 'He deserves a statue,' the fan said. I began to laugh, remembering what Clough had said during one of his furious rants against the board of directors. It was the usual thing – none of the 'useless buggers' knew anything about football, he didn't 'trust 'em', he would gladly 'stick 'em all in a boat, push it out to sea and sink it'.

And then he said this: 'When I leave here, all of 'em will be outside waving me off with their hankies, big wet tears in their eyes. The moment I'm out of the car park, they'll go back inside and have a party. Some people will say I should have a statue erected for what I've done here. Something for the pigeons to sit on. A statue? Don't make me laugh. I know exactly what I'll get from the board. And it won't be a statue, or a set of smart new gates, or even a photograph hanging in the corridor to throw darts at. The board will build a new toilet block in the main stand and name it after me. It'll be a shithouse for a shithouse.'

Clough began to grin and rock in his chair, like one of those laughing mechanical figures you used to find in gaudy seaside arcades – drop a penny in the slot, listen to it roar. He began to laugh so loudly that he went into a coughing fit, finally pulling his handkerchief from his tracksuit pocket to cover his mouth. 'I suppose,' he said when he'd recovered, 'if a toilet block is too grand for me, I might get the Brian Clough Memorial Bar somewhere in the ground . . . but I'll probably have to pay for my own drinks.' I wished I could whisper that story into the fan's ear.

Another fan, a scarf tied tightly around him, said that he thought 'Cloughie' would be bossing heaven by now. That set me thinking back to a conversation we'd had about death and dying. Early one morning on a pre-season tour, I found Clough sitting alone in the lobby of the hotel. He was wearing a white T-shirt and shorts. His arms were folded, his legs outstretched.

The author J. B. Priestley had died a day or so earlier. Clough had borrowed the paper, already more than a day old, that I'd bought containing the news of it. 'Anything in the paper?' he'd asked when I handed it over.

'Not much,' I said. 'Except that J. B. Priestley's died. He was eighty-nine.'

'Good innings,' said Clough. 'Most of us would like to get that far . . . . Blimey, the way I feel right now I won't get past sixty.'

That August morning, the two of us went for a stroll through the streets around the hotel. Clough stared up at a cobalt sky. The sun was already hot, and he let its warmth spread across his face. 'What a gorgeous day,' he said. 'You've got the blue sky. You've got the birds singing. You've got the sun on your back. You can't believe that in less than a week or so I'll be stuck in a dugout screaming like a madman to make myself heard. Hey, I must be barmy. Some people are putting it around that I *am* barmy – and for the first time, I'm beginning to think they're right. When you get a day like this, it makes you think about retirement.'

I told him about the reply Jimmy Sirrel used to give me whenever I began a conversation with the phrase 'It's a nice day, Jim.'

Clough smiled. 'Good old Jim. He's more bonkers than me.'

And that's how we got into our brief talk about death. 'It won't be so bad,' said Clough, 'if you get to see your mam and dad again. Hey, I'd love to sit down with them. Have another conversation. Tell them what I've been doing. If heaven's a collection of your favourite things and your favourite people, you won't want to move, will you? You might not want to see another football match. You'll just want to sit and chat to those you love or loved the most. Or watch the cricket on a summer's day like this one . . .'

He asked me whether I believed in an afterlife. I said I hoped I'd be able to read all the books that weren't yet published and watch whatever sport I liked. He didn't say anything in reply.

It wasn't until I read Clough's first autobiography that I discovered that he thought there was no such thing as heaven. I didn't believe it, and preferred the version he gave that morning.

When my own mother died, he offered his condolences. 'It's the hardest thing of all to lose your mam. You never really get over it. But you cope, as best you can . . . like you do with the rest of life.' He never forgot his own mother's voice, he said, or the way he'd been raised in a house which she cleaned until it glistened. 'Everyone in our street had a thing about the front step. It had to be spotless. Ours was the most spotless of all. You could have eaten your dinner off it. It was a point of pride to our mam.' I said that I remembered my own mother doing exactly the same.

'What happens in the home affects you for the rest of your life,' Clough continued. 'Our lot [he had five brothers and three sisters] were brought up by good, decent, hard-working parents who taught us the value of respect and politeness and how to behave in company. And you got a hug when you came home from school. And you knew your mam would be waiting for you. And you knew if you stepped out of line, you'd get a clip for it from your dad. Aye, I am so proud about the way I was raised – the right way.'

When I finally left the editor's office and went onto the editorial floor, a reporter asked me how much time I'd spent with Clough, and what he was like. 'He was like me dad,' I said, in a clumsy mock-Nottingham accent that I hoped disguised the significance of the answer.

I hadn't gone too deeply into it before, but it was true. He had, at times anyway, been a father-like figure to me – or at least he doled out fatherly advice, like ladles of soup. When I told him I was buying my first house, at the age of twenty-two, he said, 'That's the best thing you can do with your money. It proves that you're not as thick as you look. But pay your mortgage off. The banks rob you blind. Get yourself into a position where you owe 'em nowt – and do it as quickly as possible. Unless you can do it the way I did – get the sack after forty-four days and walk off with a big cheque – just save as many pounds as you can.'

When I told him I was about to become a father, he had this to say: 'Don't forget, whatever you do will affect your bairn. You have to start to act responsibly for the first time in your life. And do your share around the house. Don't let your missus do all the work when the bairn gets home from school. When she's a baby, get up in the middle of the night. Do the feed, change the nappies. Our Simon (his eldest son) was sick all the way down my back when he was baby. I remember it being so cold. But, hey, that's what being a father entails . . .'

And when, shortly after my mother's death, my father became terribly ill, Clough insisted that I spend as much time with my father as I possibly could. 'Bugger the job. Your family comes first. There's plenty of time to sit down at your typewriter and write your kind of rubbish. But the time you have with your dad is precious – and limited.'

My own father spent his life in the dark, back bent, hacking out coal. I watched him go off each weary day to catch the pit bus, a checked cap on his head, a bottle-blue donkey jacket hanging off his stout frame and a faded canvas bag looped over his shoulder. When he came home his clothes reeked of coal, and his stubby fingers and hard palms were stained black, the accumulation of a lifetime's grime so ingrained that no amount of washing would ever properly clean them.

His father and grandfather had been miners too. My father talked abut descending from the pit cage into that subterranean world ('like drowning', he said), where men lost fingers or limbs, and a lot – far too many – lost their lives. He saw men die, and once collected the bits of a broken corpse. But he belonged to a discreet, stoic generation that tolerated its lot, didn't complain or make a fuss and kept its emotions to itself. He was a good but taciturn man who didn't make his private thoughts public very often, not even to me.

The week Clough died, when the memories I'd boxed away like so many of my football books returned in a rush, it struck me that I'd understood this strange, famous, popular man far better than I had my own father. I had travelled the world with Clough, sat beside him, watched him operate. We had shared whisky in grand glasses. I had seen how fame and its suffocating expectations shrivelled first his skin and then his spirit. I didn't need his weaknesses explained to me: I saw them close up, unvarnished.

My father, with that amalgam of modesty and self-effacement that parents can demonstrate, was more of a closed book. He kept himself in one of those hard-to-reach places. There were things about him I would never know. But I could have pulled a dozen well-rubbed, buff-coloured folders off the library shelves and measured out Clough's life in column inches – each newspaper cutting like a thin slice of him. The cuttings, some of them yellowed and brittle, would reveal a man utterly convinced about his place in the world, his stature in his chosen profession. Through them I would be able to hear his voice, imagining the facial expressions and extravagant hand gestures that went with it. It was awful to think of him at that very moment stiffening in a hospital mortuary, eyes closed and fingers still.

249

I dwelt on my own father's death. I hated hospitals – hated the smell of them, the unfriendly echoes of ambulance sirens and squeaky trolleys, and the low ceilings and dark walls that threatened to close in around you. My father died in North Tyneside Hospital in a room that was stark white: white walls, white sheets and an off-white cover neatly folded over the end of the slim bed. Strong sunshine turned the window into a rectangle of white light and made the room inappropriately bright. A white screen had been opened like the bellows of a concertina and then left standing in the middle of the room. Beside it, two plump white pillows lay on a metal-framed chair. My father was white too, the faint outline of his body barely visible beneath a tight sheet which was pulled up almost to his chin. It was as though just his severed head had been lightly laid on the pillow. Flesh had melted from his bones. A twelve-stone man had vanished, and a seven-stone man had taken his place.

At first I didn't recognise him; I thought I'd walked into the wrong room. I called to him quietly, as though I expected an answer, confirmation that the figure in front of me truly was my father. I stared hard, trying to connect his wrinkled features with the memory of the last time I'd seen him healthy. His hair had been combed but his face was unshaven and the skin looked waxy, as though the embalmers had already done their work. My father's eyes were closed, and his mouth had fallen open into a black oval. Occasionally, soft wheezing and gasping sounds came from his throat. The first two fingers of his right hand twitched, as if he was agitated, and I took them in my own hand. I began to talk to him, telling him news from home. Frustrated, I paced the tiny room.

I didn't want Clough's – or anybody else's – last hours to be like my father's. Clough had campaigned hard for miners like him. During the pit strike in the mid-1980s, he raised money for them, made speeches, even donated his own cash without publicity. I was in his office on the day a group of miners came to see him. 'Brian,' said their spokesman, 'we can't thank you enough for what you've done. How much it means to have your support.'

Clough got up from his chair and shook each miner by the hand. 'Lads,' he said, 'for what you do, this country owes you a living. You don't deserve what's happening to you now. All the shithouses who are against you . . . let them go down the pit for a few shifts. Get some coal in their lungs. Let Maggie [Thatcher] go. She wouldn't last five minutes. She wouldn't even sweep out her own coal fire – if she had one.' He turned to me. 'Hey, this lad's dad used to be a miner. He knows everything I'm saying is true.'

When the miners had gone, fortified by a drink or two, Clough said to me, 'Always support the working man. Folk like your dad have done more for the country than any bunch of fat-arsed politicians. Just remember that when you speak to him or when you think he's getting on a bit and you've got better things to do than go and see him.'

After I left the office on the day Clough died, I went back alone to my rented flat in the centre of Leeds. The flat was on the third floor of a dull, modern concrete building. The sink was full of dishes, and the living room was piled with books – on the windowsill and all across the floor – and uneven stacks of newspapers and magazines. On my desk in the corner were a heap of paper, various pens, unwashed coffee cups and my laptop.

I switched on the laptop and began to tap at the keyboard, recording random impressions of the day. A late news bulletin was still carrying pictures from Nottingham, and I conjured an image in my mind of the city as seen from its highest point: the complicated cross-hatching of roads, streets and narrow alleys; the blocks and cubes of shops and offices; the ugly squat of the castle on its lump of sandstone rock. I thought about traffic rolling through the streets like dark blood through veins. I felt a stab of homesickness, and the sense – once more – that I was in the wrong place. I ought to have been *there*.

The next morning I collected together all the national news-papers and read the obituaries and appreciations. Matt, the cartoonist of the *Daily Telegraph*, had drawn a headstone with this inscription:

Brian Clough 1935–2004
THE GREATEST MANAGER OF
ALL TIME, EVEN IF I DO SAY
SO MYSELF

It was the end of the week before I could bring a semblance of order to my memories. I then began to work through them, with an oral retelling of each one.

Worn out by the stresses and workload of that week, and relieved that the last few days were over and a recuperative weekend loomed, I collapsed like a felled tree on the sofa at my girlfriend's house. She handed me a glass of white wine, and we began talking about Clough. Or at least I did. In fact, I couldn't stop talking.

As I spoke, moving pictures came out of the darkness, where I had consigned them so long ago. They flew at me in a torrent. I saw the first time I had met him, and the last time, and everything that had happened in between. The games I'd watched were replayed in front of me. I did my impression – a bad one – of his voice.

I didn't feel the faint tears running down my cheeks. I dabbed them with the base of my hand, feeling foolish and awkward. But I carried on talking, and laughing about many of the stories. We opened another bottle of wine, and then a third. And suddenly it was early morning.

When I awoke a few hours later, all those disparate individual images had fused into a single, coherent whole, and I suddenly realised that I was wrong.

Sport is more important than I ever gave it credit for, and athletes have a greater significance in everyday life than ninety-nine per cent of windbag politicians. Red Smith, the best sports writer of his generation and most others, believed that 'sport is life' – and I wouldn't disagree. It can move people to rapture, like a glorious spring day. It can persuade people to identify with it, and with those who participate in it, in a way that few other things can. It *matters*. It stays with us like the characters from a great novel.

There was proof of that for me on cards pinned to the many bunches of flowers left at Nottingham Forest after Clough died. One of the messages read: 'We will miss you.' You know that whoever wrote that meant what they said, for the simple eloquence of those four words conveys profound respect, perhaps love. You can't ask for much more than that at your end.

Clough's obituaries were respectful, and written with genuine regret at how he had allowed alcohol to rob him of so much. Every writer contributed their own vignette, a personal tale that demonstrated the beguiling genius and temperamentally bizarre figure that was Brian Clough.

Each story, different in its own way, underlined for me one

thing: that there is no absolute truth in biography, only judge-
ments. Every subject is posed, cropped and framed, as if in a
series of photographs that capture a lifetime of distinct, frozen
moments. As a biographer, you produce a piece of work that
honestly and accurately reflects what you witnessed, were told,
felt or discovered about the subject. You try to join the diverse
dots of a life, creating a picture that takes into account the
interpretation and the assessment of others who saw things
from a variety of perspectives. And you can only ever contribute
to an understanding of the person concerned. You can't be
definitive.

With Clough, it's still difficult to work out the complicated
wiring of his personality. He was like a Russian doll – many
other Cloughs hidden beneath the one on view. The contradictions in him distort the overall image. He is always just
out of reach – which, I suppose, is what he wanted. 'What
was he really like?' is the one question I got asked more than
any other. I still don't know, but I do know that there can never
be a last word on someone like him: he was too enigmatic for
that.

Clough the man may not have found a place in today's cor-
porate Premiership, but it is all the poorer for his uncompromising passion, his intolerance of red tape and bullshit, and his
non-stop attacks on what is wrong with the game and why.
The biggest compliment we can pay him is to paraphrase the
sentiment that Wordsworth expressed about Milton: 'Clough!
Thou shouldst be living at this hour.' But, of course, in a sense
he is. In fact, it seems as though he has been here all the time.
It's impossible to go through a football season without hearing
his name, without reading another writer quoting something he
said or a manager evoking the spirit of the way he played the
game or trying, as he did, to attain glazed perfection.

Red Smith put it well. 'Dying is no big deal,' he wrote. 'The least of us will manage that. Living's the trick.'

Brian Clough lived. He lives still.

TIMELINE

1935: Born, Middlesbrough, 31 March
1951: Signs for Middlesbrough as an amateur
1952: Signs as professional
1961: Signs for Sunderland for £42,000
1962: Injures his knee in Boxing Day collision against
       Bury
1964: Retires as a player following brief comeback after
       injury
1965: Becomes the youngest manager in the Football League
       (age thirty) at Hartlepool and recruits Peter Taylor as
       his assistant
1967: Appointed Derby County manager
1969: Derby win Second Division Championship
1972: Derby win First Division Championship
1973: Resigns from Derby with Peter Taylor in October and
       becomes boss of Brighton a month later
1974: Appointed manager of Leeds United; and sacked
       forty-four days later
1975: Appointed Nottingham Forest manager
1976: Peter Taylor leaves Brighton and joins Clough at
       Forest. Forest win the Anglo-Scottish Cup, beating
       Orient 4–1 on aggregate
1977: Forest win promotion to the First Division. Clough
       interviewed – but turned down – for the job as England
       manager

1978: Forest win League Championship and League Cup. Clough named Manager of the Year

1979: Forest win European Cup, beating Malmö 1–0 in Munich, and retain the League Cup against Southampton. In February, Clough signs Britain's first £1 million player, Trevor Francis

1980: Forest retain European Cup with a 1–0 win over Hamburg in Madrid, but lose League Cup final to Wolves

1982: Peter Taylor retires, breaking his partnership with Clough

1989: Fined £5,000 for bringing the game into disrepute by striking fans who run onto the pitch after a League Cup tie against Queen's Park Rangers. In April, Forest win the League Cup by beating Luton Town. In December, Clough marks his 1,000th match as a Football League manager

1990: Forest retain the League Cup with a win over Oldham

1991: Forest beaten 2–1 in the final of the FA Cup by Tottenham. Clough receives his OBE, which he says stands for Old Big 'Ead

1992: Forest lose the League Cup final against Manchester United

1993: Receives the Freedom of the City of Nottingham. Shortly before Forest's relegation, he announces his retirement

2002: Undergoes liver transplant

2003: Given Freedom of Derby

2004: Dies, aged sixty-nine, on 20 September

Goalscoring Record

Middlesbrough (all Division Two)
Appearances, goals:
1955/56: 9–6
1956/57: 44–40
1957/58: 42–42
1958/59: 43–43
1959/60: 42–40
1960/61: 42–36

Sunderland
(Division Two except 1964/65; did not play 1963/64)
1961/62: 43–34
1962/63: 28–28
1964/65: 3–1
Most goals in a game: 5 (Middlesbrough v Brighton, 1958)
Scored: 24 hat-tricks

England
Full:
1959 v Wales (Ninian Park), v Sweden (Wembley)

B:
1957 v Scotland (St Andrews)

Under-23:
1957 v Scotland (Ibrox), v Bulgaria (Sofia)
1958: v Wales (The Racecourse)

ACKNOWLEDGEMENTS

The cricket writer Neville Cardus was already in the high summer of his career when the cartoonist Hollowood drew two boys beside a set of stumps. One of the boys is studious looking. He is wearing round black spectacles, a hooped school cap and has a book tucked beneath his arm. The other is holding a cricket bat.

The caption reads: 'No, you be Len Hutton, and I'll be Neville Cardus.' When I saw the cartoon for the first time, I recognised myself in it. My mind went back to the early 1970s when I decided to become a journalist or, more specifically, a sports writer.

In kick-about matches, with jumpers for goalposts, my friends wanted to be George Best or Rodney Marsh. I wanted to be Hugh McIlvanney. Originally in the *Observer*, and then the *Daily Express* (the only national paper in the school library), and then back in the *Observer* again, I followed McIlvanney and regarded his words as scripture. When I had enough money to buy newspapers, I'd cut out his articles and save them in a folder.

I don't have to explain his genius as a writer. Everyone knows about it. Suffice to say that we think in generalities but live in detail; and, for me, McIlvanney's writing always picked out the critical minutiae of whatever he was reporting on. He brought out the human facets of sport beautifully.

I suppose it's peculiar to begin an acknowledgement by paying tribute to someone you flatly don't know. But if McIlvanney hadn't inspired me, I doubt whether I'd have become a journalist at all. Growing up, I admired a lot of newspapermen and women: Ian Woooldridge, Arthur Hopcraft, John Arlott, David Lacey, Brain Glanville – the list could easily become an Oscar-like procession of thanks. I read no one, however, more eagerly than McIlvanney.

A lot of people turned me into a journalist. Foremost among them was Matthew Engel. I was a trainee fortunate enough to share a stamp-sized office with him. He was always patient and very generous with his time.

Specifically for sage advice/ unfailing support/ good judgement on *Provided You Don't Kiss Me*, I'd like to thank Grainne Fox at Ed Victor and Ben Dunn and Jack Fogg at Fourth Estate. I am very grateful for John Woodruff's copy-editing and his knowledge of the period. Material from *The Unfortunates* is granted by kind permission of the Estate of B.S. Johnson.

Finally – and most importantly – this book wouldn't have been written if it hadn't been for my fiancé Mandy.

It happened like this:

I'd already told her all the stories about my years as a football reporter. When I complained – I admit, not for the first time – that no one had depicted Brian Clough the way I saw him, she said: 'Instead of moaning about it, why don't you write a book yourself.'

I protested that no one would read it.

'Just write it,' she said.

And, of course, I always do whatever she tells me.

PHOTOGRAPHIC ACKNOWLEDGEMENTS

The publishers would like to thank the following sources for supplying photographs for this book: *Empics* 2t, 2b, 3t, 3b, 13t, 15; *Nottingham Evening Post* 1, 7, 10, 11t, 12, 14; *Popperfoto.com* 4t, 4b, 5, 6, 9t, 9b, 11b, 13b, 16; *JMS Photography* 8.

TEXT PERMISSIONS

'Fly Me to the Moon' by Bart Howard © 1959 Hampshire House Publishing Corp., USA assigned to ESSEX MUSIC LTD of Suite 207, Plaza 535 Kings Road, London SW10 OS2. International copyright secured.

'Let's Face the Music and Dance' Words and Music by Irving Berlin © 1936 Irving Berlin Music Corp. All rights administered by Warner/Chappell Music Ltd. London W6 8BS. Reproduced by permission.